Lectures on Greek Philosophy 1928

by
John Anderson
Challis Professor of Philosophy
University of Sydney 1927-1958

Introduction by Graham Cullum
Senior Lecturer in English, School of Humanities
Faculty of Arts Australian National University

Edited by Creagh McLean Cole
and Graham Cullum

SYDNEY UNIVERSITY PRESS

SYDNEY UNIVERSITY PRESS
Print on Demand Service
SETIS at the University of Sydney Library
University of Sydney
www.sup.usyd.edu.au

Texts digitized from manuscripts held in the University of Sydney Archives of lectures delivered at the University in 1928.

© 2008 Sydney University Press

Reproduction and Communication for other purposes
Except as permitted under the Act, no part of this edition may be reproduced, stored in a retrieval system, or communicated in any form or by any means without prior written permission. All requests for reproduction or communication should be made to Sydney University Press at the address below:

Sydney University Press
Fisher Library
University of Sydney
NSW Australian 2006

E-mail: info@sup.usyd.edu.au

```
National Library of Australia Cataloguing-in-Publication entry
Author:           Anderson, John, 1893-1962.
Title:            Lectures on Greek philosophy 1928 / John Anderson;
editors: Creagh McLean Cole and Graham Cullum.
ISBN:             9781920899073 (pbk.)
Series:           John Anderson series
Notes:            Includes index.
Subjects:         Philosophy, Ancient.
Other Authors/Contributors:
                  Cole, Creagh McLean.
                  Cullum, Graham
Dewey Number:     180
```

ISBN 1-920899-07-3
978-1-920899-07-3

Foreword to the John Anderson Series

In 2006 a senior academic advisory committee was established at the University of Sydney to oversee the publication of a series of books which would present the intellectual achievement and development of John Anderson, Challis Professor of Philosophy 1927–1958. In 2006-08 the committee members are Emeritus Professor David Armstrong, Emeritus Professor Paul Crittenden, and Professor Stephen Gaukroger. The committee is convened by the John Anderson Senior Research Fellow undertaking research into and publication of the papers of Professor Anderson.

To some extent a proper appreciation of Anderson's work requires an experience of his lecture room. From the notes in the University Archives we may be able to provide something of this experience. Many of these lecture notes have been transcribed and are available at the John Anderson Archive along with Anderson's previously published writings, allowing researchers and students to access the chief resources and to follow the course of his thinking over many years.

The published series to be selected from this material aims to provide scholarly editions of the most complete and significant lectures now available and will include works devoted to Anderson's metaphysics, logic, ethics, politics and aesthetics. The series will help younger students and scholars to understand why John Anderson was the most important, the most controversial and the most influential philosopher ever to have worked in Australia.

Ongoing research into Professor Anderson's unpublished writings and the series of books drawn from this research has only been possible due to the generous bequest to the University of Sydney by his son, Alexander (Sandy) John Anderson (1923-1996).

Dr Creagh Cole
John Anderson Senior Research Fellow
University of Sydney 2007

Table of Contents

Foreword to the John Anderson Series	i
Introduction	iii
Note on the Text	xv
Lectures on Greek Philosophy 1928	1
Part I: Pre-Socratics	3
I. Introductory Lectures	5
Lecture 1: Science, philosophy and mythology	5
Lecture 2: Mythological thinking continued	8
Lecture 3: Foundation of science	11
II. The Milesians	13
Lecture 3 continued: the Milesians	13
Lecture 4: Common quality as unity within diversity	15
Lecture 5: Thales on the nature of things	19
Lecture 6: Anaximander and the unlimited or boundless	22
Lecture 7: Anaximander continued: influence	25
Lecture 8: Anaximenes	28
Lecture 9: Anaximenes continued: notion of substance	31
Lecture 10: Main difficulties in Milesian thinking	34
III. Xenophanes	36
Lecture 10 continued: Reactions to Milesians	36
Lecture 11: Xenophanes' rejection of speculation	37
Lecture 12: Xenophanes continued	40
IV. Pythagoras	44
Lecture 13: Pythagoras and the conception of units	44
Lecture 14: Units applied to music and harmony	48
Lecture 15: The theory of the mean: division of reality	51
Lecture 16: Division of reality continued	54
V. Heraclitus	58
Lecture 17: The particular importance of Heraclitus	58
Lecture 18: All things in process	61
Lecture 19: Things as attunements - exchanges	64
Lecture 20: Fire as process not substance	68
Lecture 21: Systems and cycles	72
Lecture 22: Each thing a cycle	74
Lecture 23: Personal identity	78
Lecture 24: Ethical theory	80
Lecture 25: Modern misunderstandings of Heraclitus	84
VI. Parmenides	88
Lecture 26: Parmenides – early Pythagoreanism	88
Lecture 27: The question of pure Being	90

Lecture 28: Parmenides' criticisms of Heraclitus	93
Lecture 29: Eleatic paradoxes	95
Lecture 30: The Way of Truth – change impossible	98
Lecture 31: Pythagorean units corrected	100
Lecture 32: Criticisms of Parmenides	102
Lecture 33: Criticisms continued	106

VII. Empedocles and Anaxagoras 108
   Lecture 33 continued: So-called Pluralists 108
   Lecture 34: Pluralists' reactions to Parmenides 109
   Lecture 35: Difficulties in Empedocles and Anaxagoras 112

VIII. Melissus and Zeno 115
   Lecture 36: Eleatic responses to Pluralists: Melissus 115
   Lecture 37: Eleatic responses to Pluralists: Zeno 118
   Lecture 38: Zeno continued: the paradoxes 120
   Lecture 39: Zeno continued: the simple dilemma 123

Part II: Socrates, Plato and Aristotle 127

I. Introductory Lectures 129
   Lecture 40: Socrates: Pythagoreans and Eleatics 129
   Lecture 41: Doctrine of imitation: being and becoming 132
   Lecture 42: Knowledge and opinion 135
   Lecture 43: Influence of the physicists 138
   Lecture 44: Socrates continued: the dialogues 140

II. The Euthyphro and Apology 145
   Lecture 45: Euthyphro on piety 145
   Lecture 46: Euthyphro continued 149
   Lecture 47: Euthyphro - stages in the argument 152
   Lecture 48: Euthyphro contined 156
   Lecture 49: The Apology 159

III. The Phaedo and the Parmenides 162
   Lecture 50: The Phaedo – on soul and body 162
   Lecture 51: Proofs of immortality – forms as external 165
   Lecture 52: The treatment of forms as predicates 168
   Lecture 53: Socratic consideration of propositions 171
   Lecture 54: The testing of hypotheses 173
   Lecture 55: Phaedo continued 175
   Lecture 56: Socratic theory of approximations 179
   Lecture 57: Phaedo continued 182
   Lecture 58: Socrates on nature of forms incomplete 185
   Lecture 59: Socrates twin doctrines in conflict 188
   Lecture 60: Two conceptions of forms continued 191
   Lecture 61: The Parmenides – division of reality 194
   Lecture 62: Universality and particularity 198

IV. The Republic 203
   Lecture 63: Introduction to the ethical theories 203
   Lecture 64: Virtue and the arts 206
   Lecture 65: The Republic continued 209

Lecture 66: Thrasymachus on justice 213
Lecture 67: The art of ruling 216
Lecture 68: Justice and the form of the good 220
Lecture 69: Forms and natural kinds 224
Lecture 70: The nature of the state 227
Lecture 71: Goodness as fulfilment of function 230
Lecture 72: Parts of the state and parts of the soul 234
Lecture 73: Consequences of the theory of justice 238
V. Aristotle's Nichomachean Ethics 243
Lecture 74: The good life as that which is aimed at 243
Lecture 75: Aristotle on the practical and happiness 247
Lecture 76: Aristotle's theory of the mean 251
Lecture 77: The goodness of character 254
Lecture 78: Aristotle's emphasis on activities 257
Lecture 79: Socratic philosophy and Butler's Sermons 261
Lecture 80: Comparisons with Butler continued 265
Lecture 81: Butler concluded 269

Appendix: Books on Greek Philosophy in the Anderson 274
Family Collection

Index 279

In memory of Kimon Lycos

Greek Philosopher

Introduction

The new age begins with the return to the Greeks.
—Friedrich Engels[1]

In 1928 John Anderson delivered his first full-year lecture course as Challis Professor of Philosophy at Sydney University—a course on Greek philosophy with a coda consisting of several lectures on the ethics of Bishop Butler. Anderson began with a detailed account of aspects of the thought of the PreSocratics (as they had survived in fragments and doxological writings), moved on to address a number of the Socratic Dialogues of Plato—focusing on aspects of *The Euthyphro*, *The Apology*, *The Phaedo*, *The Parmenides* and *The Republic*, with passing references to some of the other Dialogues—and concluded the Greek section of the course with an account of aspects of Aristotle's ethical philosophy with particular reference to the *Nicomachean Ethics*. While not, in any sense, being an exhaustive account of these works or the history of early Greek philosophy, the course was both comprehensive and critically, philosophically engaged. Like Hegel[2], Anderson took the history of philosophy to be part of philosophy itself, and took seriously the need to engage with prior thought as a condition of working out his own philosophical position.

As an undergraduate at Glasgow University, Anderson took two honours degrees, one of them in mathematics and natural philosophy, the other in logic and moral philosophy. All four of these fields or 'subjects' inform his engagement with Greek philosophy in these lectures. Equally important is the work of John Burnet, Professor of Greek in the University of St. Andrews from 1892–1926, the year before Anderson arrived in Australia. In his Preface to the third edition of his *Early Greek Philosophy* Burnet had written

> My aim has been to show that a new thing came into the world with the early Ionian teachers—the thing we call science—and that they first pointed the way which Europe has followed ever since, so that, as I have said elsewhere, it is an adequate

---
[1] F. Engels, *Dialectics of Nature* (Lawrence and Wishart: 1946), translated and edited by Clemens Dutt with a Preface and Notes by J.B.S. Haldane, p.218.
[2] See, in particular, Hegel's General Introduction and the Introduction to Part I of *Hegel's Lectures on the History of Philosophy* (abridged), translated by E.S. Haldane and Frances H. Simon (Humanities Press International, Inc.: 1996).

description of science to say that it is "thinking about the world in the Greek way." That is why Science has never existed except among peoples who have come under the influence of Greece.[3]

Such was Anderson's engagement with and esteem for Burnet's work that he paid tribute to it at the beginning of 'Socrates as an Educator' (1931), claiming that owing especially to that work "it is now possible for us not only to recognize the Greek philosophers as the founders of modern science, but to distinguish and appreciate the contributions of Socrates and Plato to science and general culture."[4] In a much later essay, 'Classicism' (1960), Anderson recognized his continuing indebtedness to Burnet:

> On the Socratic philosophy I very largely follow the view of John Burnet, whose work on Socrates and on Greek philosophy generally, neglected though it is in these days, seems to me to make a remarkable contribution both to classicism and to philosophy, and whose wholeness of view provides a striking contrast to the piecemeal "philosophies" which are now in vogue.[5]

Anderson's lectures strive for a comparable "wholeness of view" to that which he praised in Burnet when, in a later footnote, he talked of Burnet's "striking combination of philosophical and historical insight" which, in the case of the views of individual thinkers and the course of philosophical thought, "can help us to arrive at philosophical truths (to learn philosophy)."[6] On the evidence of the lectures, Anderson's knowledge of the PreSocratic corpus was largely limited to Burnet's book and his translations. Even so, some of the most interesting moments in Anderson's lectures are those when he critically disagrees with, and the many instances when his own analyses and arguments take him well beyond, Burnet.

Reflecting on what he saw as "the renascent interest in ancient thought," in 1954, Erwin Schrodinger wrote of being "swept along... as happens so often, by a trend of

---

[3] John Burnet, Early Greek Philosophy (Adam & Charles Black: 1920), p.v. This work survived in Anderson's library.
[4] 'Socrates as an Educator' in John Anderson, Studies in Empirical Philosophy (Angus and Robertson: 1962), p.203. Henceforth referred to as SEP.
[5] Ibid, f.n. to p. 193. It is interesting to note that Anderson seems to have been unaware of the remarkably original insights in John Burnet's lecture given as The Second Annual Philosophical Lecture to the British Academy of January 26th 1916, 'The Socratic Doctrine of the Soul'. The case put forward there for the Socratic notion of the soul or psuche is more complex and nuanced than that of Anderson in the lectures below.
[6] Ibid, f.n. to p.201.

thought rooted somehow in the intellectual situation of our time."[7] It is true that a literal 'return to the Greeks' is hermeneutically and culturally impossible—for all of the labours of recuperative scholarship we cannot escape the fact that what passes for our knowledge of them is inescapably *our* understanding of *their* meanings, *our* belated understanding of *their* understanding of themselves. But it is also true that re-engagements with Greek thought have characterized much of what was most original and significant in the thought of the last century. Detailing, exploring and accounting for this in the fields of Philosophy, Literary Theory and, to go no further, Historiography is an important project for the present.

In these lectures, Anderson's 'return to the Greeks' was inseparable from his own working out of the contours of his Realist, Empirical philosophy. In the Introductory Essay to Anderson's *Studies in Empirical Philosophy*, John Passmore characterized that philosophy in the following way.

> No total scheme, no simple units, no first principles, no ultimate objectives, no modes of being, no necessary truths—these, not the rejection of God, are the fundamental negations of Anderson's philosophy. To put it positively, there is, on his view, a single way of being: the complex activity of a spatio-temporal occurrence, within which discriminations can be made and which is itself discriminable within a wider system. To explain, to prove, is to draw attention to relationships which occur between such occurrences; to assert a proposition is to take something of a certain kind to occur; any proposition can be false; science proceeds by the critical examination of hypotheses; any objective has a variety of characteristics and it can always be pursued as part of a procedure for getting something else.
>
> These are definite and general doctrines. In taking it to be his task as a philosopher to enunciate, and to argue for, propositions of such a kind, Anderson is in total opposition to the view that philosophy is simply analysis, or that its object is purely therapeutic. So far he is an untypical figure in recent British philosophy.[8]

---
[7] Ernst Schrodinger, *Nature and the Greeks* (Cambridge University Press: 1996), p.4.
[8] *SEP*. p.xxiii. It is not clear to me that Anderson would have agreed that he was a "British" philosopher. See also J.L. Mackie, 'The Philosophy of John Anderson' in *Australian Journal of Philosophy*, vol. 40 no. 3 December 1962, pp. 265–82. For a more comprehensive account of the scope and thematics of Anderson's Realism see A.J. Baker, *Australian Realism: The Systematic Philosophy of John Anderson* (Cambridge University Press: 1986). For Anderson's views on education, and other views on them, see D.Z. Phillips (ed.), *Education and Inquiry* (Basil Blackwell: 1980). For Anderson's fundamental views on Aesthetics see Janet Anderson, Graham Cullum and Kimon Lycos (ed's.), *Art and Reality: John Anderson on literature and aesthetics* (Hale & Iremonger: 1982).

Engaging with early Greek philosophy was, for Anderson, a way of defining and engaging with what he took to be the central questions of philosophy. As he put it in his later essay 'The Place of Hegel in the History of Philosophy' (1932), "the nature of philosophical problems remains the same now as it was in 500 BC."[9] From the perspective of Anderson's understanding of his Realist position, the early Greek thinkers would always be, in one way or another, deficient.

Perhaps the central feature of Anderson's position could be found in his insistence on what the Greeks called 'the common measure of things'—one sense of the word *logos* as it is used by Heraclitus. Kirk and Raven translate one of the Heraclitean fragments (their *198*) as follows: "Therefore it is necessary to follow the common: but although the *Logos* is common the many live as though they had a private understanding."[10] Anderson links this to his insistence that "there is only one way of being,"—that of ordinary things in space and time. As J.L. Mackie put it, for Anderson

> There are no different degrees or kinds of truth. His propositional view of reality implies that things are irreducibly complex, that we can never arrive at simple elements in any field.[11]

Anderson made an analogous claim for Heraclitus in arguing that "he solved the problem of Pythagorean dualism and asserted a common measure of reality, a coherent logic of being as one" (p.58). This insistence, and the logical reasons for it, are central to Anderson's treatment of much in early Greek philosophy, particularly to the lectures on Pythagoras, Heraclitus and Parmenides. Indeed, he takes Logic to be not merely a formal quality of successful arguments but connected to the very question of being. This, too, emerges in Lecture 17 on Heraclitus when he reflects that what the

> Milesians were concerned with was the different types of explanation which are applied to physical phenomena and the insoluble problems that arise if explanation is made in terms of another way of being than the phenomena themselves.

---

[9] *SEP*, p. 80.
[10] G.S. Kirk and J.E. Raven, *The PreSocratic Philosophers* (Cambridge University Press: 1975), p. 188. Robin Waterfield translates it as his F.6: "And so one ought to follow what is common, the majority of people live as though they had private understandings" in *The First Philosophers* (Oxford University Press: 2000), p.40.
[11] Mackie, op. cit., p. 265.

In other words, if a distinction is made between ultimate and immediate being or between reality and appearance, and however indefinitely this problem is formulated, it is at the basis of all these investigations and it is a problem of logic. In fact the determination of the character of *what is*, or of the conditions of existence, is the whole object of the science of logic.(p.58)

Anderson's account of the emergence of philosophy is at the same time a particular kind of investigation into what philosophy is, and how it relates to what he (perhaps loosely) refers to, and means by, 'science'. In the first lecture he argued "it is important to have a general idea of what distinguishes the work of the early philosophers. Thought becomes philosophic when it ceases to be mythological", when it ceases, that is, to give an account of things in terms of 'higher powers' or when it ceases to be 'animistic'. Animism, he goes on, is

> the theory which postulates an "anima" for every observable occurrence. The result of this animistic thinking is that anything in the nature of science is impossible. Inquiry can proceed only by reference to observation of facts and verification by means of these facts of theories formed in relation to facts. Now under conditions of animist thinking, it is quite impossible for this inquiry to proceed. (One person attributes an event to one spirit, another to another. There is no way of deciding.)
>
> This fact indicates what is fundamentally necessary for scientific thinking, and the investigation of what is necessary for scientific thinking is a fairly accurate description of the work of philosophy. What is necessary is that explanations of facts should be of the same order as facts themselves. (p.5)

As Anderson saw them, the relationships between philosophy and science are manifold. He raised the possibility that "until scientific thinking has begun there can be no philosophy," (p.8) but also saw that science is consequent upon a need to work out certain practical affairs, just as it is in a sense enabled by certain philosophic conditions in the sense that "if once a distinction is made between what is ultimately real and what is apparently real, then science,... can't be thoroughly carried out." (p.10). More importantly, the relations between them might be thought of as complementary and symbiotic:

... in terms of scientific thinking we are no longer concerned with two types of reality, namely, ordinary facts and things, as opposed to powers of a higher order. What is implied is that throughout our investigations we are dealing with things and activities which are all of the same order—the order of fact. And it is in relation to this necessity of science that philosophy comes forward as the explicit study of what constitutes this single order of events—of what is implied in belonging to this order. Or, alternatively, science depends on there being some common denominator of things, on there being no fundamental division of reality but everything being real in the same sense. Philosophy then inquires into what this common denominator is. And this inquiry in its most general form is inquiry into what we mean when we say of anything that it *is* or exists, or what we mean by calling anything a *thing*. (pp.6-7)

Some qualifications to this account might be appropriate here. While there is widespread agreement that the early Greek philosophers of nature practiced ways of thinking which are analogous to many of the practices of modern science, and while the conceptual domains of *phusis* or nature which are formulated in the writings that have survived have consonances with modern scientific conceptions, it would be misleading to imagine that these philosophers had any conception of what is thought of as the scientific method, that is the testing and refuting, or provisionally confirming, of hypotheses in terms of empirical data or facts. Nor do we have any evidence, or reason to suppose, that they saw themselves in terms that are at all congruent with the self images of modern science. The great historian of science, G.E.R. Lloyd, and others, have made it clear "just how strained it is to assimilate" what the practitioners of *phusike* did "under that rubric with what we now think of as physics." Lloyd has pointed to the many ways in which these early thinkers, including the theorists and practitioners of medicine, did not have a conception of the scientific "way ahead," or of the paths that later thought would take.[12]

In lecture 17, commenting on Heraclitus, Anderson linked what he saw as "a coherent theory of existence" with "an attempt to formulate a logic." This important connection

---

[12] G.E.R. Lloyd, 'The Invention of Nature' in *Methods and Problems in Greek Science* (Cambridge University Press: 1991), pp.417-8; 422 and 432. For further measured views on the 'scientific' status of early Greek thought see G.E.R. Lloyd, *The Ambitions of Curiousity* (Cambridge University Press: 2002) and J. Brunschwig and G.E.R Lloyd (ed's.). *The Greek Pursuit of Knowledge* (The Belknap Press: 2003).

can be seen in Anderson's philosophy as well as in that of Heraclitus. We wish to avoid contradictions, Anderson claims, "because we recognise that there is no contradiction in nature."

> And again, if a proposition is to be significant, it must signify that which exists. So that inquiry into the conditions of coherent and significant thinking is in reality an investigation of the conditions of existence.... The attempt therefore to give a coherent theory of existence is really an attempt to formulate a logic, and that is what Heraclitus undertakes, and he recognizes as the first condition of that theory that there should be only one way of being and correspondingly only one way of signifying. (p.59)

Understood in this way, logic takes us to the question and nature of being, as Parmenides saw in Fragments 4 and 5 (which Anderson discussed in lectures 27 and 28): "thou canst not know what is not—that is impossible—for it is the same thing that can be thought and can be." One consequence of this deep connection, as Anderson saw it, was that "things are not to be thought of as prior to propositions, but it is only in propositions that we know things at all." (p.90) So that, when commenting on Socrates' attitude towards the need for propositions in reasoned dialogue, Anderson further claimed that "What we know when we know a proposition, may be described as *a thing having a character.*" (pp.134–35) This 'logical' relationship between the proposition and the way things are was central to Anderson's thinking, and he brought out part of its importance in lecture 43, arguing that

> the most important implication of the recognition of the possibility of error is that all that we know must be considered as taking the propositional form: that the proposition must not be regarded as our peculiar way of dealing with things which are not in the propositional form, but as the way in which these things actually occur. For if we assume that things occur in a different form, then we cannot solve the problem of showing how the propositions we formulate apply to these things. (p.139)

It is for this reason that Anderson criticises Socrates for not fully grasping the consequences of the propositional method in lectures 53–56.

That said, it is important to see how at one level, and for all of their differences, the concerns of Socrates and

Anderson merge: in their preoccupation with the nature and conditions of meaningful discourse. That lies at the heart of Socrates' use of the dialectic, just as it is central to Anderson's engagement with early Greek philosophy.

> It is only by reference to speech or discussion that we can understand the raising of any problem whatever, and therefore the solution of any problem must be equally expressible in terms of ordinary speech. In other words, the question of the conditions of existence can only be approached by a consideration of the conditions of intelligible discussion or of significant speech, since in any investigation and in any expression of things we require to use speech not merely to convey our views to others, but even to enable ourselves to understand at what point exactly we have arrived, and whether we have solved the problem or not. (p.172)

In these lectures, and despite that focus on 'speech' as the site of what is now commonly called 'inter-subjectivity', Anderson pays little attention to the fact that Plato's Socrates exists for us as a dramatic figure in written dialogues, characteristically engaged in speech with others. It seems that Anderson was uninterested in, or deaf to, the artistry of Plato in his philosophical deployment of the Dialogue form—unaware of the kind of philosophical exercise that these dialogues embody, and occasion in and for the reader. On several occasions Plato's Socrates expresses detailed and serious doubts about the philosophical effectiveness and adequacy of the written word. The critique of *poiesis* (works of literary imitation or representation) in *Republic* is such that Socrates provisionally concludes that 'poets' or literary imitators should be politely banished from the philosophically just city until and unless "the kinds of poetry and representation which are designed merely to give pleasure can come up with a rational argument for their inclusion in a well governed community."[13]

Further, and perhaps more challenging, is the case against writing *per se* that Socrates relates in *Phaedrus*, that it will "atrophy people's memories"

> Trust in writing will make them remember things by relying on marks made by others, from outside themselves, not on their own inner resources, and so writing will make the things they have learnt disappear from their minds. (275a)

---
[13]Plato, *Republic*, (Oxford University Press: 1993), translated by Robin Waterfield, 607c, p.361.

Against that dismissal of the written word (where Plato's own writing paradoxically preserves the question and difficulty in philosophical memory), Socrates points to another, better use of words, a figurative form of 'writing' which emerges from but goes beyond the dialectical engagement in speech, its "legitimate brother."

> It is the kind that is written along with knowledge in the soul of the student. It is capable of defending itself, and knows how to speak to those it should and keep silent in the company of those to whom it shouldn't speak. (276a)[14]

It is part of Plato's artistry in the Dialogues to have them show, or enact rather more than what Socrates explicitly says by way of propositions or sustained logical argument.

For one thing, they seldom result in anything that resembles a formal conclusion or final resolution of a problem or question: in anything, that is, which amounts to coherent or settled *doctrine*. Characteristically, they record a certain dialectical process of examination, of question and attempted answers, wherein one or more of the 'characters' comes to recognise that they did not know what they thought they knew: Phaedrus in his dialogue, Euthyphro (on piety) in his, Laches (on courage) in his and Thrasymachus (on justice) in *Republic*, for example. In the face of Socratic questioning one character or another faces a certain kind of *aporia* where he is not only unable to give an account of what he thought he knew, but is also brought to see, so long as he continues the dialogue, that he faces certain real difficulties (of definition) if he is to *think more coherently* about, say, courage, piety, justice, moderation and wisdom or *sophia*. Now not all of the interlocutors are able to do this, and that is shown to be a philosophical failure on their parts. Thrasymachus angrily leaves Book II of *Republic* and Polus (in *Gorgias*) is shown to be unable to continue the *elenchus*, and so on.

It is this *aporia*, or intuition of an inability—a kind of ignorance—which faces the reader of the dialogues as he, in his soul as he reads, participates (or fails to) in the process of self-examination. The fully responsive reader faces a kind of test or *agon* (trial) commensurate with that described by Nicias in *Laches*:

---

[14] Plato, *Phaedrus*, (Oxford University Press: 2002), translated by Robin Waterfield, pp.69-70.

> ...whoever comes into close contact with Socrates and has any talk with him face to face, is bound to be drawn round and round by him in the course of an argument—though it may have started at first on a quite different theme—and cannot stop until he is led into giving an account of himself, of the manner in which he now spends his days, and of the kind of life he has lived hitherto; and when once he has been led into that, Socrates will never let him go until he has thoroughly and properly put all his ways to the test. (188a)[15]

Nicias tells us that he delights in such philosophical discourse. Much less comfortable with its insistent logical and moral pressure is Alcibiades in his complex, moving speech—rich with contextual, dramatic significance and irony—in the *Symposium* (215a-222b). He says of other great speakers (including Pericles) that "they never disturbed my mental composure or made me dissatisfied with the slavishness of my life," whereas Socrates has "made me think that the life I lead isn't worth living... to admit that I busy myself with Athenian politics when I'm far from perfect and should be doing something about myself instead." Alcibiades does not, and cannot, do so at the deepest level of discourse, and so he speaks as a failed lover (*erastes*) and one who is incapable of philosophy—"I make myself block my ears and run away".[16]

Part of what the dialogues represent, then, is an *exemplary* life and it is in terms of that life, which 'grounds' and illuminates the propositions and discourse of Socrates, that his full ethical significance is to be found and evaluated. Even the notorious Socratic paradoxes—that wisdom (*sophrosune*) is bound up with knowing that one does not know; that no-one commits evil knowingly; that it is better to suffer injustice than to act unjustly—gain much of their force and significance from their 'dramatic' contexts, from the fact that Socrates' discourse (as Plato presents it) is informed by the desires and drives, the motives and incapacities of his interlocutors and antagonists.[17]

Nonetheless, the Socratic life is characterised by its ability to "give an account" (*didonai logon*) of itself. In

---
[15] Plato, *Laches, Protagoras, Meno, Euthydemus* (Loeb Classical texts no. 165, 1924), translated by W.R.M. Lamb.
[16] Plato, *Symposium* (Oxford University Press: 1994), translated by Robin Waterfield, p.61.
[17] A detailed and comprehensive account of the philosophical dynamics of this is provided by Roslyn Weiss, *The Socratic Paradox and its Enemies* (University of Chicago Press:2006).

an illuminating comment on the passage from *Laches* I quoted above, Michel Foucault observed:

> ...giving an account of your life, your *bios*, is...not to give a narrative of the historical events that have taken place in your life, but rather to demonstrate whether you are able to show that there is a relation between the rational discourse, the *logos*, you are able to use, and the way that you live. Socrates is inquiring into the way that *logos* gives form to a person's style of life, for he is interested in discovering whether there is a harmonic relation between the two.[18]

Laches, who has not as yet heard or entered into discourse with him, prefigures the kind of harmony which is the philosophical virtue (*arête*) of Socrates.

> I have but a single mind, Nicias, in regard to discussions, or if you like, a double rather than a single one. For you might think me a lover, and yet also a hater of discussions: for when I hear a man discussing virtue or any kind of wisdom, one who is truly a man and worthy of of his argument, I am exceeding delighted; I take the speaker and his speech together, and observe how they sort and harmonize with each other. Such a man is exactly what I understand by "musical"—he has tuned himself with the fairest harmony, not that of the lyre or other entertaining instrument, but has made a true concord of his own life between his words and his deeds, not in the Ionian, no, nor in the Lydian, but simply in the Dorian mode, which is the sole Hellenic harmony. Such a man makes me rejoice with his utterance, and anyone would judge me then a lover of discussion, so eagerly do I take in what he says: but a man who shows the opposite character gives me pain, and the better he seems to speak, the more I am pained, with the result, in this case, that I am judged a hater of conversation.[19]

Socrates is presented as just such a man: there is a harmonic relation between his words (*logoi*) and his deeds (*erga*), the quality and bearing of his life. Or, to put it another way, there is no discrepancy, no asymmetry, between what he says and what he does. He is the *mousikos aner*—one whose discourse and life are in perfect accord. In that way alone does he become "worthy of his argument."

Here we find aspects of Heraclitus' cosmic "attunement" (which Anderson considers in lecture 19, pp. 64ff.) embodied as qualities of the ethical life. Moreover, that life has affinities

---

[18] Michele Foucault, in his account of *parrhesia* in early Greek thought, *Fearless Speech* (Semiotext(e): 2001). Edited by Joseph Pearson, p.91.
[19] Plato, *Laches*, op.cit., 188c-189a.

with the Pythagorean view (as Anderson put it) that 'goodness' is related to the different elements of the soul being in right relationship with each other—that it "consists in a harmony or attunement of the parts of the soul" (p.54). Yet even for the Pythagoreans, that theory was inescapably linked to ethics and to conduct.[20] In his treatment of Pythagoras, Anderson argues that "according to him, philosophy is a way of life and what the philosopher seeks is a right way of living." More generally, a student of Anderson's philosophy would find it illuminating to consider the importance that he places on "ways of life" in *Studies in Empirical Philosophy* in relation to these lectures.

Yet it might also be argued that in them Anderson underestimates the nature and concern of early Greek philosophy with "ways of life". One of the most eminent of contemporary Classicists, Pierre Hadot, has reminded us that ancient philosophy "is, at the same time and indissolubly, a discourse and a way of life which tend towards wisdom without ever achieving it," so that philosophical discourse was always part of, and anchored within, particular ways of life. To that extent, he argues, it is misleading to

> oppose discourse and way of life, as though they corresponded to theory and practice, respectively. Discourse can have a practical aspect, to the extent that it tends to produce an effect on the listener or reader... Insofar as way of life is concerned, it cannot, of course, be theoretic, but it can be theoretical—that is to say, contemplative.[21]

This, however, should not be seen as a contradiction of Anderson's view of, and engagement with, the early Greek philosophers. Both they and he were, in their different ways, in agreement that to "be thoroughly philosophic one must accept the consequences of any view which one holds" (p.192)—and that was to live them out, as it were.

Graham Cullum
June 2008

---

[20] For a recent account of the Pythagorean legends see Arnold Hermann, *To Think Like God: Pythagoras and Parmenides* (Parmenides Publishing: 2004).

[21] Pierre Hadot, *What is Ancient Philosophy?* (The Belknap Press: 2004) translated by Michael Chase, pp.4–5. See also, Pierre Hadot, *Philosophy as a Way of Life* (Blackwell: 1995), translated and with an Introduction by Arnold I. Davidson. Relevant ancillary material may be found in Marcel Detienne, *The Masters of Truth in Archaic Greece* (Zone Books: 1999), translated by Janet Lloyd; and Jean-Pierre Vernant, *The Origins of Greek Thought* (Cornell University Press: 1982).

Note on the text

There are two versions of the 1928 lectures on Greek Philosophy. The version in Anderson's handwriting held by the University of Sydney Archives is the source for this book (Personal Papers of John Anderson, Series 3, Item 4). There is also a typed version of student notes taken by Gaius McIntosh in the Philosophy III (Day) course of 1928. The typed notes correspond very closely to Anderson's handwritten notes and have been used to check against unclear passages in the handwriting. There are also informal statements made by Anderson included within the student notes which have been incorporated into the lectures presented here. Following the practice of earlier books in this series these informal comments appear in slightly smaller font and indented from the left. Three figures illustrating Pythagorean unit figures are adapted from the student notes rather than the handwritten notes and appear on page 47 below.

The McIntosh notes are in two sections. The section on the Pre-Socratics is 177 pages of typed lectures beginning in Lent Term 1928, Lecture 1 dated Tuesday 13th March. The course continued to meet on Tuesdays, Wednesdays and Fridays until Friday 6th July. This typescript section of the course was among the papers included within the Anderson Family Library at the University and has been transferred to the University Archives. The second section on the Socratic dialogues and on Aristotle's ethics was originally found at the Anderson family home at Turrumurra. A copy has been transferred to the University Archives. This second section is missing pages 178 to 201 and begins with Lecture 21 on Plato's dialogue *Euthyphro*. This lecture corresponds to Lecture 45 in Anderson's handwritten notes and in this book. That is to say, Lectures 40 to 44 introducing the Socratic dialogues are missing from the student notes.

The second section of the student notes also includes a handwritten covering note by Ruth Walker who speculated on the provenance of the notes. Missing the first section on the Pre-Socratics, Walker could only suggest that the notes may have been taken by G. F. McIntosh but then remarked

"McIntosh did not *sit* Philosophy III until 1929". She also remarked upon the odd numbering of the lectures in this section. The first section, however, is clearly attributed to McIntosh.

Marginal notes by Anderson in his handwritten lectures, notes which do not appear in the student notes, have been captured as footnotes prefaced by the identification "JA". The handwriting in these notes is particularly difficult to decipher and is occasionally marked in the book as "unclear".

The first complete typed copy of these lectures was produced by Ms. Julie Bishop to whom the editors are very grateful. The quality of her work on a very difficult manuscript was exceptional.

A list of books on Greek philosophy in the Anderson Family private library is included as an appendix to the lectures.

Lectures on Greek Philosophy 1928

Part I
Pre-Socratics

I
Introductory Lectures

Lecture 1

Early philosophy—science and mythological thinking—science and scepticism

It is important to have a general idea of what distinguishes the work of the early philosophers. Thought becomes philosophic when it ceases to be mythological. The character of mythological thinking is that it gives an account of things by reference to certain powers; a certain power commonly described as a spirit and sometimes as a deity is regarded as that which is responsible for bringing about a natural phenomenon. We have references to spirits which bring about storms and thunder, which inhabit trees and rivers, and these spirits are supposed to be the occasion of the behaviour of these things, that is, "Animism"—the theory which postulates an "anima" for every observable occurrence. The result of this animistic thinking is that anything in the nature of science is impossible. Inquiry can proceed only by reference to observation of facts and verification by means of these facts of theories formed in relation to facts.[1] Now under conditions of animistic thinking, it is quite impossible for this inquiry to proceed. (One person attributes an event to one spirit, another to another. There is no way of deciding.)

This fact indicates what is fundamentally necessary for scientific thinking, and the investigation of what is necessary for scientific thinking is a fairly accurate description of the work of philosophy. What is necessary is that explanations of facts should be of the same order as facts themselves. That is, they should be capable of being discussed and examined in exactly the same way as the facts. If what is offered as an explanation of a fact is something of a higher order than fact, then we find that it really gives no explanation. It is of no practical significance because we can see what difference this discovery makes only if we can question it and examine it in detail. To say, on the other hand, that a certain event

---
[1] [Ed.] The manuscript here has "in relation to (facts? practice?)."

has come about merely because there was in existence a power sufficient to bring it about is not really adding to our information. It does not show us how to bring about the event in case we should wish to do so. We may endeavour by placating the power; but since by hypothesis the power is beyond our observation we can't observe the effect our appeal has on it and we are therefore no nearer knowing how to bring the event about. Even if it comes about, we have no justification for saying that it was in any way due to the making of the appeal. In fact animistic thinking resolves itself into guessing. Having no means of determining that a certain action causes a certain event, or, in general, of determining the conditions under which the event comes about, we have simply to rely on guesswork. We can suggest that anything at all might be the determining factor and so come no nearer to systematising our views on the subject.[2]

Science, the working out of theories by means of strict verification of hypotheses and actual observation of facts, develops from (into) practical interests; and it is when men enter into new undertakings of a practical kind that they find it necessary to develop a more accurate science than they hitherto have had. Periods of expansion of trade for example are generally accompanied by considerable scientific progress and it is remarkable in that connection that philosophy first developed in Ionia—a trading centre having connections both with Persia and so forth to the East, and Greece and Italy to the West.

The working out of practical affairs makes accurate information necessary and makes it necessary to deal with observed facts by means of other facts which can likewise be observed instead of setting up abstract powers, the nature and types of activity of which could never be adequately investigated. Now this means that in terms of scientific thinking we are no longer concerned with two types of reality, namely, ordinary facts and things, as opposed to powers of a higher order. What is implied is that throughout our investigations we are dealing with things and activities which are all of the same order—the order of fact. And it

---

[2][JA] But we have "conviction"! (Passion as an *argument*. N.B. Importance of the Milesians: in suggesting it *might* be anything at all, water or what not. No truths *prior* to inquiry, that is, prior to hypothesis. *Cf.* David Hume.)

is in relation to this necessity of science that philosophy comes forward as the explicit study of what constitutes this single order of events—of what is implied in belonging to this order. Or, alternatively, science depends on there being some common denominator of things, on there being no fundamental division of reality but everything being real in the same sense. Philosophy then inquires into what this common denominator is. And this inquiry in its most general form is inquiry into what we mean when we say of anything that it *is* or exists, or what we mean by calling anything a *thing*. Whatever differences things may have from one another, they are all called things, all are said to be, and it has to be considered just what is conveyed when these statements are made; and what is at least indicated in the first place is that there are not higher and lower orders of being, that being means precisely the same no matter what different things it may be applied to.[3] Or, to put it in relation to human activities, nothing is above discussion: everything which is capable of being asserted is likewise capable of being questioned. Anything which can be used as an observation to verify or falsify a supposition can likewise be regarded as a supposition to be verified or falsified by other observations. That is to say, what is implied by the very existence of science and inquiry is that there are no privileged truths, no truths which stand above other truths and in relation to which the latter are to be judged. Now this tendency to elevate certain truths above others (put them in a privileged position) is one which recurs even among scientists. In recent science, it was customary to treat the laws of nature as standing over and above the facts of nature, as somehow guiding and controlling them. To take this view of a law like the law of gravity is to treat a fact (namely, the fact that bodies do behave in a particular way in relation to one another) as if it were a power of the animistic sort—as if it were a certain spirit operating on the bodies and of a quite different order of reality from bodies themselves. And then arises the difficulty of determining exactly how these objects of higher and lower reality are related to one another. In order to recognise them as related at all, it

---

[3][JA] "Law of Identity"!

is necessary to consider them as falling within the same reality. Now when contradictions of this kind arise we have a natural tendency in the direction of scepticism (the view that there are a large number of problems simply insoluble and which leave our thinking incapable of systematisation and without any common basis). So that we may regard the object of philosophy as being to protect science from attacks of scepticism (scepticism being fundamentally the view that there is no common denominator of things, and philosophy standing for the opposite view). And science in the course of its development itself from time to time leads up to scepticism, and it is just at these times that philosophy is required to re-establish science on a sound footing.

Lecture 2

Philosophy and mythological thinking continued

In the case of mythology,[4] explanation is by entities which are supposed to be at a higher level than the facts and not subject to the same interpretation. On the other hand, in science an account is given of facts in terms of other facts, so that there is no point at which a question or doubt cannot be raised: there is nothing which may not be made the subject of scientific investigation. Now until scientific thinking has begun, there can be no philosophy (cf. Burnet) but once we do have scientific thinking, our very scientific procedure immediately leads us on to philosophical problems. If explanations are of the same order as things they explain, it is immediately suggested that all things belong to this single order, that there is a common denominator of things, namely, what is implied by calling them things. There must be some fundamental character conveyed by the term—a character which is common to all things in spite of the many ways in which they differ from one another. Again, we may ask—"what is implied when we say of anything that it is?" If we can give any further description of a thing, we must at least be able to say that it is. And the philosophical question is precisely "what is conveyed by that fundamental statement?"[5]

---
[4][Ed.] Lecture 2 in Anderson's handwritten notes corresponds to Lecture 3 in the McIntosh student notes dated Friday March 16th 1928.
[5][JA] "Being" means having *place and character or* active complexity (occurring).

Now in the history of Greek philosophy, many very different answers were given to this question. The Milesians who founded philosophy in Greece considered that the common denominator of things, that which was conveyed by saying that a thing is, was some particular quality or substance, out of which things are made. Thus we find Thales, first of the Milesians, maintaining that everything is composed of water. Anaximenes considered that everything is composed of air. These of course are very crude early theories, but what is important about them is the way in which they attempt to deal with the question of the nature of what is, and the fact that whatever answer they give, they do raise the question. Now the Milesian way of thinking, although it was modified by subsequent philosophers, did very definitely influence all the Greek philosophers up to the time of Socrates: and thus the last of the pre-Socratic schools, namely, the Atomists, still maintained a view of the nature of what is which is very similar to the Milesian. But they no longer specify any particular quality or substance, such as water or air, but say that things are composed of what may be called substance in general or "matter". Now that view, while it depends on the Milesian theory of a primary substance, is also influenced by theories of the Eleatic school (founded by Parmenides of Elea) who maintained that all that could really be said about what is, is simply that it is: that if we say anything more about it, we are describing it in terms of what it is not, that is, erroneously. And from this he derived the conclusion that there can't be many things but only one thing, namely, being itself. The atoms in which Leucippus and his followers believed were simply separate parts of *being*, each being composed entirely of this fundamental matter, but all being separated from one another by intervening space. Now it may be argued that on this question Parmenides is correct, that is, if we once admit the existence of things whose sole character is being or matter, then it is strictly impossible to distinguish one from another, so that we can't maintain that there are many beings but are reduced to saying that there is only one. This difficulty brought out in the history of Greek philosophy is one which necessarily arises in connection with any theory of matter, so that it may be said of modern physics that when it speaks of matter, it is speaking of the abstract being into which the early Greek philosophers inquired and is faced with the same difficulties as they were. Accordingly, if it can be said that the Atomists fail to find a solution for difficulties raised by Parmenides, then the same can be said of modern physics. In fact in taking atoms as the fundamental reality the Atomists are making their science mythological: they are taking the character of indivisibility as being of a higher order than all other characters and as giving an explanation of these other characters but not itself requiring or being able to have any explanation. The type of view current among modern philosophers and physicists, namely, that there are certain primary qualities of things which constitute their fundamental reality and, on the other hand, secondary qualities which do not belong to the things, or do not belong to them in the same sense—this doctrine is of a mythological nature. It distinguishes a higher from a lower reality and it raises some objects above discussion. If, on the other hand, there is to be a common measure or denominator of things, then this will have to apply as much to the supposed accidental qualities as to supposed fundamental qualities, and accordingly it is for philosophy to point out the division in reality which will follow from accepting these scientific theories. And once a division in reality has been formulated, then scepticism is inevitable, because only by taking the standpoint of acquaintance with a reality more fundamental than either of the two kinds of reality which have been distinguished, would it be possible not merely to find a connection between the two but even to assert their distinction. And this, on the assumption in question, would be impossible. And this implies that we could not know in what sense to take any assertion whatever, since it might be supposed to be the assertion of a fact of higher order or again of lower, and unless there were a common order this question could never be resolved. Or, putting the matter in a slightly different way, if once a distinction is made between what is ultimately real and what is apparently real, then science, the investigation and discussion of all phenomena, can't be thoroughly carried out. If it be asked how it happens that science leads on to scepticism in this way, the answer is that any science is concerned with a particular set of phenomena, and any scientist with a particular set of problems. That is, before investigation can proceed, certain things have to be regarded as important and other things neglected, and in consequence there is the danger of the former things being taken to be actually superior to the latter, instead of being merely more useful for a particular purpose. And again, when a particular explanation has been found to fit a large number of cases, there is always the danger of its being applied universally, so that those cases which in reality it does not fit are misrepresented so as to make it apply to them.

Lecture 3

The foundation of science

Scientific thinking develops after, and is opposed to, mythological thinking; leads to scepticism, and new form of mythology. Philosophy, therefore, leads to setting up a single order in which science can exist.

Philosophy states what is the foundation of science in determining a common nature of things, a common measure or common denominator. Whatever differences may be between one thing and another, they must have in common whatever is implied by the statement that they both exist. It is necessary that they should have these common characters and conditions in order that they should all be subject to discussion, should all be capable of being asserted or known, and in order that these assertions may be tested and if possible proved.

Now we find, as a matter of fact, that this theory that everything is to be subject to discussion and that nothing can be taken as certain but can only be affirmed if in our experience we find it to be the case—this theory is itself denounced as sceptical. And it is the endeavour to utilise the theory for sceptical purposes that is the mark of the school of Sophists and that is directly opposed by Socrates. It is argued that if we are to have knowledge at all (scientific knowledge) we do require some ultimate criterion or principle, and in the absence of such a principle, since we can have no certainty, we are at liberty to believe what we like. The general answer to that view is that in the mere fact of belief we already have all that is required for founding science, because to believe anything is to believe that it is true. Whatever we believe is taken by us to be an absolute fact. And so to say that it is a mere opinion of ours, where opinion is treated as something unrelated to fact, is to misrepresent the very nature of opinion. In other words, unless there are facts, there can't be opinions. We can't tell in advance, apart from experience, whether a given opinion is true or false. But even if it is false, this implies that its contradictory is true. In other words, it implies that there is some fact to which the opinion is related. And it may be further pointed out that to say that anything is a mere opinion is in itself to advance a statement which we take to be actually true, to be a matter of fact. So that to deny that absolute facts can be known is a self-contradictory or incoherent position, and is inconsistent with the possibility of making any statements at all. This is part of the case that Socrates brings against the Sophists.

II
The Milesians

Lecture 3 (continued)

The Milesians—the common denominator as a fundamental substance

The work of the Milesians was done mainly in the early part of the sixth century B.C. There are difficulties in determining their precise dates. We shall take Burnet's dates as sufficiently correct for our purposes. (Thales 624-546; Anaximander 610-546; Anaximenes 585-528).

Anaximander was a pupil and follower of Thales, Anaximenes a follower of Anaximander. Each developed the theory of his predecessor in a new direction.

Each of these men in seeking for a common denominator of things set up a particular kind of thing as being what is real, that is, as being the substance of which things are composed, whatever differences they may have from one another. Thus Thales says things are composed of water: whatever else may be said of any given thing, we can always at least say that it is water. Similarly in the case of Anaximenes, we can always at least say of a thing that it is air. Anaximander has a more complicated theory according to which the substance of which all things are composed is a certain *boundless* or *unlimited being*[1] which is not correctly described by any one of the characters we ordinarily find in things, and which may even be said to be identified in his theory with *space*—on the understanding that space is taken to be a thing of some sort, and not as we should more naturally say, a medium or region in which things exist. Now this type of theory in which a fundamental substance is set up, has been interpreted in the course of the history of philosophy in terms of subsequent theories. Thus Aristotle describes the position of Thales as being that water is the "material cause" of things. That is, he expresses the matter in terms of his own philosophy.[2] Again it is suggested that this substance is something out of which

---
[1] [Ed.] *apeiron*, unlimited, indefinite.
[2] [Ed.] Metaphysics Book I, Chapter 3. 983a24–983b27.

things come; that it is a source or origin of things[3] and still further it is suggested that the substances of the Milesians are to be taken as in each case descriptive of the whole of reality of which any particular thing is a part or aspect. Now if we take the substances of the Milesians as being a source or origin, then we are representing their theory as of a mythological character, and as setting up an opposition between different kinds of reality—the reality of source, and, on the other hand, the reality of things which come from it. If this source is represented as an explanation of the things we find in ordinary experience, then it is not itself subject to the same sort of examination, and thus the fundamental assumption of science is destroyed. It is the particular merit of the Milesians that in the main at least, they abandoned questions of origin, of how things came to be constituted as they are, and took up the question of how things are constituted now or at any time. And strictly on that theory, if there were a particular state of things from which a second state of things had arisen, the question is not to explain the second by the first but to show what the two have in common, to show what is characteristic of any state of things, whether it is an origin or result. Because the fact that we can discuss both shows that they are both subject to conditions implied by affirmation and investigation.

Secondly, the setting up of a common substance of things is not to be taken as implying the conception of a total reality of which various things are forms. The latter view is *monism*, the view taken by Parmenides. It may be argued that the Milesian position, if fully worked out, would result in monism—would result in the view that ultimately there is only one real thing which we may describe as the whole or the universe (the "One"). But even if, consistently with some of their views, the Milesians ought to have gone on to draw the conclusion that there is only one thing that really exists, still that was not their intention. They were concerned to show what were the characters of any particular thing that did exist, but the mere fact that a number of things have common characters does not imply that they can or need be united. If, for example, we take the character of humanity, then we

---

[3][Ed.] *arche*, beginning, starting point, principle, ultimate underlying substance.

know that there are a great many individuals who have this character but although they all have this in common, it does not follow that they constitute a whole, that they can all be taken together as making up one being. There might be men in different places who had no sort of communication with one another, and accordingly to treat them all as parts or constituents of a single entity to be described as *mankind* would really be misleading.

To say then that things have all something in common does not imply that they can be summed up or united, that there is any aggregate of things. And we can't maintain that it was the intention of the Milesians to investigate any such aggregate, but only to consider properties of any particular thing wherever it might be. At the same time their actual procedure makes a result of this kind almost inevitable, for if water, for example, is to be taken as the real character of a thing, as its fundamental reality, and if any other property that might be assigned to it does not really give us information about the substance of the thing, then any two things are substantially identical, so that we are not in a position to distinguish one thing from another—so that, as Parmenides argued, we can't avoid the conclusion that all things are one. But in spite of these inconsistencies, it is still important to remember that the Milesians set out neither to explain the origin of things nor to reduce things to one, but simply to indicate what is meant by a thing or what is to be understood by existence. (Clearly, then they were wrong in thinking that existence is substance or quality.)

Lecture 4

Common quality as unity within diversity—no real diversity possible—the question of change

The attempt to find a substance of things may be described as the search for unity amid variety, and this is commonly taken to be characteristic of science. Science pursues this method when it establishes general laws, for example, the law of gravitation is held to be particularly important because of the great variety of phenomena of which it enables us to give an account. It enables us to account for such diverse occurrences as the motions of the bodies in the solar system, tides in the ocean, and it applies alike to a stone falling to the ground and a balloon rising into the air. Now the difficulty about this establishment of a common denominator of things is that it may lead us to *reduce* everything to this common denominator, that is, not to show unity amid variety, but to argue that there is no real variety at all, that all things are in the end the same. And this is a conclusion which cannot be avoided if we take what is common to all things as a particular quality, such as that of being water. Then, that particular quality appears to have nothing in common with any other quality (*cf.* Forms as Ultimate) so that if that quality conveys what is meant by existence, other qualities must be said not to exist. The position is different in the case of a limited class of things. We may say that by the term *man* we intend to convey qualities common to all men and no others. But this does not mean that the other qualities of men are explained away, because an individual who belongs to the class of men may at the same time belong to many other classes. But what we are investigating (in the case of the Milesian's philosophy) is that which is conveyed by saying that a thing belongs to any class whatever. And if we identify that with a particular quality, then we are undoubtedly putting it on higher level than other qualities and suggesting that the latter are unreal or illusory. The setting up of a common measure of things is not intended to involve their *reduction* to the common measure, so that there is really no difference between them. But it does in the end involve this, if the common measure is identified with some particular quality or some particular kind of actual thing. If we say that all is water, then we can be confronted with the fact that in ordinary experience some things are said to be water and other things not to be water. If we say that the latter really are water all the time, we would appear to be saying that they are presented to us in an inaccurate or illusory way. (Question of what *illusion* is.) This result is inevitable if a measure of such kind is set up, although this was not Thales' intention.[4]

One of the most important questions for the Greek philosophers was the question of *change*. In our observation of things we seem to be confronted with a number of things

---
[4][JA] X is = X is water. (Or Water is *being*—of things.)

that change and a number of things that do not change. And the question is: "What have these different classes in common?" We speak of states and, on the other hand, of processes. We speak of situations and also of events, and yet we say of all of them that they occur or exist. Now any attempt to reduce either of these classes of phenomena to the other would seem to misrepresent the facts; as, for example, the doctrine of the Eleatics that change is unreal and that whatever exists exists permanently. Any solution of this kind is really a denial of the problem. But it may be said that Thales in taking water to be the common measure of things was endeavouring to combine that which is in a particular state with that which is in process. Water is a particular sort of recognisable thing: it has a certain character. At the same time it is particularly unstable or restless; it is always passing from one place to another, and also from one condition to another. For these reasons water seems to be a kind of thing in which state and process are united and therefore to be capable of measuring states and processes in general. While in this way we may find reasons in support of the fundamental contention of Thales, it does not immediately appear why he should ever have formulated this theory. There seems to be no obvious reason for taking water to be more important than any other kind of thing that we observe. Now here it is to be remembered that philosophy and science arise as a result of practical research. The Ionians were at the commercial centre of things in those times and it is just because various practical activities were of great importance in their public life that their need of theory as a solution of practical problems arose. Now what these practical problems were may be gathered from the stories narrated about Thales even though we do not accept them as literally true. It is said that he diverted the course of a river, measured the distance of ships at sea, predicted in one year an exceptionally good crop of olives and made a fortune. Without accepting these stories as historical we may take them as indicating that Thales in particular and the men of his time and country in general, were interested in military, naval and agricultural matters. Now in connection with all these, the cycle of the seasons is of importance, and this is also a matter of great concern to primitive men in general. Variations of weather are of special importance in agriculture, but they are for the most part incapable of being controlled by men. And it was natural in consequence of this that we should have among the primitive men mythology instead of science, and the attempt to propitiate powers which could not be affected in any other way. But as commerce develops and the various other arts which enter into the life of cities, we find that even where it is impossible directly to control such conditions it is possible in various ways to adapt ourselves to them. It is possible if not to predict with absolute accuracy what the weather is going to be, at least to be prepared to meet a number of alternative contingencies which we might reasonably regard as possible. Just as the consideration of the seasons is of prime importance in this connection, so the primitive theory of elements is of importance in dealing with these situations. As Burnet points out, the actual term "element" does not appear in Greek philosophy until the time of Empedocles (born 490) and also he was the first to describe those elements as earth, water, air and fire. But among the Milesians we have a corresponding doctrine of the *opposites* (the hot and the cold, the wet and the dry) and as we find in the theory of Anaximander the character of a particular thing is determined by the proportion of each of these four opposites which it contains. Now this theory does not appear to have been so explicitly stated by Thales but it indicates the kind of question he was concerned with. In saying that all things are water, or that water is the common measure of things, he would appear to suggest that we can determine the character of things by the amount of moisture that is present in them, and that one season is distinguished from another by the position which water, or the moist, has at that time. If we can describe the character of seasons by the position in which water is found in them, then we may be able to show at what times and under what conditions one season will give place to another. We may say that a certain season will be maintained so long as evaporation is taking place, or another, so long as freezing obtains. That is, we are not to think simply of water as having a given character, we are also to think of it as having different states and passing naturally from one to another. These processes of evaporation and solidification are to be regarded as natural characteristics of water or stages in its history and by means of these variations, taken to be characteristic of water itself, we are to account for seasonal changes—in fact for the whole of what we now call meteorology. (There was no distinction between meteorology and astronomy for the Milesians.)

Lecture 5

Thales (624–546) and the beginning of philosophy—on the nature of things

Considering the beginning of philosophy in the work of *Thales* (624–546) we find it arises out of the concurrence of several lines of inquiry, out of the need for arriving at a conclusion on certain practical affairs and need at the same time for finding a method of settling any dispute that might arise on these particular matters. That is, the notion of a common measure of things (of all things being commensurable) indicates the possibility of finding some way of settling any disagreement, namely, by applying or referring to this common measure. At the same time the existence of a common measure is suggested by the fact that several lines of investigation are found to run together; by the discovery that the separation of life and human interests into different spheres supposed to be independent of one another—this separation which is made for practical purposes—does not satisfy a number of equally practical requirements. In practice we may suppose Thales found that certain elements were of importance alike in military, naval and agricultural questions, just as at a later time Socrates found that similar questions arose in the working out of mathematics and, on the other hand, of ethics. And what Thales found to be important in each case was the question of what are now called the four elements and of what the Milesians took to be the fundamental opposites, namely the hot, the cold; the wet and the dry, a question which was closely related to that of the seasons. We will find that Heraclitus, who brought the theory initiated by the Milesians to its greatest perfection, was also fundamentally concerned with such phenomena as the seasons; that in fact he took seasonal or cyclic recurrence to be in effect the common measure of things or their fundamental nature. Thales, finding that his various investigations led him in a common direction, considered that his problem was to formulate a theory of the nature of things (or their common measure). The particular way in which he did so led to difficulties in the subsequent history of philosophy. That is to say, in taking the nature of things as a certain quality or substance, he not only raised the difficulty of finding what was common to such a quality and to that which *had* the quality, or again what was common to the quality in its own nature and its existence in a particular place, but he also raised the difficulty involved in the opposition of static and dynamic, the difficulty of finding something which was common to states and processes. And it was as a result of these obscurities in the theory of Thales that the essentially sceptical theory of Parmenides, according to which there is only one being to which nothing ever happens, came to be formulated.

According to Thales, then, the single substance out of which all the variety of things are made, or more precisely of which they are all at any time composed, was water. And this is connected with the theory of the seasons in so far as any season would be defined by the extent to which water was present in it and by the forms which it took, and the processes which it was undergoing. The solutions offered by Thales are not to be regarded as simply static, that is, as characterising any given thing or phenomenon by the proportions which it contained of water in its three different forms, solid, liquid and gaseous. But on the contrary we are to think of the *processes* of solidification and evaporation as going on all the time. And these are to be considered as natural characteristics of water, so that to some extent Thales may be held to have anticipated the doctrine of Heraclitus that what was fundamental to things was a cyclic succession of changes through various distinct states. And again in holding that what is fundamental to things is something of a fluid character, Thales takes up a position which is in line with the statement attributed to Heraclitus, that everything flows, $\pi\alpha\nu\tau\alpha\ \rho\epsilon\iota$. If then we interpret the doctrine of Thales as being simply that everything is fluid or that it involves changes and succession, then we may find in his theory as in that of Heraclitus the establishment of a common measure of what are ordinarily called states and, on the other hand, what we call processes. But the fact that Thales called his substance *water*, that is, introduced the consideration of a special quality in addition to the general character of fluidity, he may be said to have failed to solve the problem which he had set himself, because in our ordinary observations we call some things water and say that other things are not water. Now if the meaning of the term is to be broadened so as to include everything, then it becomes correspondingly vague. And in saying that the nature of things is to be water, we are merely saying that the nature of things is to be real. If, on the other hand, we retain for the term water something of the particular meaning which it has in ordinary speech, then either in saying that all things are water we are maintaining what is obviously false, or we are putting forward what is really a mythological theory, namely, that water is in some way superior to all other substances or qualities, that it somehow dominates or determines them.

Fragments of Thales' Doctrine.

(1) The earth floats on the water.

(2) Water is the material cause (Aristotle) of things.

(3) The magnet is alive, for it has the power of attracting iron.[5]

Anaximander (610–c.546) appears to have realised the difficulties to which the theory of Thales led—namely, the difficulty of giving a common description to states and processes, and the difficulty of saying that what was apparently water and what was apparently not water were really the same. Now the former difficulty arose only because Thales had chosen a particular substance like water as the common denominator of things and not because there was any real difficulty in reconciling states and processes. Accordingly Anaximander is really going further wrong than Thales when he proceeds, as he does, to give two quite independent accounts of states and processes or, to put it in the terminology of the time, of being and becoming. And

---

[5] John Burnet, *Early Greek Philosophy*, 4th edition, London: Adams and Charles Black, 1930 (1st ed., 1892) pp. 47–48. [Ed.:] Anderson omits in the 3rd fragment on the magnet "All things are full of gods."

as regards the second point, Anaximander is certainly right in saying that we can't call everything water while the term water stands for a particular sort of object. But in solving this difficulty Anaximander decides that no particular quality can be taken as common to all things, but retains the notion of Thales that what is common to all things must be some substance. And accordingly he formulates his theory of the boundless, that is, of a substance with no particular form of its own (unqualified "matter") and that is a conception which can solve no practical problem and which leads directly on to the negative theory of Parmenides.

Lecture 6

Anaximander (610–546)—the unlimited or the boundless

Any attempt to say that a certain nature is the real nature of things must necessarily fail because it must be contrasted with other qualities. The same applies if substance be substituted for quality for it is a character, for which an adjective could be used. It does not apply to everything. *Cf.* Idealism in modern philosophy (the only ultimate reality is mind). The same problems are still affecting philosophy.

To consider the way in which Anaximander (610–546) developed the theory of Thales: he appears to have believed that Thales, in regarding all things as forms of water, was taking as a common character of things what was in reality a special form or particular kind of thing, or, as it may be put in terms of the opposites, that Thales was exaggerating the moist at the expense of the dry. Accordingly he formulated the theory of the *boundless* or *unlimited* from which the various things that we know (hot, cold, moist, dry) are supposed to be separated out and into which as their common ground they afterwards pass. That is to say, any difference which we find in ordinary inspection of things has arisen from what was undifferentiated, and this difference will in time disappear and be replaced by the undifferentiated. Now in taking this view Anaximander has departed to some extent from the fundamental line of inquiry which we take to be characteristic of the Milesian school and in fact of philosophy in general—inquiry, that is, into the nature of things, into what things *are* anywhere and at any time. In raising the question of the origin and destiny of things, he is making a division between what things *were*, what they *are* and what they *will be*, instead of trying to discover what is common to things in all their states; that is, what is characteristic of things whether in the past, present or future.

Now it is possible that Thales also thought of water in this way, that is, as something out of which things have come and into which they return, as a form which any particular thing has at one time but not as characterising things at all times. And this view is supported by the fact that in Milesian theory in general we have a definite order among the four elements—fire, air, water, earth. That order was expressed in terms of density, earth being the most dense and fire the least in the theory of Anaximenes, and in the theory of Anaximander it was expressed in terms of distance from the centre of any particular *world*. In all the theories it is recognised that things pass from one of these forms to another, and this is the order in which the passage takes place; that is, before earth could turn into air, it would require to go through (the form of) water. We see then that both Thales and Anaximenes take one of the intermediate forms as the measure of things, the fundamental form, and they consider that by means of processes of solidification and evaporation the mean or intermediate form passes into the extreme. So far we may say that these three philosophers are in agreement in taking as fundamental something intermediate between the things that we find to be definitely different. But the difficulty that Anaximander seems to have seen is this—that if we say that earth is simply solidified water or that fire is simply air in a less dense form, the question is: What sort of air or water is air or water itself? Why should one sort of thing be described as air without qualification and another as air with a qualification (when they are all equally *air*)? In what way does the common term help us to understand this distinction or to understand under what conditions one form gives place to another? Objections and difficulties of this type seem to arise on any view which takes as the common denominator of things something specific. In terms of this criticism Anaximander set up as the common denominator of things something which was not any one of the four opposites or of the four elements. What is common to the moist and the dry can't be either moist or dry unless the whole distinction is unsound. Similarly with hot and cold, and with earth and air etc. Since then it cannot have any one of these specific characters what is common to things must be unspecific or indeterminate. It is sometimes argued that the *unlimited* or *boundless* of Anaximander doesn't mean anything indeterminate but means that which is infinite in space. But we find it necessary to argue that in the theory of Anaximander, the *boundless* has both of these characteristics, that is, that it is both indeterminate and unlimited in extent. For in order to say that it is limited in extent we should require to be able to distinguish it from that which surrounded it and therefore we should require to recognise it as having some specific character. We find also that in the theory of the Pythagoreans, the *unlimited* is regarded as being indeterminate and infinite. In fact some of the difficulties of Anaximander's theory would be avoided if the boundless were identified with space itself. In space we have something which by itself has no specific quality and which is also infinitely extended. But if that view were adopted it would no longer be possible to think of the boundless as the origin or source of things.

Accordingly since what is common to the moist and the dry cannot be either of those characters, it must be regarded, Anaximander thinks, as something intermediate between them, something which is a mixture of both but has not the definite characters of either. As against Thales, then, Anaximander will maintain that there are certain things which are not water and that the common ground of the two is something from which water and what is not water may be separated out: something which may be divided into moist and dry. In order to account for the occurrence of differences we have to assume an initial separation. In order to account for change, that is, for the fact that observed differences are not permanent, we have to assume that things so divided can be united again, and go to form a piece of this indeterminate matter from which they arose. In accordance with this view, the moist and the dry are not to be thought of as entirely apart from one another but they are to be considered as differences within the boundless, as potential differences which can be made actual or can cease to be actual and thus the *unit* of being, the least that we can observe as a specific (actual) thing, is not any single object that might be moist or dry, hot or cold, but it is a system within which opposition holds between these opposites. And any such system is surrounded by the boundless. If this were not so, then when the moist was separated from the dry they might become entirely apart from one another and accordingly we might have entirely different kinds of reality. But since they must be thought of in relation to one another, they must be incapable of this complete separation and accordingly they must be surrounded by the boundless. And since any such system is surrounded in this way, it can always be added to by further separation from the surrounding mass and can always be diminished by the fusion of opposites (their "encroachment on one another") and their return to the undifferentiated mass in which they exist.

Lecture 7

Anaximander continued—astronomy advanced—influence upon the Pythagoreans

The position of Anaximander involves these four conceptions

(1) the boundless, or indeterminate and infinite mass;

(2) the conception of a *system* existing within that mass;

(3) the processes of separation whereby opposites come to be out of what was intermediate;

(4) the process of fusion whereby opposition ceases to be by encroachment of opposites on one another and their return to the intermediate and indefinite form.

And in the boundless are innumerable systems of this kind which are constantly emerging from the boundless and returning to it, constantly increasing and diminishing.

Now when this theory of division and fusion has been set up we no longer have a common measure of things. We have on the contrary two kinds of states (namely, the boundless itself and the world or system) and two kinds of processes (separation and fusion) and no common character or common description of any two of these has been given, let alone of all four. We can say that the boundless exists, that the systems exist, and that the processes of separation and fusion exist, but we have no way of enumerating what is meant by existence in each of these four cases. If the boundless really expressed the common nature of things, expressed, that is, the nature of existence, then it would have to be applicable not only to itself but also to the systems and again to the two kinds of process. So that Anaximander just like Thales seems to be applying a given term both to itself and to its opposites. Alternatively, if the boundless is really distinguished from the systems, then it must be a *specific kind* of thing and not the common ground of things, and we should have to inquire what was common to the boundless and the systems. And further it may be said that if specific things do come from the boundless, then for that reason also it must have a specific character of its own.[6] Anaximander has become involved in these difficulties because he has departed from the question of what things *are* and has substituted for it, or confused it with, the question how things come to be. Now if a separation is made between being and becoming (state and process) we have the insoluble problem of showing what is common to the two; what is involved, that is, in calling them both *real*. The result of this division is that those who called one of the two real were bound to say the other was not real. Those who said that reality was static had, in the end, as Parmenides showed, to deny that there was such a thing as motion or change. And this denial had to be combined with the denial of any differences between things. On the other hand, Heraclitus, in denying the static, in arguing that all things were processes, did not in taking up that position maintain that only becoming was real and being was unreal: he maintained on the contrary that being and becoming are identical, or that all existence takes the form of process, but that this does not prevent it from being quite specific.

We may say, however, that though Anaximander does not succeed in finding a common measure of things, the theory

---

[6][JA] Solution of *problem*: what is "difference" between places where a system arises and where it does not?

which he does propound is of scientific importance, and as a result of his investigations, astronomy in particular is notably advanced. We have seen that in his theory each system is constituted by the interrelation of the opposites. Now he contends that within each system the cold and the moist tend towards the centre, while hot and dry tend towards the circumference. Taking the earth as centre, we find that evaporation leads to rising and solidification to falling. Accordingly Anaximander came to the conclusion that each system is encompassed by fire, this being again surrounded by the indeterminate boundless. It is in the heavens, which appear to encompass the earth, that fiery bodies (in particular, the sun) are found. Now this gives the notion of a spherical system with earth at the centre. This notion arises from the conception of space as infinite and that again arises from the fact that we can't think of it as limited. Thus when once our attention is drawn to the notion of space, we are bound to come to the conclusion of Anaximander that there is in reality no absolute up and down—that "up" merely means away from a certain body, arbitrarily chosen as point of reference, and *down* means in the direction of that selected body. Now, when once this has been recognised, it is easy to suppose that the earth has an opposite side to that on which we are. And this conclusion was drawn by Anaximander though he formed the theory that earth was not a sphere but a cylinder. Once the conclusion has been arrived at, it is supported by various astronomical phenomena and in particular by the rising and setting of the sun, which if it is the same body from one day to another, we must assume to have passed under the earth during the night. Now this theory led directly to the discovery in the Pythagorean school of details of the solar system. The Pythagoreans, pursuing these inquiries and distinguishing planets from fixed stars, arrived at the notion of a planetary system containing earth but of which earth was not the centre. And actually at about the birth of Plato, the theory was put forward in Pythagorean circles that the centre of the planetary system was the sun. As a result, however, of the influence of Aristotle, the view that the earth was the centre again became accepted, and it was not until the time of Copernicus that the true theory of the solar system was rediscovered.

That was one of the influences which Anaximander had upon the Pythagoreans. But he also influenced them by his doctrine of the separation of the worlds and the boundless, that is, making them different kinds of reality, and by the division he set up between being and becoming. As a result of this we have the Pythagorean division of reality, or of the ultimate principles of reality, into the limit and the unlimited, and though this theory did not prevent them from pursuing astronomical and mathematical investigations, it led them in the end to insoluble problems even within those special spheres. The problems which arise, according to this type of mathematical theory, a theory, that is, dependent on the rejection of processes, were pointed out by Zeno in his famous paradoxes. What these paradoxes showed was that mathematical theory could not be pursued beyond a certain point on the basis of any ultimate division in reality and that what was required was a new philosophy which would show that this supposed division did not really exist. And in default of such a demonstration the only possible outcome was a purely sceptical position. That is what Zeno showed, and the sceptical position involved in Eleaticism itself was further developed by the Sophists, while the philosophic theory required to solve these difficulties was introduced by Socrates and more fully and satisfactorily worked out by Plato. What Socrates and Plato gave was a new statement of the foundations of science.

Lecture 8

Anaximander criticised—Anaximenes (585-528)—primary substance air

The system in which we live, that is, our particular world (it being allowed that there are innumerable other worlds) has the cylindrical earth in the centre, and the fiery heavens round about. According to Anaximander's theory, the first separation that is made is that between fire and not-fire, that is, out of the boundless comes a moist mass with fire fitting closely round about it like bark round a tree. This being the primary state of things, where what is hot and dry

The Milesians

is opposed to what is cold and moist, further developments are occasioned by the interaction of these opposites; the heat of the fire breaks up the inner mass into vapours and something solid, the vapours lying between the fire and the central mass, which consists of both earth and water. These vapours in turn have a certain effect on the heavens; they cause *it* to be broken up into a number of rings of fire in place of a continuous fiery surface. And Anaximander contends that these rings consist of fire enclosed in vapour, but that they have a certain aperture through which the fire can be seen; so that what we call the sun, for example, is simply the fire shining through this opening in the ring. The earth surrounded by these rings swings free in the centre of the system. That is to say, Anaximander's clearer conception of space indicates the weakness of those theories according to which the position of a body in a particular place is to be explained by something supporting it. That is no explanation because we have to go on to say what supports this secondary body, and so on indefinitely. And the very notion of supporting implies the conception of an absolute up and down. But if we think of infinite space, then when two bodies are in contact we might say indifferently that either supports the other, and by a further continuation of these processes of interaction, opposites will gradually encroach on one another, their opposition will disappear, and the system will return to the boundless.

Now in this theory, as we have seen, there is a certain incoherence in that the assumption is made that there is a substance from which all things originate and into which they all return, and we can find nothing in common between the universal substance and the particular systems. At the same time, it is of the greatest scientific importance to point out that there is a question of the origin of the solar system as much as of anything in it; and also it is of the greatest importance to have formulated the conception of a solar system, even if earth is taken to be its centre—a system from which the fixed stars are excluded. Now these important astronomical results are the result of the removal of certain prejudices, of certain conceptions which will not stand logical examination—in particular, the conception of an absolute up and down.[7] But what was required in order that these prejudices might be removed, was the original willingness to discuss all things in the same way, to place them all on a common level, and not to look for special agencies beyond the objects which we can actually observe. So that, even although this standpoint has not been fully formulated, there is an implicit philosophy in these investigations, and it is this which makes discovery possible, even though in the actual working out of these theories the common measure is lost sight of and a mythological element introduced. Philosophy, that is, the attitude of opposition to mythology, is what makes science possible, even when all the implications of this opposition are not realised.[8] Anaximander is of particular importance among Milesians because of his influence on the Pythagoreans.

Anaximenes (585–528) was the third of the Milesians. For him the primary substance is not something indeterminate but is definitely to be described as air. But though he differs in this way from Anaximander, he accepts his predecessor's view so far as to consider air to be that which encompasses all things and out of and into which all things pass. It is, of course, a natural criticism of Anaximander that if the boundless is really something substantial, as it must be, if things have come from it, then it must have just as definite qualities as they have. And accordingly Anaximenes gives it the particular quality of air. In so doing he is approaching what would have been the solution of Anaximander's difficulty, the consideration of the boundless or the universal condition of existence, not as having any particular quality or being itself a substance and an origin of things (since that makes it just as much a thing as anything else) but as *space* itself, that in which things are contained. Now if we say that the common denominator of things is their existence in space, we have a position which is not far removed in terms of the thinking of the time, from that of Anaximenes, though the difference is still sufficiently important to lead to many difficulties and false conclusions. But at that time no real distinction was made between air and space. As Burnet points out, darkness was identified

---
[7] [JA] Philosophy as *removing* prejudices: clear your mind of cant.
[8] [JA] *Cf.* Burnet's; *Early Greek Philosophy*, op. cit., pp.50–71.

with a particular kind of vapour and in a similar way air was regarded as that which occupies space; and there was no conception of empty space, that is, there was no real distinction between a particular space and the thing which occupied it.

Now this being so, this distinction not having been made, Anaximenes was constrained to call his primary substance by a special name and to regard it as having a special quality, namely, *air*; and thus to reintroduce a theory like that of Thales with all the difficulties that Anaximander had tried to overcome. If we think of the primary substance as surrounding the various particular things, then we have to be able to distinguish it from these things, and it itself becomes a particular thing. But if we think of what surrounds things as *space*, then this general condition of existence is not something separate from actual existing things, since space not merely surrounds things but actually penetrates them through and through. While then Anaximenes removes one inconsistency of Anaximander's theory, he does not remove the basis of the Milesian inconsistency—the taking of what is common to all things as being a particular substance or a particular kind of thing.

Lecture 9

Anaximenes continued—the notion of substance

The same criticism that Anaximander had applied to Thales could also be applied to Anaximenes, namely, that taking air as some specific substance or qualitative existence, we have to recognise that there are some things which are not air. Anaximenes certainly supposes a substance which penetrates the various systems as well as encompassing them and so he comes nearer the solution which would be arrived at by taking the universal condition of existence to be space. But also in describing his substance as air, he is able to formulate the theory of the maintenance of the systems by the breathing in and out of air from the boundless mass surrounding them, that is, any system subsists, not merely as might have appeared from the theory of Anaximander, by the interaction of elements within itself, but also by its interaction with its environment. The whole system is, as it were, nourished by the surrounding substance. The criticism remains, however, that fire and earth are not air; and the method employed by Anaximenes to overcome this difficulty leads to the loss of a common measure or common denominator. According to Anaximenes, air is always in motion, "otherwise it would not change so much as it does". It changes by going through various forms, as fire, earth, water, air, but by making the underlying form a specific quality, Anaximenes is reduced to explaining away apparent differences of quality. Fire and earth, he says, are really air. And thus we have the formulation of the distinction between appearance and reality which has created so many difficulties for philosophy. Since these substances are really air, since they do not differ from what we ordinarily call air in quality or in kind, they must differ only in degree.

Thus Anaximenes arrives at the theory that things differ from one another only in density, that is, everything is air but some air is more dense than other portions of air. Earth is more dense than water, water than air, and air than fire. So what exists is made up of various forms of rarefied and condensed air. And the changes in things are to be explained as changes in density and not as changes in quality. The main agent of change will therefore be *pressure*. And thus the particular form that a given portion of air takes is determined principally by the densities of the other portions with which it is in contact. Thus Anaximenes gives us relative density as a common measure whereby we may account for all change. But this leaves us with two utterly different kinds of measurement, namely, measurement by the common substance, air, and measurement by reference to density and the processes of condensation and rarefaction. That is to say, we have the two types of character applicable to things—being air and being more or less dense. And these two characteristics cannot be put on a common footing; they have no common measure. In dealing with density we have simply to neglect quality, as in fact we must do if all qualities are the same.

This seems to have been what determined Anaximander's conception of the boundless as indefinite, since if we attribute the same quality to all things, we might as well attribute none at all. If there is nothing that is not air, how do we know what is conveyed by calling things air. The statement can have no significance for us, and thus we are reduced to a purely quantitative measure. But the objection to this—and the same objection applies to the theory of the atomists, the foundation of which was laid by Anaximenes—is that if there are no differences of quality, then there is nothing to measure. We cannot say what is greater and what is less, if *greater* and *less* are to be the only characters of the things in question. In other words, a purely quantitative theory is impossible but in order to have quality, so as to make the theory possible, we require to have difference of quality. We only recognise qualities as appearing in certain definite regions and therefore not in others. In order to have a common measure of things, we require not to treat it as a common *quality*, since this is equivalent to no quality, and that means no things to measure. According to Burnet, Anaximenes

> "makes the Milesian cosmology consistent for the first time; since a theory which explains everything as a form of a single substance is clearly bound to regard all differences as quantitative".[9]

But this depends on what we mean by substance. We regard all men as having a common humanity but this doesn't imply that men differ only quantitatively. A man may have humanity and also, say, artistic gifts, and we could not distinguish men who were artists from men who weren't, in any merely quantitative way. But when it comes to the class of all things and to the question of what is meant by their existence, we can't answer this question by setting up a particular quality, since thereby we are depriving all other things, and other qualities, of existence.

> This raises the question of what is meant by substance in Milesian theory, and does seem to suggest something essential. A return to mythology—power, dominance over other things. The question the Milesians raised is still important.

---

[9] John Burnet, *op.cit.*, p. 74.

Lecture 10

The main difficulties in Milesian philosophy

The point to be explained in regard to those things which we do not ordinarily call air is not merely that whatever other appearances it may have it has air or airiness as one of its characters, as in the case of men we say that an individual has humanity as one of his characters and at the same time has others. What has to be explained is that earth, for example, doesn't appear to be air at all, and those specific characters in which it differs from atmospheric air are not explained by what it has in common with air—no matter how much that may be. We may say then that in endeavouring to substitute a single term for all qualitative descriptions whatever, Anaximenes is bringing out one of the main difficulties of the Milesian theory. But he is also passing away from the really important line of inquiry which Thales had initiated, namely, the general inquiry into what is meant by existence, as contrasted with the specific inquiry as to what a particular thing is composed of. And in taking water as the common measure of things, Thales at least indicated the possibility of considering what is common to things as *fluidity*—in other words, as process or motion—this being distinct from any quality a given thing may have and indicating that whatever else may be said about a thing, at least it must be said if it exists at all to be in *space* and *time*.

Similarly, Anaximander was led to formulate the conception of the fundamental substance as being intermediate between the opposites, precisely because he did not wish to do away with the differences between things; that is, because he recognised to some extent what was defective in the theory of Thales. In describing this general or indifferent condition of things as a substance, in thinking of the condition of existence as itself existing, Anaximander was led into inconsistencies, but it is not possible to avoid these inconsistencies by insisting on the conception of substances and dropping the theory of the nature of existence—and that is what Anaximenes does.

Again, we have the question of what is meant by the difference between quantitative and qualitative. Density is at least a character of things, just as being composed of air is a quality (character) of things; and since different things have different densities, their common character of being composed of air doesn't explain these differences. We may say then that what Anaximenes has done is to take up the special problem of density and to give up the general or logical problem of the nature of existence. Anaximenes in fact is concerned particularly with meteorology and while not developing a general philosophy or logic, he also fails to follow up the lines of astronomical inquiry on which Anaximander had entered. For example he gives up the theory that the earth swings free in space and thinks of the earth as a flat disc floating on the air, just as Thales had said that the earth floats on the water.

With Anaximenes we return to the conception of an absolute up and down which Anaximander had rejected from a consideration of the nature of space. In developing astronomy further, therefore, the Pythagoreans took up the problem precisely where Anaximander had left it, the only conception which they borrowed from Anaximenes being that of *breathing*, as that which sustains the systems within the boundless. At the same time while these general criticisms may be passed, it has also to be recognised that Anaximenes practically identified the boundless with space, the fact being that in the time of the Milesians there was not a clear conception of space itself, everything being treated as in some way substantial as for example darkness was treated as a form of air or vapour. Accordingly the way is prepared for the theory of the Pythagoreans that the various worlds or systems are units of light against an infinite background of darkness which may be indifferently identified with air or with space. And thus all existence is thought of on the analogy of the heavenly constellations, which enables the Pythagoreans to make progress in astronomy and in the mathematical sciences, even though they find themselves in certain *philosophical* difficulties.

III
Xenophanes

Lecture 10 (continued)

Two reactions to the Milesians—Xenophanes and Pythagoras

There were two main reactions to the Milesian philosophy, namely, that of *Xenophanes* and that of *Pythagoras*. Pythagoras develops the mathematical side of the earlier theories, while the theory of Xenophanes is a sceptical reaction to the Milesians, an insistence on the difficulties of other theories with the suggestion that it is impossible to solve their problems, impossible to find a common denominator of things but that things should be accepted as they come without any inquiry. Xenophanes represents the anti-philosophical attitude of the plain man—the man who objects to "all this theorising and speculation", who "doesn't see any good in it". This attitude is only possible because the person who adopts it has not observed the mythological elements in his own thinking, the way he separates reality into divided regions and thus is bound to come to insoluble problems. But as far as ordinary practice is concerned, it is possible to continue while these problems remain unsolved. It is evident, if only from the difference of opinion among those who speculate on these subjects, that it is possible to conduct these inquiries without arriving at a solution; and so there is a certain plausibility given to the reaction of Xenophanes and in a later time of the Sophists, who held that inquiry into the nature of things could produce no valuable result. In denying that there is any common nature of things, Xenophanes is the first *pluralist*.[1] As we saw in connection with the Milesians, the theory that things have a common nature is not necessarily and in fact can't consistently be monistic in the sense in which the term is commonly employed. In the sense, that is, that *ultimately* there is only one real thing and that the various things which we recognise are merely parts or aspects of this whole and are not to be considered separately from them. When monism is

---
[1] [JA] *logical* "pluralist" (i.e., sceptic).

Xenophanes 37

taken in that sense, then all who seek for a common nature of things must be opposed to monism because, unless things are definitely different from one another, there can be no question of finding what is common to them. But this still leaves it possible to hold that there is a common nature of things, that being real has one and only one meaning, and to hold that this theory is necessary if any inquiry is to be made—to hold that all things must be subject to the same kind of examination as, otherwise, insoluble problems regarding the relations of the different kinds of reality are bound to arise. In our ordinary thinking these problems are obscured; and the contradictions which naturally arise are evaded owing to the refusal of the persons concerned to formulate their theories of knowledge and action. And it is even easy for them to make out that those who try to set up a general logic are themselves dividing reality into what is fundamental and what is erected on that foundation. Now this charge has a certain amount of justification in relation to a theory of the nature of things as consisting of a common substance, in relation to a theory like that of Anaximenes. But it does not follow from the rejection of such a fundamental or *ultimate* nature of things, that we are bound to reject a common nature of things or a common medium like that of space and time in which they all appear.

Lecture 11

Xenophanes and the rejection of speculation

To consider the general bearing of the theory of Xenophanes: his rejection of speculations was due to the belief that they raised artificial problems which could not be solved; any suggested solution of which could not be verified. And he considered that there was no need for inquiry or speculation, that we should simply take things as they are presented to us.[2]

Now this attitude is valuable as an objection to the postulation of metaphysical entities or powers for the explanation of natural phenomena. At the same time this attitude is a mistaken one in that it suggests that things are presented to us in a simple and direct manner; and that

[2][JA] Xenophanes 565–470?; Pythagoras 570–500?; Heraclitus 540–470?; Parmenides 515–450.

we do not require to form suppositions and hypotheses in order to deal with things practically as well as theoretically. If this were so, then no explanation could be given of the fact that there *are* speculations, even if these speculations are mistaken. Criticism of any view is not complete unless it can be shown not merely that the view is false but how it is possible for anyone to hold this false view. Now it certainly is possible to raise artificial problems and to formulate speculative theories which cannot be verified, that is, it is possible to put forward a theory in which the processes of things are explained by ultimate powers, but this type of theorising wouldn't be possible if we could take things simply as presented and require nothing more of them. According to the theory of Xenophanes we have two types of cognition, namely, observation of immediately presented facts and speculation about what lies behind them. And it would be impossible to show how two such diverse modes of thinking could both be undertaken by the same person and could be applied to the same things. The solution is then that we do not in our observations simply have things presented to us which we know completely and in regard to which no question or doubt can be raised. On the contrary, in all observations there is present an element of expectation or anticipation and it is only on account of this element that it is possible not merely to form hypotheses but also to show their relation to what we call observed facts.

Xenophanes considered that in ordinary life speculations are not required. But he also considered that it was possible to speculate even though we can get no verification. We see that attitude in the following two fragments:

> "There never was nor will be a man who has certain knowledge about the gods and about all the things I speak of. Even if he should chance to say the complete truth, yet he himself knows not that it is so. But all may have their fancy" (Fragment 34).

> "Let these be taken as fancies something like the truth" (*these* being his own speculations) (Fragment 35).[3]

Even if we accept the contention of Xenophanes that on these subjects no certainty is to be obtained (that is, "this (for example gods) is *certainly* not a matter on which we

---
[3] John Burnet, *op.cit.*, p. 121.

can be certain"), we should also have to remember that in accordance with this view no certainty could be obtained on any subject, because if we divide the world of reality into matters of certainty and matters of uncertainty, we are assuming that we ourselves can determine with certainty the distinction between these two classes of things. Again, it would be impossible to say that we can have a fancy or a speculation which is something like the truth unless there is a definite truth in question. And if there were not, our speculation would not only be unverifiable, it would be meaningless. That being so, the distinction is not between matters which are themselves certain and those which are themselves uncertain but between subjects which we are capable of investigating and those which we are not. In other words, a view of this kind must be based on a criticism of our capacities. But this criticism can only be undertaken by our cognitive faculty or faculties; that is, we are presuming that we can know things by simple inspection, for the purpose of upholding the view that in certain cases we cannot do so.

We find further that when Xenophanes comes to deal with his predecessors' theories in detail, his rejection of them places him in as great difficulties as their acceptance of them could possibly do. For example he refuses to accept Anaximander's theory of the earth swinging free in space and the sun passing round it. This, as we saw, was a direct result of the consideration of space in its proper character. If once we begin to take space seriously, we find that we can place no limit to it; and we also find that the conventional notions of up and down have no general application. Now Xenophanes wishes to show that Anaximander's theory is mere guesswork, that we can't possibly know that the earth has another side, seeing that we have never seen it, or that the sun goes under the earth, seeing, again, that we have never observed it doing so. But once this question has been raised, it is impossible for Xenophanes to settle it without formulating theories which he himself admits are fancies or guesswork and which differ from those of Anaximander precisely in that they are incapable of being verified or in that they do not enable us to make any anticipations. As we know, in astronomy, the foundations of which were laid by Anaximander, it is possible to predict with remarkable accuracy the positions and appearance of the heavenly bodies at any given time. Whereas if we simply regarded them as so many lights on a heavenly dome placed over the earth, then we should never know what to expect—we could form no theory of the position of any given body at any given time. We should have the rough general knowledge that the sun passes across the heavens from east to west and that its path varies in certain ways at different seasons of the year. Similarly we could have a general knowledge of phases of the moon. But if there were any apparent deviation from the regularity of these processes, we should simply accept this as being in the natural course of things and thus we should never be able to give any explanation of it (to find "differences"). If, for example, the moon was concealed by the clouds, we could not, on the basis of this type of thinking, have any theory of what its actual state was, or even (for that matter) whether it was present in the sky or not. We could not on the basis of that way of looking at things make any differentiation between astronomy and meteorology. The separation is not made in primitive thought, and it was not clearly made even by the Milesians, but Anaximander's theory of the boundless made it possible for that theory (distinction?) to be made and the Pythagoreans were able to develop an astronomy quite distinct from meteorology.

Lecture 12

Xenophanes continued—a reaction to philosophy

Xenophanes' was not a philosophic position, but a reaction to philosophy. He lived in Ionia when the country was conquered by the Persians.

Primarily Xenophanes was a *satirist*. His position is that of the civilised man whose country has been occupied by the barbarians and who satirises both the weakness and effeminacy of his own countrymen and the superstitions and barbarity of the invaders. And this attitude of Xenophanes as the representative of civilisation explains to some extent his attitude to speculation. Speculation, he seems to suggest, is useless: it is not a thing that can keep the barbarian out, and it is just as detached from the facts of practical experience as are the barbarian superstitions. In fact we may sum up the position of Xenophanes by saying that it is fundamentally an expression of the attitude of a superior class in a particular community. His attitude to speculation could be expressed in our terminology by saying that a *gentleman* does not theorise but concerns himself with the demands of practical life (that is, does what "his position" demands). In brief, his standpoint is that of *urbanity*. What is to be pointed out in relation to this attitude is that the position taken up by Xenophanes is just as mythological as that of the barbarians and as he represents that of the philosophers as being. That is, the distinction which he makes between those things that we can be sure about and those we can't be sure about is one which would require theoretical justification but for which no such justification can be given. That is to say, *the division between certainties and uncertainties can never be made with certainty.* And equally the certainty of familiar beliefs is just as mythological, just as much a matter of fancy, as the superstitions of the barbarians. Xenophanes says that the Thracians have gods who are conceived in the likeness of the Thracians, and if oxen had gods, they in turn would be conceived in the likeness of oxen. And he seems to suggest that, in the same way, a theory like Anaximander's merely shows what Anaximander's preferences are, or the sort of things which fit his fancy, whereas, Xenophanes maintains, what we tread on is the solid earth. And we move about in the air, and that is all we can know with certainty about the things above and the things below. But in returning in this way to the conception of an absolute up and down Xenophanes is compelled to *answer* the contentions of Anaximander. The question of infinity having once been raised, we can at least understand the question how far down the earth goes and how far it extends laterally. If we say that it extends in these directions to a limited distance, then we must be able to give an account of this boundary and of what lies beyond it. Xenophanes being unable to give any such account is forced to take up the position that the earth extends to an infinite distance in all these directions. Now this is certainly guesswork, but it does not show the position of Anaximander to be guesswork. Xenophanes contradicts himself by combining infinite extension with an absolute up and down, and further his speculations can lead to no new discoveries, whereas those of Anaximander can and do.

It may further be said that unless we admit that anticipation is combined with observation, that everyone has to make some suppositions, we can give no account of our knowledge of developing things, and so can give no account of our treatment even of those earthly things that we meet with in everyday life. Xenophanes formulates his supposition that there is a new sun every day, since having passed from east to west it has no way of getting back to the east without our observing it. But if we insist on mere observation in this way, we should have to say that there is a new sun every time we looked at it, since we had not observed it passing from one position to another. The fact that we don't take up this view, shows that we consider things to have a history, to have continuity and identity independently of us. In fact we could not think of things at all except as having a continuous history, and when we do think of them in this way, when we take time as well as space seriously, we find ourselves capable of recognising the same thing under new circumstances. Now as far as observations of the sun on two successive days are concerned, there is nothing in these observations by themselves to prove that it is the same thing we observe and not simply another thing of the same sort. It is conceivable that they are different things—we can't be absolutely certain that they are the same, but we have to make some supposition one way or the other. But when it is recognised that this type of supposition is made in all our experience, that we constantly do recognise individual things, then it appears that even our familiar beliefs could not be maintained as absolutely certain but involve some supposition. We believe that we meet the same persons on different occasions and that we find ourselves in the same surroundings on successive days, for example. But it is conceivable that what we call the same isn't really the same thing but is only something very like the thing we saw before. Now when these admissions are made, we see the justification for the assumption of the Milesians that all statements should be subject to discussion and we see at the same time that the division made by Xenophanes between the familiar and certain and the unfamiliar and uncertain is not justified. In terms of the demand of Xenophanes, on the contrary, for statements which involve no speculation and which could never be questioned, it would be impossible to make any statements at all. We find then from a consideration of this position that theorising is not something cut off from practical life but is absolutely bound up with it. But we find also that the admission of mythological elements into our thinking would, if consistently carried out, lead to the complete disintegration of thought, to absolute scepticism. The arguments of Xenophanes refute the first sceptical attack on philosophy as a result of the concentration of philosophers on special scientific questions without at the same time working out a logic or a general theory of the nature of things, to serve as a foundation for the special sciences. And thus the Eleatic reaction to the Pythagorean development of Anaximander's position has a similar basis, and so has the reaction of the Sophists, later, to the speculations of all the schools of philosophy, Pythagorean, Eleatic and Ionian.

IV
Pythagoras

Lecture 13

Pythagoras (570–500)—the conception of units applied to mathematics, music, medicine and ethics

Note on Xenophanes: distinction between matters of fact and opinion, or settled and unsettled questions. Led to scepticism. The attitude recurs even among scientists, who then become unphilosophical when they divide reality like this. Facts themselves cannot either be certain or uncertain, probable or improbable; but must simply be true or false, even if we cannot at the moment determine which. Followers of Xenophanes derived this tendency, particularly the case with the Pythagoreans, in the limited and unlimited in their two kinds of reality. Also an attempt is made throughout science to make all ordinary things built up of elements. Two different orders of being, *elements* and *constitution* whereby things are built up. Leads to the same difficulties as in Xenophanes. All scientists are more or less of the Pythagorean way of thinking. Why sceptical reaction of the Sophists also became possible. The problem which faced Plato was to show that all things were on the same level. Had already been attempted by Heraclitus (the only one not to extend Pythagoreanism—the Eleatics opposed the Pythagoreans in the terms of the Pythagoreans, brought out the inconsistency in the Pythagoreans.) It is the search for elements that has been very characteristic for science: leads to scepticism and these difficulties.

We find that Pythagoras (roughly 570–500) came from Ionia and that he had absorbed some of the teaching of Anaximander and Anaximenes, but the school which he founded in southern Italy developed along different lines and was more particularly concerned with astronomy and with mathematics, with the working out, that is, of particular sciences, than the Milesians had been. It is also to be noted that in the Pythagorean school the subject of ethics was first definitely treated.

There are difficulties about distinguishing the doctrines of Pythagoras from other members of his school, because, like Socrates, he left no writings, and divergent tendencies arose within the school, and each sect tried to make out that it had the true theory of Pythagoras himself. Burnet suggests a method of distinguishing early theories and later ones. The Eleatics bring certain objections to their views, and we find in Pythagorean theory certain views that seem like attempts to answer Eleatic criticism. Doctrines, therefore, which show no traces of an attempt to answer Eleatic criticism can be said to be early. Secondly, doctrines more closely related to the Milesians may be said to be early, and those more closely related to Empedocles as late.

Pythagoras adopted the theory of Anaximenes that there is a boundless air which encompasses the worlds. And like Anaximander he considered that there were innumerable worlds existing within the boundless. And as we have already noted, the air of Anaximenes was identified with darkness and also, in a general way, with space. In terms of this theory we may infer that the original interest of the Pythagoreans was in astronomy. Now in the heavens we find a great number of stars, or units of light, against a dark background to which no definite character can be assigned. And some of these units of light form constellations, or rather a constellation consists of certain units of light with certain intervals of darkness between them. And it is by means of these arrangements that we recognise the stars.

On this basis, then, Pythagoras formulated the theory that any existing thing is a system of units arranged in a certain pattern or configuration and having the indefinite boundless substance between them. This theory was applied to mathematics, to music, to medicine and to ethics. In all these fields, Pythagoreans employed the conception of units and of arrangements of units, and it sometimes appears doubtful in which of these fields the theory was first developed.

But considering Anaximander's theory of the innumerable systems surrounded by the boundless and of the way in which the systems depended on the maintaining of certain relations between the opposites, considering further that Anaximenes regarded the boundless as air, the suggestion that the necessary relations are maintained in each system by means of a process conformable to breathing seems a natural one and is in accordance with what we otherwise know about the Pythagorean doctrine about the limit and the unlimited. The general position is that all things or systems are in configurations or arrangements of units at certain intervals and that these arrangements depend on the interrelation of the two ultimate forms of reality—the boundless and the unit.

Now this means that whatever progress might be made in the study of configurations or figures there was nonetheless a fundamental dualism which rendered inevitable the appearance of contradictions. The difficulty of finding a relation between the unit and the interval between units was emphasised by Zeno, and this is connected with the further difficulty of finding any relation between the complex and the simple which was emphasised by Parmenides. That is, if we have certain ultimate realities, then no amount of manipulation can give us any other sort of reality. If in the last resort, the reality of any thing or system is made up by the reality of certain units, then there can be no distinction between the system and the units themselves and any appearance of complexity must on this view be accounted a delusion. That is the Eleatic argument. But it may be said, on the other hand, that if we cannot account for complex things by means of a theory of ultimate units, then we should have to dispense with the ultimate units. That is the line followed by Heraclitus. Again, the difficulty may be also put in this way, that if we are going to deal with things simply as configurations, then we are reducing all differences to differences of quantity or extension and we can give no account of differences of quality. As regards the unit itself, Pythagoreans certainly seemed to think of it as having the definite quality of *light*, whereby alone it can be contrasted with the indefinite *darkness*. But this would mean that there are two ultimate qualities, and that there is no way of finding a relation between them. And whether in any case we begin with one quality or two, it is impossible on this basis to account for the very diverse qualities which things exhibit and, just as in the case of the Milesians, the result of this theory is that differences are neglected and the supposed common quality becomes quite indefinite.

Pythagoreans treated numbers as configurations or as we may alternatively put it they distinguished configurations numerically. In taking up this position they identified arithmetical and geometrical considerations. By arranging units or unit-points in different figures, we obtain different series of numbers. Thus, we have the triangular numbers formed by successive whole numbers or integers:[1]

Pythagoras

1, 3, 6, 10...
1, + 2 + 3 + 4...

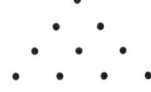

Figure 1.

On the other hand, we have the square numbers by adding successive odd numbers:

1, 4, 9, 16...
1, + 3 + 5 + 7...

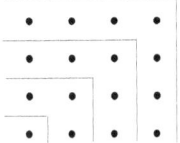

Figure 2.

And, in the third case, oblong numbers arrived at by adding successive even numbers:

2, 6, 12...
2, + 4 + 6...

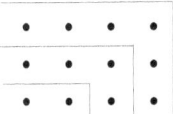

Figure 3.

These are three types of configurations which generated series of numbers in particular ways, and the Pythagoreans arrived at the conclusion that all actual configurations could be represented by means of these elementary figures. In terms of this view, for the general statement that things are configurations, Pythagoreans were prepared to substitute the statement that things are numbers. That statement taken by itself seems very strange to us, but when we take it as

---
[1][Ed.] The following three figures are taken from the student notes.

meaning that things are particular arrangements of units with certain intervals between the units, we find that it is not so far removed from our ordinary ways of thinking. (The atomic theory of bodies is derived from this position of the Pythagoreans.)

Lecture 14

Pythagoras continued—music and harmony

These figures are composed of unit points arranged at certain distances from one another. And things being identified with these configurations, the generation of a thing consists of the marking out of its figure by means of these units against the indeterminate background, that is, a certain region which was previously indeterminate is now marked out, or limited, by means of the units. And that is what the Pythagoreans mean when they say that configurations (or limited things) are generated by the application of the limit to the unlimited. The unlimited is simply the general region in which things are, and it appears in the resulting configuration as that which intervenes between one point and another. On the other hand that which limits or marks out these figures is the unit point. It is of course necessary for the Pythagorean theory that there should be many such units—in fact that there should be any number of them; but except as regards position they are indistinguishable from one another.[2] And that raises the difficulty emphasised by Parmenides—namely, how if the many units are indistinguishable, we are able to say that there are many: that is, if we say they are indistinguishable, are we not identifying them all and reducing them to one?

Music. In the musical instruments which the Greeks used a great range of sounds was not possible. In fact prior to Pythagoras only the seven-stringed lyre was used and according to Burnet it was as a result of the researches of Pythagoras that the eighth string was added. Now these strings had to be tuned in relation to one another and they form what we now call an octave. The question which the Pythagoreans considered then was this question of *tuning*,

---
[2] [JA] A figure marked out by units from indeterminate background: the application of the limit to the unlimited. *Units differ only in position.* Criticism that they are really indistinguishable.

of making the different strings harmonious, that is, securing that there would be the correct intervals between the different notes. Thus in the notion of intervals we have something which connects the theory of music with the theory of numbers and constellations. We now know that a note an octave higher than a given note is connected with a vibration twice as fast. However, as Burnet says, Pythagoras had no means of recording these vibrations and he must have proceeded by considering *length of string* instead of considering rate of vibration directly. He presumes that Pythagoras worked with the monochord.³

What we find then is that if we have two similar wires such that one is twice the length of the other, then the note emitted by the latter is an octave higher than that emitted by the former. If we express this in terms of vibration, we find that the octave corresponds to the ratio 2:1. So, that ratio is spoken of as *the figure of the octave*.

Again if we take two wires such that one is one and a half times the length of the other then the note emitted by the shorter wire is a 5th higher than that emitted by the longer wire, that is, 3:2 is the figure corresponding to the interval of a 5th (C to G); 4:3 equals a 4th, C to F. Just as 3/2 x 4/3 = 2/1, so the 5th together with the 4th make up the octave. In tuning the lyre we first of all secure that the two extreme strings give an interval of one octave. Then if we tune the middle strings so that one of them is a 4th above the lower and a 5th below the higher, and the other is a 5th above the lower etc., we have the four basic notes:

C–F G–C.

This central interval is the *tone*: and to complete the scale it is required to insert two notes within each half. In the tuning of the Greek lyre that was done in different ways, and according to the way it was done we have a different scale, that is, a different configuration of notes. There is this fundamental configuration of the four basic notes which applies to all the scales, and then there are the various figures in which the other four notes can be arranged in relation to the given four.

---

³[JA] *Music*: note tuning. (1) Octave 2:1 (2) 5th 3:2 (3) 4th 4:3 Thus four fundamental notes: different arrangements of intermediate notes. Difficulties in both numbers and music. Indefinite $\sqrt{2}$ comes into geometry: also $\sqrt{5}$ in pentagon. Similarly, cannot divide *tone* equally: again come on $\sqrt{2}$.

Roughly speaking, if we call the difference a tone, then the fourth is two and a half tones. (There are no quarter tones in our music, so that Greek music is very different from ours.)

Note that the theory of figures is applicable to the different arrangements of the strings in a lyre, and as a result of this connection, these ratios themselves came to be known as harmonious, and the term harmony was applied even in astronomy. That is the origin of the expression "the harmony of the spheres". It refers to a Pythagorean theory of the arrangement of heavenly bodies on the surfaces of a number of concentric spheres—the radii of the spheres having to one another the fundamental ratios of the octave.

Now in connection both with the theory of numbers and with that of music, there are difficulties arising out of this attempt to measure things by means of ultimate individual units. In attempting to treat geometry in terms of whole numbers we find it impossible to give an account of the important figure, the isosceles right-angled triangle; we can't in terms of whole numbers solve the problem of the duplication of the square (to find a square whose area is twice the area of another square); we cannot in terms of whole numbers find the ratio between the diagonal of a square and its side.

This number ($\sqrt{2}$) which is what we call a surd, was important in Pythagorean geometry, but could not be determined as any sort of ratio between whole numbers. Again we know that in Pythagorean theory the pentagon was important (in fact it was the Pythagorean symbol) but the construction of it and the measurement of the different lines used in that construction involves $\sqrt{5}$ which likewise cannot be expressed as any ratio between whole numbers.

Problems of an exactly similar character arise in connection with the octave. If we take the difference between the 4th and the 5th as the *tone* or unit, then we can't measure the 4th (and correspondingly the 5th and the octave) as an exact number of tones. The same problem can be expressed as the problem of the division of the tone. We can't by means of any manipulation of the fundamental intervals discover a method of dividing the tone into two equal parts. In fact this is the same problem as the duplication of the square. For if we take the four fundamental notes, then we find that their ratios in terms of vibrations, or in the reverse order in terms of lengths, are as 6:8:9:12, that is, 8/6=12/9=4/3 (4th) and 9/6=12/8=3/2 (5th).

In order to divide the tone equally we should have to find a number x such that

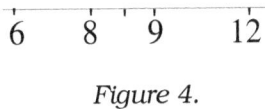

Figure 4.

9/x=x/8 (x=6√2).

(N.B. Problems are not *quite* the same, though both involve √2, that is, the 4th/the tone might be rational, say 5/2, but the square root of the 5th/the 4th need not, that is, √(7/5).)

Lecture 15

Pythagoras continued—the theory of the mean—the division of reality into rational and irrational

This question of the division of the octave introduces the theory of the mean which was to play a great part in Greek philosophy and which we find was an important conception in the ethical theory of Aristotle. In modern terminology, if we take these numbers 6, 8, 9, 12—9 is the arithmetic mean between 6 and 12, 8 is the harmonic mean and the problem of dividing the octave is the problem of finding the geometric mean between 6 and 12, which is also the geometric mean between the arithmetic mean and the harmonic mean. From the theory of music then the Pythagoreans received a certain support for their doctrine of configuration. The most important way in which any system or thing can be determined is the determination of the ratios or proportions which hold among the elements. Now we also find in the Pythagorean application of this theory an explanation of the weakness of Pythagoreanism. The Pythagoreans in setting up their theory of ratios or proportions introduced a division of reality into different realms—the *rational* and the *irrational*.[4] The problem of the Milesians had been to find a common measure of all things. Xenophanes had opposed this view by contending that there

---
[4][JA] In effect, *Sophistry* founded by Pythagoreans.

were some things which the human mind could not measure but could only guess at, and the Pythagoreans supported Xenophanes by what they consider to be a scientific theory of the division of reality into the *rational* and the *irrational*, that which is exact and that which is not exact, the *limited* and the *unlimited*. And this division depends on the theory of the *limit* or *unit*, that is, of *ultimate elements* of things, in terms of which alone anything is intelligible. (Just as Xenophanes took familiar objects as ultimate elements of reality.)

Now the admission that certain things cannot be accounted for by means of these units indicates that the theory is false, that these units are not the constituents and foundations of all things. But instead of drawing this conclusion, Pythagoreans concluded that those things whose nature could not be expressed in terms of units were not really things in the same sense as those which could be so described. And thus, instead of recognising their failure to account for reality, Pythagoreans affirmed the failure of certain entities to be real or to be determinate beings.

By setting up this distinction between reality and appearance or between higher and lower reality, Pythagoreans developed the first *rationalistic* theory and they introduced ethical considerations into regions where they could have no exact application. To regard the impossibility of dividing the tone as a defect of the musical system itself, as a failure on its part, instead of a positive and important characteristic of it, is an introduction of ethical considerations which cannot be justified by the facts of the case. That is to say, it is really the case that the semitone cannot be represented in terms of integral ratios. Now, granting that this is so, it is meaningless to say that the semitone *ought* to be capable of being so represented, and that in an ideal rational world it could be represented in some such way.[5] The fact that the octave as a whole, apart from the three dominant ratios, cannot be rationalised, merely shows that rational numbers are not capable of expressing the nature of everything that is real. And if we assert (as the later Pythagoreans certainly did, and earlier Pythagoreans may have done) that such a number as $\sqrt{2}$ is not to be

---

[5][JA] Pythagorean *ought*: return to superstition—fetishism: away from Ionian "pessimism", that is, Pythagorean *reaction*.

regarded as a number in the same sense as the integers but that it is, so to speak, trying to be a number or tending towards numerical reality—that way of speaking can only result in falsification, since it is impossible to say what rational number $\sqrt{2}$ is tending towards.

That problem, which cannot be solved arithmetically, can immediately be solved geometrically: $\sqrt{2}$ is the ratio between the hypotenuse of an isosceles right angled triangle and either of the sides. What is shown, then, by the defects of the Pythagorean theory, what enabled the Eleatics to bring unanswerable objections to it, is that it is impossible to base geometry upon arithmetic, to base the theory of space upon the theory of numbers; but it is quite possible to base the theory of numbers on the theory of *space*. It is also shown that it is impossible to base a knowledge of things upon a knowledge of ultimate elements, or to account for the *continuous* in terms of the *discontinuous*. And most important of all, any attempt to do so must be derived from some general conception of a superior reality to which other things are subordinate—as in the case of the reality of the units as found with the reality of the unlimited, as well as the various configurations themselves. Now to mention the theory of a superior reality is to restore the animistic doctrine of power which philosophy was designed to remove: and as Parmenides shows, having asserted the existence of a superior reality, we can't consistently assert the existence of anything else: the other things which are supposed to exist are, in so far as they are inferior, unreal, so that they cannot be said properly to exist. The doctrine of the unlimited is used by Pythagoreans as a convenient way of explaining away difficulties, but if we are going to introduce the two conceptions of the limit and the unlimited into our theory, we must be able to indicate the relation between them—we must be able in some way to measure or *limit* the unlimited. The defect of Pythagoreanism, then, is that according to it there are different modes of being which cannot be brought to a common denominator, namely, that of the *units*, that of the *unlimited*, which constitutes the intervals between the units, and that of the *configurations* or arrangements of the units within the unlimited. If we cannot find a common denominator for all these, (modes of being) then we have no means of connecting them and of introducing them all into the same theory.

On the other hand, it is the merit of the Pythagoreans that they discovered that certain facts could be expressed by means of ratios, and the search for proportion among things, while it cannot give us all the information that we may desire, at least gives us important information in many different fields. The question of harmony in music being the question of finding the right ratios or concordant intervals, so, according to Pythagoreans, the question of health in medicine is the question of finding the right proportion among the different elements which constitute the body. And similarly in ethics, Pythagoreans hold that goodness is constituted by the existence of the different elements of the soul in right relation to one another. Or, as we may put it, it consists in a harmony or attunement of the parts of the soul, a theory which is worked out in some detail in Plato's *Republic* but which is substantially a Pythagorean theory. We find references to it even in Heraclitus so that the doctrine of the parts of the soul and their harmony must have been an early Pythagorean doctrine and may well have been the theory of Pythagoras himself. For according to him, philosophy is a way of life and what the philosopher seeks is a right way of living; and in accordance with (the Pythagorean) statement that philosophy is the higher music, we may take it that this doctrine of harmony dominated the whole philosophy. And the main defect consisted in its dividing reality into parts, or in contending that only the harmonious is truly real, and the discordant comparatively unreal.

Lecture 16

Pythagoras continued—the division of reality—Pythagoreanism

Applications of Pythagoreanism in early state: tonic—substance to be applied to the human body to bring it to the right tune; *cf.*, temper, temperance. The aim of medicine is to find the right proportions of the opposites in the body (harmony or health). Harmony of different elements in the soul also: desire, spirit, reason—the three elements of the soul in Plato's *Republic*; corresponds to the theory of the three lives; *cf.*, the three types at the Olympic Games: 1, lookers on; 2, competitors; 3, traders. 1, the spectators, represents the best condition, contemplative attitude, theory and reason; 2, the competitors come next, emulation, spirited element; 3, the traders come lowest. *Cf.*, the *Republic*, legislators, soldiers and traders. The analogy of tuning is kept in mind - the harmonious soul

The Pythagorean theory divides reality into the rational and the irrational. In so doing, instead of finding a common denominator of things, it puts the two classes of things on an entirely different level, so that the reality of the one is of an entirely different nature from that of the other. And this raises the fundamental difficulty of how we are to know not merely the connection but even the distinction between the two spheres of reality. (*cf.*, the *Parmenides*.) Whether that connection or that distinction belongs to the higher or lower level of reality, we are presented with an insoluble problem.[6] If for example the connection between higher and lower itself belongs to the higher order, then it would seem that it could not penetrate to the lower order so as to make the connection. The suggestion is that such a connection or distinction belongs to a common or neutral order of reality: but in that case the whole distinction between the different spheres breaks down. Now this difficulty is specially exemplified in connection with the problem of becoming. Suppose that a thing has a certain configuration and that it changes or goes through a process so as to have a different configuration, then in order to speak of this process, we must regard it as being determinate, as having a certain character or configuration of its own. And the question raised by the Eleatics relates directly to this problem, namely, by what configuration can we represent the passage from one configuration to another? If it is possible to represent it by a configuration, then it would seem that we merely have a third configuration between the other two, and that we require to find further relations to complete the connection; just as in space, if we conceive it to consist of unit points, we can always find a unit between any two units, and the connection or continuity between any two points is never completed.

On the other hand, if we regard it as possible to have a determinate process, then we can no longer think of the beginning and end of that process as being an absolutely

---

[6][JA] Eleatic type of argument: dilemma.

fixed and unchanging figure. And so the Pythagorean theory of ultimate configurations of things would have to be given up. Putting the matter quite generally, we have a theory of different ways of being or kinds of reality represented by the units, figures marked out by units, and the unlimited which fills the intervals between them. And we can find no common denominator of these three ways of being. But unless intervals between points are exactly measurable, that is, just as exactly as points themselves can be enumerated, we are not in a position to compare one figure with another. And again, if the reality of any figure is entirely constituted by the various units which it contains, then it would appear that we can speak only of the units and not at all of the figures. This is the objection to all theories of ultimate elements—not merely to Pythagorean, but also to those of Empedocles and the atomists who were supposed to have found an answer to the Eleatics, and likewise to a large extent even to the doctrines of Socrates.

To take the theory of Empedocles, if a particular thing is completely described as so much fire, air, earth, water, then we could never regard it as one particular complex and historical thing, we should simply speak of the different amounts of the four elements which were found together in a particular place. So that having begun by making these fundamental distinctions, by saying that there were ultimately four sorts of things, we should be unable to make any further distinctions—a certain amount of fire simply remains so much fire, even if it is present along with different entities of the other elements.[7]

What we find then in philosophers who followed Pythagoras is a criticism of this theory of a multiplicity of ultimate or elementary beings which presided over the appearances of things, just as the powers or spirits were supposed to do in the animistic theory. And the two types of answer to the problems presented by this philosophy were those of Heraclitus and Parmenides. According to Parmenides there can't be a multiplicity of units of being, because there would have to be a multiplicity of distinctions between these units and so on indefinitely: and if these distinctions are not

---
[7][JA] Socratic forms really *animae*.

ultimately real, then ultimately, or in reality, there are no distinctions between one unit and another; and so there is only a single being. On the other hand, if we allow that connections and distinctions are just as real as the things which they connect and distinguish, then we have no reason for calling any particular thing more ultimate than anything else, and this is essentially the solution of Heraclitus. According to him we don't require to invoke something of a lower order than the ultimate forms of things in order to account for the passage from one to another. We do not require to call the changing unreal in comparison with what persists. There is, he contends, nothing which persists indefinitely, but even so long as a thing persists and appears not to change, it is going through processes, just as much as a thing which is obviously changing—the fact being that in the case of the persisting thing we have different changes which balance one another. He uses as his chief illustration the case of a fire which appears to be burning steadily: it lasts through a definite duration. But all the time that it is burning, all the time that this apparently unchanging flame persists, a certain amount of fuel is being supplied, and a certain amount of smoke is being given off, and so long as these two given sets of processes balance one another, so long as supply and demand are equal, the flame remains as it was. All the time something that was not fire is becoming fire. And something that was fire is ceasing to be fire; and it is only because of the balancing of these exchanges that the fire persists. In this way in terms of equality and inequality of exchanges, we can give fundamentally the same account of change and persistence. So that the difference which Pythagoreans emphasised between being and becoming is not a fundamental difference in the kind of reality which the two things have but is a minor difference, a difference expressed in terms of quantities, but resting on an underlying similarity.

V
Heraclitus

Lecture 17

Heraclitus—the particular importance of Heraclitus in the history of philosophy—the logical character of his doctrine

Heraclitus is of particular importance in philosophic history. He indicates the methods of solution of the Pythagorean problems, which were not to receive any precise solution until . Apart from Heraclitus, all the philosophers from Pythagoras to Socrates were dominated by Pythagorean conceptions. Heraclitus stands apart from this development. In particular, he solved the problem of Pythagorean dualism and asserted a common measure of reality, a coherent logic of being as one.

To understand the position of *Heraclitus* we have to view it as being of a fundamentally logical character. According to Burnet's view, the doctrine of Heraclitus is not to be considered logical, but merely a particular physical theory conformable to the physical theories of the Milesians and their successors. But even the Milesians developed their theory in terms of certain general considerations. The mere observation of a number of physical facts could not have prompted the view that there is a common denominator of things. On the contrary, the differences among things would have appeared so obvious that any attempt to attribute a common nature to them would have been regarded as absurd. We find then that what Milesians were concerned with was the different types of explanation which are applied to physical phenomena and the insoluble problems that arise if explanation is made in terms of another way of being than that of the phenomena themselves. In other words, if a distinction is made between ultimate and immediate being or between reality and appearance, and however indefinitely this problem is formulated, it is at the basis of all these investigations and it is a problem of logic. In fact the determination of the character of *what is*, or of the conditions of existence, is the whole object of the science of logic. This question is sometimes confused by making logic refer specially to thinking and to theory as held by individuals; and by considering it as the attempt to determine how thinking is to be coherent and how discussion is to be significant. But the question is—what criterion of coherence and significance can we obtain? What is it that is to be signified, and why should we desire that our thoughts should be coherent? We desire it only because we consider that things themselves are coherent: that is, we wish to avoid contradictions simply because we recognise that there is no contradiction in nature. And again, if a proposition is to be significant, it must signify that which exists. So that the inquiry into the conditions of coherent and significant thinking is in reality an investigation of the conditions of existence. We are concerned all the time with what is objective in these processes, that is, with what is thought or said, and not with acts of thinking and speaking on the part of any individual. The attempt therefore to give a coherent theory of existence is really an attempt to formulate a logic, and that is what Heraclitus undertakes, and he recognises as the first condition of that theory that there should be only one way of being and correspondingly only one way of signifying. Thus he defines the object of his search as wisdom, and he says:

> "Wisdom is one thing: it is to know the thought by which all things are steered through all things." (Fragment 19).[1]

In other words, the logic or wisdom of Heraclitus is an account of processes and it applies to all phenomena whatever. And he maintains (Fragment 17) that as contrasted with this wisdom, the wisdom claimed by Pythagoras and other contemporaries is only a knowledge of many things and an art of mischief.[2]

The point is that in Pythagorean theory, fundamentally different types of explanation are given in different cases, and accordingly we have to suppose that there are different kinds of truth and reality. The units have one kind of being, the unlimited has another and figures have a third. And similarly a different type of being is attributed to the harmonious and to the discordant. The ultimate units and fundamental harmonies are eternal but the various things which appear to us are merely transitory. In other words, the eternal world of

---
[1] John Burnet, *op.cit.*, p. 134.
[2] [JA] *Cf.*, familiar and unfamiliar; or rational and irrational.[Ed.:] Anderson diverges from Burnet who prefers "imposture" to "mischief" in Fragment 17.

numbers is contrasted with the transitory world of what we regard as physical processes.

Now accepting a theory of that kind, we may be able for a time to solve problems in some particular field, but disconnections and incoherences are bound to appear. And it is because of the necessity of explaining away these inconsistencies that the Pythagorean theory is described by Heraclitus as mischievous. As against this art of giving special explanations of particular cases, understanding, according to Heraclitus, consists in the recognition of the fact that the same categories apply to all things, that there are not different kinds of being, eternal and transitory, but that all alike are historical or in process. Now this does not mean that Heraclitus is explaining away any appearance of permanence among things or that he is saying that there is no such thing as being but only becoming. According to him each process has determinate being, in being the peculiar sort of process that it is and in being placed among other definite processes. And the notion of permanence merely indicates an inaccurate way of considering things which persist for a certain period of time but nonetheless are definitely historical and are constituted by processes. Thus, process is for Heraclitus the common measure of things and recognition of it enables us to understand things, to find the connections and distinctions between things by placing them all on a common basis. That this understanding is not given by mere inquiry is shown by the work of Pythagoras and other thinkers of the time. That it is not given by mere observation is shown by the errors that are made in ordinary life, by the mythological explanations of phenomena which are offered and by the assumption of permanence or fixity merely because the changes that are going on are not immediately obvious. Heraclitus does not condemn observation nor does he condemn inquiry. He considers that they are both necessary and that there is no other way of arriving at truth. But they do not safeguard us against errors because in our observations and inquiries we employ certain fixed ideas, certain fixed expectations, we demand that nature should conform to our wishes and so we are often misled into supposing that it actually does so. Now in order to avoid error as much as possible, in order to develop understanding to its fullest extent we require, Heraclitus says, to hold fast to what is common to all, that is, we require to conduct our investigations on the basis of the common nature of things and not to invent explanations in order to arrive at the result we want. Thus it is an essential part of the theory of knowledge that what leads men astray is desire; it is desire that provides the basis of all mythological thinking, a type of thinking which is specially exemplified in dreams (*cf.*, Freud, whose theories are approached by Heraclitus—for example *Totem and Taboo*).

> Psycho-analysts and Freud: objects in dreams satisfy latent unrealised desires. Dualism of satisfied and unsatisfied desire. The world of permanent realities is a way of conceiving the world without dissatisfaction or discord.

Lecture 18

Heraclitus continued—all things in process—contrast with Pythagoras

The difference between Heraclitus and Pythagoras: the former thought it necessary for the sake of consistency to reject dualistic doctrines, and supported a single way of being, namely, process, change, persistence and acquisition [and] process and interaction; admits a many. Heraclitus did not set up a different method than ordinary observation. Though this is fallible, yet we have no other means of obtaining facts. Observation is combined with anticipation. We must have a logical outlook and not admit distinct sorts of reality, but hold that all is of a single sort. Heraclitus condemns dualism and shows its source. Of our desires or demands on reality some are satisfied and some are not; we imagine states in which they would be satisfied in dreams, in thinking, and imaginings generally, where they get their unobtained satisfaction. There is a division between the dream worlds, or rational worlds, and the actual unsatisfactory world which does not correspond to preconceptions, and unless we expect the unexpected we do not find truth. We are deceived if we lay down laws for nature. The result is the higher and lower realities of dualism; the higher reality satisfies particular desires in imagining that which is persisting.

Taking the fundamental contention of Heraclitus to be that all things are in process, we find that there are certain objections brought to this view, similar to objections brought by Eleatics to the Pythagorean theory of *becoming*. For example, the criticisms of Heraclitus advanced by Socrates in the Platonic dialogues assume that Heraclitus, in spite of his deviation from Pythagoreanism, is committed to certain Pythagorean assumptions. The statement that nothing is but all is becoming could only be taken to be representative of the position of Heraclitus if we accepted the Pythagorean conception of *being*; if being meant permanence, independence of all change and relation, then Heraclitus would certainly deny that anything *is*. But what he maintains is that this is a false view of the nature of being, that there is nothing fixed and permanent but that *what is, is in process* and *what is in process, is*. Similarly the suggestion of Socrates that according to Heraclitus things cannot even be named since they do not stay to let us name them, since by the time we have named them they have become different, and thus no name could have any clear and definite meaning—that suggestion implies that naming and speech in general involves something fixed and permanent, and it also neglects the fact that Heraclitus has endeavoured to give an account of persistence as well as of change, in terms of processes. Now if it were true that in order to be named and understood a thing had to remain constant, then everything that we now recognise as process or as change would be perfectly indescribable.[3] The fact is that we can name different species of motion, and if the motion had to stop to allow us to identify it, it would clearly not be the motion itself that we were identifying. And similarly if, according to Socrates, changes are only describable in terms of other elements in the situation which do not change, then it would appear that changes are not describable. On the theory of Heraclitus naming is just as much a process as the thing which is named, and thus there is no more to prevent our naming a particular phenomenon than to prevent any one process from being related to any other. Thus if the argument of Socrates were to be accepted, it would follow not merely that the view that all things are processes is false but that there can be no such thing as a process at all. In modern philosophy, the theory of Bergson is of a similar character to that of Socrates. He argues that changing reality in some way escapes the concepts that we apply to it. The suggestion is that we try to tie it down by means of these

---

[3][JA] According to the Socratic view, terms "process", "change", "motion" etc. would be meaningless.

concepts but that in so doing we falsify its nature. But this is to assume that our concepts do mean something fixed; in other words that we can only conceive the unchanging, an assumption which contradicts the previous description of reality as changing. We may say then that Heraclitus understood the difficulties of Pythagoreanism and that he is not to be refuted by a mere return to Pythagoreanism. As we have seen, he criticises Pythagoras for attaining only a knowledge of many things but not to understanding. He also makes reference to Pythagorean theories when he says:

> "the hidden attunement is better than the open". (Fragment 47).[4]

He objects, that is, to the Pythagorean theory of harmonies, because those harmonies are represented as mere results, they are simply states of connection and distinction holding between certain units or elements. Now in the Pythagorean account of this attunement the elements are simply taken for granted and the connections and distinctions between them are externally affixed to them by a subsequent act of thought. Now this means that we have a knowledge of many things, many units and arrangements of units, without being able to give a general account of their interrelations because we have no fundamental theory of *being*. Now according to Heraclitus it is quite possible to have an attunement of things, that is, to have things arranged in a certain way, but it would be impossible if the things themselves were mere units without individual character and without a history. In order to have continuity in our thinking we require, Heraclitus thinks, to give an account of the supposed elements similar to the account we give of configurations. That is, we have to regard what previously was taken as elemental or simple as being itself an attunement, as being itself a complex of interrelated elements and in this process of analysis, according to Heraclitus, we can never arrive at ultimate elements, since this would lead again to all the difficulties of Pythagoreanism. But we must consider everything we deal with as being complex, as having parts or constituents connected with and distinguished from one another. Thus Heraclitus speaks of things as being attunements of opposite

---
[4] John Burnet, *op.cit.*, p. 136.

tensions. He considers that such must be the character of anything whether we immediately observe it or not; and that is why he says that the hidden attunement is better than the open. The Pythagorean arrangement of things might have been taken to have simple or elementary constituents, were it not for the fact that we must recognise all things as complex, since otherwise they could have no history.

This theory of Heraclitus is naturally expressed in such a way as to be in accordance with his general theory of becoming. Since all things are processes, to say of anything that it has constituents is to say that it is a *complex of interrelated processes or activities*, or in general, all things are complex and active. Now in this way Heraclitus claims to be able to account alike for constancy or persistence and for change. Each thing has within it various tendencies and is brought into relation with similar tendencies in other things, and according to the way in which these processes work out, things come to have new constituents or to retain those that they already have. It is because in terms of this theory of the hidden attunement we are no longer compelled to regard constancy and change as incommensurable, that the hidden attunement is said to be better. And similarly it is precisely because things are active and complex that we should *expect the unexpected*. Since everything has constituents and these constituents have constituents, since in fact everything is infinitely complex, we can never profess to know all about a thing or situation and to predict exactly what its outcome will be. Heraclitus does not mean that it is impossible to make correct predictions but it is impossible to make complete predictions, and thus with the existence of unknown factors there is always at least a possibility of error; there is always a need for further observation and inquiry.

Lecture 19

Heraclitus continued—things as attunements—doctrine of exchanges

When Heraclitus declares that the hidden attunement is better than the open, he means that attunement or configuration must not be something which simply holds between units and is, as it were, affixed to them from without. It must arise from their own nature and they themselves must be attunements. Thus corresponding to the conception of outward change we have that of inward tension, of changes going on within a thing in terms of the different tendencies which constitute the being of a thing as a historical entity. Now such tendencies may be so related as to balance one another, so that we have a condition of constancy. This would not be describable from the point of view of Heraclitus as apparent constancy, but it would be the only sort of constancy that there is—constancy as it appears in historical situations. And those who think that constancy means fixity, that it excludes all change, are misconceiving it. If the same interrelation among different tendencies is maintained throughout a period of time, then we have a persisting thing. But it is not to be supposed that there is anything which persists for an indefinite time. The general position of Heraclitus in relation to the Pythagoreans is that they have failed to give an account of change in terms of fixity and therefore an attempt must be made to give an account of what is called fixity in terms of change. This is an attempt to work out to a satisfactory conclusion the theory of the Milesians. It is an attempt to restore the doctrine of fluidity as the common denominator of things, which was implicit in the speculations of Thales, and to remove the inconsistencies into which the philosophy of Anaximenes fell owing to the dualism of qualitative and quantitative treatment of things—as consisting of air, and, on the other hand, simply in terms of density. This being the fundamental position, it is erroneous to suppose that Heraclitus presents a theory analogous to that of earlier thinkers but merely chooses a different element as fundamental. It is not correct to say that just as Thales regarded all things as forms of water, and Anaximenes as forms of air, and just as Xcnophanes considered earth to be the fundamental reality, so Heraclitus selected the fourth element fire as that by which all other phenomena could be explained. It must be admitted that fire occupies a prominent place in the theories of Heraclitus and that his insistence on its primacy leads him into a number of difficulties. But the theory of change and exchange which he formulates is quite independent of any special theory about fire and if we consider fire to have been simply a convenient illustration of his theory of exchange, we will be misrepresenting the position of Heraclitus less than if we present it in the form "All is fire".

Now taking it as an illustration of his fundamental doctrine of exchange—a doctrine which he calls his *word* or λογος—we find that it exemplifies the hidden attunement of things according to which they are to be regarded as complexes of interrelated activities instead of compounds or arrangements of so many elements. That Heraclitus did not confine his theory to the consideration of fire is shown by many of the fragments, for example:

> "You will not find out the boundaries of soul, so deep is the measure of it." (Fragment 71).[5]

This is clearly a protest against the Pythagorean treatment of soul as a certain fixed figure or arrangement of elements. Now on the Pythagorean view, there is an incommensurability between things and elements. If this is to be avoided, then we must treat the "elements" as themselves complex and active and not merely fixed and static things which can be moved about into different positions and thus provide different figures. If that were so, we should require to suppose the existence of forces capable of moving the units about and thus we should at once be re-introducing animistic conceptions and at the same time recognising the existence of some real thing whose nature could not be expressed in terms of units. That is the difficulty which is to be found in the theories of Empedocles and Anaxagoras.

> Attempt to answer Eleatics on Pythagorean basis—certain elements in existence—four elements, with love and strife causing combinations (Empedocles). According to Anaxagoras—the mover of seeds in the complexes was mind—dualistic position—the seeds are what are real and the others cannot be so—if the latter are, there is no reason to say that all things are constituted of the elements.

The position of Heraclitus in this connection implies that we can never know *all* about a thing. Any description of it that we give implies the possibility of further descriptions, any activity or tendency which we find in it has itself further tendencies or constituents. But this does not mean that we cannot know *something* about a thing. Allowing that further knowledge

---
[5] John Burnet, *op.cit.*, p. 138.

is allowable (possible?)[6] we can still have definite and direct knowledge in the meantime. The really sceptical position is that which assumes that there are certain things that we know all about, because in that case we can never study relations between these things, and we can never think of a thing as having a history. But if discovery is impossible, then we are reduced to a position of scepticism. In place of this discontinuity between units or ultimate modes of being, the theory that active complexes are made up of active complexes retains continuity and makes it possible for us to recognise things, even if they have changed in certain particulars so long as a certain interrelation among tendencies persists. And this is what is conveyed by the Heraclitean formula that "strife is harmony". If we regard the units as perfectly indifferent to one another, and we must do so if we have a theory of pure and simple units, then we cannot take them in relation to one another; and so we can give no account of configuration and harmony. On the other hand, if we realise that things are always interacting, then we can find a formula for their interaction. We can describe the way in which that interaction takes place. Thus in Fragment 59 we have another suggested criticism of the Pythagorean theory of figures.

> "Couples are things whole and things not whole; what is drawn together and what is drawn asunder; the harmonious and the discordant." (Fragment 59).[7]

This would appear to mean that the Pythagoreans cannot consistently treat a couple or pair of things as a single thing. To say, on their view, that there is a pair means that there are two units, each absolutely distinct from the other. But unless we can also consider the couple as one thing, unless we can also treat it as a unit, then we cannot speak of *a* couple or *a* pair; we cannot say *one couple*, because in terms of ultimate units, the fact that it is two precludes it from being one. Now according to the theory of Heraclitus, on the other hand, according to which there are no ultimate units, we can recognise a thing to have two constituent units, each of which is treated as one, but this does not hinder us from taking

---
[6][JA] available? attainable.
[7] John Burnet, *op.cit.*, p. 137. [Ed.:] Anderson omits the final sentence: "The one is made up of all things, and all things issue from the one." It is included in the student notes in parentheses.

the two together and treating the aggregate as one. Since the possibility of enumeration depends on the possibility of treating the same thing as one and as many, it is not possible to work out a mathematical theory, as the Pythagoreans had attempted to do, on the basis of pure units. Now the fact that Heraclitus works out these criticisms and puts them forward as essential to his own theory shows that that theory is not limited to a consideration of fire, that it is not a purely physical theory, but that it is a logical theory, dealing with the general conditions of existence and describing them as change and exchange; or, implicitly, as *complex activity*.

Lecture 20

Heraclitus continued—the conception of fire—process not substance

Coming then to the actual position of the conception of fire in the doctrine of Heraclitus, we find that Heraclitus represents fire as illustrating that system of exchanges which is his fundamental conception of the nature of being. As he puts it:

> "This world, which is the same for all, no one of gods or men has made, but it was ever, is now and ever shall be, an everliving Fire, with measures of it kindling and measures going out." (Fragment 20).[8]

Now this in itself indicates an objection to the position of Anaximander wherein a distinction is made between the being of things and the origin of things. And Heraclitus brings out the fact that it is not the function of philosophy to distinguish phases in universal history, or cosmic eras, but to show what is the nature of things at any time that we like to consider them. Because, however different any phases of historical development might be, they must be capable of investigation and description, and this implies that they all have something in common. Now it is this common way of being, constituting the conditions of investigation and description, that is the central object of philosophic inquiry. We find also in the reference to measures kindling and measures going out that Heraclitus is primarily concerned with the phenomenon of exchange and only secondarily with

---
[8] John Burnet, *op.cit.*, p. 134.

any particular exchange. He is concerned to account for constancy in terms of equal changes in different directions, to account for stability in terms of the balancing of tensions. Now if we take the case of a fire or flame we find that in order that it may continue for any length of time it must always have fresh fuel, that is, at any time so much not-fire is becoming fire (or certain physical processes are acquiring the fiery character). At the same time other processes are *losing* that character (or so much fire is becoming not-fire), that is, we have the passing out of smoke from the flame. What we call a flame, even when it is burning steadily and might be taken to be a fixed and unchanging light,[9] is in reality a process of combustion. Now, generalising on this basis, we arrive at the theory that anything that exists requires to be supported or nourished by certain material, just as the fire is fed by the fuel, and at the same time this thing provides material which sustains or nourishes other things. And so long as there is a balance between what a thing receives and what it gives off, the thing remains constant. Heraclitus sums up this theory of opposite exchanges and the balancing of tendencies by maintaining that harmony is based upon strife. It is not static, as the Pythagoreans supposed, but dynamic.

> "We must know that war is common to all and strife is justice, and that all things come into being and pass away through strife" (Fragment 62).[10]—and, it should be added, *persist* through strife.

Now this doctrine is put forward as an answer to "Anaximander" who had argued that the encroachment of one thing upon another is an act of injustice for which reparation must be made; that by encroaching on one another things returned to the boundless, that is, they are all reduced to the same dead level. Heraclitus argues, on the contrary, that but for this encroachment, but for the way in which things opposed and passed through one another, but for the general phenomenon of change and opposition, things would never persist and exhibit their distinctive character. And he argues that interaction between things is possible because each thing is a complex of interacting forces, or that the connection and distinction of things are made possible

---
[9][JA] For example a *star*.
[10] John Burnet, *op.cit.*, p. 137.

by the fact that each thing has connections and distinctions in it. In terms of this theory of outward and inward tension Heraclitus regards strife as the distinctive way in which things exist.[11] Thus we have a further demonstration of the fact that the theory of exchanges is not limited in its application to the phenomenon of combustion. But, at the same time, Heraclitus does most frequently illustrate his theory by reference to fire. Thus he says:

> "All things are an exchange for Fire and Fire for all things, even as wares for gold and gold for wares." (Fragment 22).[12]

Also,

> "Fire lives the death of air and air lives the death of fire"—but "water lives the death of earth, earth that of water". (Fragment 25).[13]

So that, principally, the reference is to the general theory of the way in which things are nourished or maintained, to the fact that one thing comes to be or continues to be only because other things cease to be. And this is connected with the general doctrine referred to by Socrates in the *Phaedo* of the generation of things from their opposites. Thus we have the statement,

> "Cold things become warm, and what is warm cools; what is wet dries and the parched is moistened." (Fragment 39).[14]

Now what all this implies is a theory of the existence of things in certain cycles, that is, in processes which proceed regularly through successive phases, returning again to the starting point, as in the case of the seasons; day and night, phases of the moon, and so forth. So that we find a further illustration of the fact that Heraclitus is endeavouring to work out the Milesian theories to their logical conclusion.

What the illustration of combustion and the general theory of exchanges are supposed to convey is something of the nature of cyclic activity. Not only does a particular thing depend upon the activity of other things in the cycle in order that it may be maintained, but the cycle itself depends for its continuance on the activity of the thing. And just as in the case of the theory of the constituents of things it

---
[11] [JA] The thing's internal tensions being links in various chains of tension going beyond the things: having, in fact, a place in a cycle, which is a tension in something else etc.
[12] John Burnet, *op.cit.*, p. 135.
[13] John Burnet, *op.cit.*, p. 135.
[14] John Burnet, *op.cit.*, p. 136.

Figure 5.

was found necessary to regard what is complex as having complex constituents, so it is necessary to regard the things which recur in a particular cycle as being themselves cyclical, as having a cyclical activity within them. The illustration which would be most natural in modern times and one which Heraclitus actually employs is that of the individual and society. The individual depends for his continuance on the society of which he is a member and the society depends for its continuance on the operations of individuals. Thus, in terms of this illustration, we can understand what is meant by the existence of a thing in a system which maintains it, and by the assistance given by the thing to the continuance of the system and we can also understand how it is possible to regard these things, the constituents of the system, as themselves systems having constituents. The theory can be further illustrated by developing the reference to economics. Taking the system of money-exchanges, it may be said that we require to produce or to supply or offer goods in order to obtain money and we require to offer money in order to consume goods. Or, leaving aside the consideration of money as a mere intermediary, it can be said that we require to produce in order to consume and to consume in order to produce; to demand in order to supply, and to supply in order to demand. Applying the economic metaphor to the existence of things, we can say that any particular thing is a sort of market upon which exchanges take place at certain rates and the market persists so long as the exchanges balance one another; so long as supply and demand are equal. And similarly a system or cycle continues so long as it can *produce* what it requires, though it does not follow that each member of that system must produce exactly what he requires: as long as the general production satisfies the general requirements, the system pays its way and continues to exist.[15]

Lecture 21

Heraclitus continued—the theory of systems and cycles

We can sum up the economic expression of the theory by saying that things persist so long as they pay their way, so long as their products can be exchanged for their requirements. But the theory further implies that everything in the long run becomes, so to speak, bankrupt, that it ceases to pay its way and that instead of receiving nutrition from other things and providing nutrition for other things, it in its turn becomes food or fuel for the upkeep of some other thing or system. That is what is meant by the statement that fire lives the death of air etc. Now apart from this consideration of the *ultimate*[16] bankruptcy of any thing or system, the important point is the way in which things occupy places in a system and the way they contribute to one another, the fact that while a thing receives from the system what is required to keep it going, it must at the same time produce something that helps to keep the system going. Now this theory of things persisting in cycles and cycles passing through things is immediately applicable to the phenomena of the seasons, which as we have seen were of so much importance in Milesian thought. But it has many further applications not merely to human activities of an economic and social character but also to physical facts. Thus Heraclitus uses the illustration of a river to support his theory that all things flow. In the case of a river we have obviously something which is continuously changing. At any given part of its course it may have a similar appearance on two successive occasions, but we know that the water which was there on a former occasion has now passed downstream and its place has been taken by water coming in from further up. Hence we have the Heraclitean statement that

> "You cannot step twice into the same river, for fresh waters are ever flowing in upon you." (Fragments 41 and 42).[17]

---

[15][JA] "produce": really *get*; certain conditions external to the system are necessary: certain *appropriateness*.)
[16][JA] ("ultimate": *eventual*)
[17] John Burnet, *op.cit.*, p. 136.

What this means is not that it is impossible *in Heraclitean terms* to speak about "the same river", but that it is impossible to do so if sameness means identity of *substance* as it was understood by the Milesians. What enables the river to persist, that is, to be a continuous feature of some particular landscape is the equality of exchanges, the fact that what is passing downwards from a given point is balanced by what is coming down to a given point. Taking the river as a whole, it remains one describable and identifiable thing because the amount of water that passes out from it into the sea is balanced by the amount that is received from the source. Being the same thing, then, means *not* being composed of an unchangeable and fixed substance *but*, as Heraclitus says, being an attunement of opposite tensions. And this river, which we can describe as a single thing, and which exhibits these exchanges, has a place in a wider system, in which clouds are produced by the evaporation of water and rain produced by the breaking-up of the clouds and thus the river is continually furnished with the water that is required to maintain it. We have then a cycle of rainfall, the flowing of the river, and the formation of clouds by evaporation from the water that thus flows. Now, in the same way, Heraclitus contends that mind and body form a cycle, the mind being maintained by means of the nutrition of the body and itself directing the body in its activity of finding nutrition.[18] The mind has, of course, additional properties and activities, but it is in this particular way that the cycle of mind and body is maintained.

Now this theory of systems or cycles does not imply that a given thing must always remain in the same cycle: it is possible to have passage from one cycle to another, since otherwise one cycle could not help to maintain another.[19] At the same time a thing cannot pass from one system into another system completely unrelated to the former and this implies that the two systems and the things which constitute them are included in some still wider system. And in the second place this theory does not imply that any system persists for ever. Every describable system, every system having a definite history, must contain discords as well as

---

[18][JA] (cf. metabolism.)
[19][JA] Need only be passage of *tension*: wave-motion (a ripple passing from one to other).

harmonies and must be capable of passing away in the production or maintenance of another system. It would appear from some of the fragments that Heraclitus supposed that there must be an ultimate and all-inclusive system. But this assumption is inconsistent with his general theory, because this supposed total system, having nothing outside it from which it could be nourished, could have no history and consequently would not be describable. Taking this system as a whole we should have to say that it was absolutely static; but if once this admission were made, then its constituent systems would also have to be regarded as static, so that in the end we should arrive at the notion of the Eleatic One, which implies that there is no such thing as history but simply a permanent and unitary being. In so far as Heraclitus suggested that there must be a cycle of all cycles or a total system, he lays himself open to Eleatic criticism. But this suggestion could only be regarded as a failure to work out to its logical conclusion his general theory of the nature of being as an attunement of opposite tensions and as involving existence within a system. For if we assume a totality of things which is not within a further system, then we cannot say that it *is* in the same sense in which particular things are said to be. And consequently we are brought back to the duality of being which characterised the Pythagorean system, and the fundamental conception of Heraclitus that what is, is in process and what is in process, is, would have to be abandoned.

Lecture 22

Heraclitus continued—each thing a cycle

What is required to complete this theory of the existence of things in cycles is the theory that each thing is itself cyclical, that we cannot describe a thing by any simple formula of absolute equality between what is supplied to it and what it supplies. We must recognise that variations in the exchanges are possible, but that the system persists, so long as these variations take place according to a regular formula. Thus at any given time the exchanges may be unequal, but if they balance one another throughout a certain period, then the cycle persists. If we return to the example of the river, we find that there is a variation in its appearances from one season to another and from one time to another. There is a rainy season at which what the river receives is rather more than it has been giving out, and so there is a greater volume of water at any point along its course. Then at the dry season the river receives rather less than it has been giving out and accordingly it shrinks. Now in spite of these variations, though we have floods at one season and drought at another, we still say that it is the same river. And this is because though these changes do definitely take place, they balance one another throughout the year, so that the cycle of increase and diminution is maintained. If change continued indefinitely in any one direction, there would come a time when we could no longer say with any significance that this was the same thing. We could no longer speak of that river with any precise meaning. And similarly with things in general, they persist in their cyclic activities so long as (to return to the economic metaphor) they can balance their accounts for a certain period. Taking the year as the most noteworthy period, we can say that if yearly revenue and yearly expenditure are equal, then whatever may be the state of the exchanges at different times of the year, we can say intelligibly that the thing or system in question has a continued existence. Now as in the case of the Milesians, Heraclitus was particularly interested in the yearly cycle but at the same time he pointed out many other instances of this cyclical variation. Thus we have day and night, and, in the case of man, sleeping and waking: and Heraclitus further applies this conception to such oppositions as those of youth and age, life and death, and even good and bad. His position is expressed in Fragments 35 and 36 in what appears to be a mystical form, but in light of his general theory we can see how these statements are to be interpreted. Thus he says:

"... (Day and night) are one. (Fragment 35)"

"God is day and night, winter and summer, war and peace, surfeit and hunger." (Fragment 36).[20]

---

[20] John Burnet, *op.cit.*, p. 136. [Ed.:] The fragments in Burnet are:
"35. Hesiod is most men's teacher. Men are sure he knew very many things, a man who did not know day or night! They are one.
"36. God is day and night, winter and summer, war and peace, surfeit and hunger; but he takes various shapes, just as fire, when it is mingled with spices, is named according to the savour of each."

What this supposed identification of opposites really means is that these things are taken as opposites precisely because they occur in the same cycle. "Day and night are one" means that day and night belong to a definable cycle, that they are phases in a recurrent process. So that if we wish to give an account or explanation of either we find that we are at the same time giving an account of the other, because the only way in which they can be dealt with historically is by reference to the cycle in which they appear.[21] Now modern astronomy has justified Heraclitus as far as his theory of day and night, and the seasons, is concerned. It has shown the place of day and night and similarly of seasons in a certain cycle. It has given an account, in terms of the motions of the bodies in the solar system, of these different phases. So that even if Heraclitus gave a wrong account of these cycles—as he did, in terms of fire and water—he at least showed the logical conditions which any account of the phenomena must satisfy. And the same applies to his other theories, to his other descriptions of cyclical recurrence in terms of fire and water. Thus in the case of youth and age, youth is considered to be that period in which we are on the way up to the height of our powers, in which, as Heraclitus would put it, we are becoming more fiery. And in that connection it has to be remembered that Heraclitus identifies fire with understanding, so that to say that the fiery element in a person increases means that he is acquiring greater understanding. Naturally this is a process in which the person requires nourishment, in which he is sustained by the operations of a certain system, which would be, broadly speaking, the system of education. On the other hand, age is taken as the period in which we are on the way down, in which the fiery element, or understanding, is gradually being diminished until it is extinguished at death. Now the fact that Heraclitus expressed the phenomena of human life in terms of the Milesian elements does not imply that he was ignorant of these phenomena, but merely that he found a connection between these phenomena and the phenomenon of combustion, a connection which as a matter of fact does not exist. At the same time there is the real similarity implied

---

[21] [JA] To find the *difference* of PM is at same time to find difference of not-PM.

in the conception of things as existing in a cyclical manner. We can say therefore that the account which Heraclitus gives of human nature may be substantially correct, even if he expresses it in peculiar terms. In fact we may say that the greatest interest of Heraclitus was in human life, that he lacked the astronomical sense which was most notable in Anaximander, and it was in consequence of this that he was ready to assume the existence of a total system and that he even appears, like Anaximenes, to have accepted the common conception of an absolute up and down.[22] We can say then that owing to the limitations of his outlook Heraclitus was unable to make definite advances in astronomy. Nonetheless the logical method which he formulated is the correct one for astronomy as well as for any other sort of investigation.

Coming then to the cycle which constitutes the existence of a person we find that Heraclitus places the mind as the fiery element at the apex of the cycle and the body as the watery element at the base of the cycle; and we should presume that the two communicated with one another through the medium of air, but this is a matter which Heraclitus does not work out. The main point is that in human life there are two tendencies, upward and downward, the downward tendency being that of desire and the upward being in the direction of understanding. This being the general formula of the human cycle there are still variations within those limits. We can presume for example that one individual differs from another: that some men have greater understanding, that is, more of the fiery element. And again we have the minor cycles, sleeping and waking, which corresponds to the astronomical cycle, day and night, youth and age, and others of a like character within the general cycle which constitutes a life. In sleep the fiery or understanding element is reduced to a minimum whereas in waking it is at a maximum. And we have a general comparison between a person's mind and the sun. We could roughly express the theory of Heraclitus in its astronomical application, by saying that the sun sleeps at night. The fragment in which Heraclitus says that the sun is new every day has to be interpreted in relation to this general position.[23] It is similar to the statement that we cannot step

---

[22][JA] But doesn't "up and down same"... really *contradict* this? Of course, there could be "up" within a particular system, as Anaximander admitted.

twice into the same river, that is, the sun on successive days belongs to the same cycle and is a persistent thing as far as anything can be. And similarly a person is the same person from one day to another. In a certain sense we can make an absolute distinction between the two. Considering reality, as Heraclitus does, as consisting of processes or activities, we are bound to distinguish between a person's activities on any one day and his activities on any other day. They are definitely different. And if we were to assert that there is a permanent self which is behind all these activities, then we should be reintroducing the Pythagorean dualism, and we should be unable to explain how a thing which was the same in all respects should have different manifestations on different occasions.[24] The problem is to be solved by reference to the continuity of the cycle. No activity of any one day is identical with an activity of any other day, but there may be continuity between them; the exchanges may be maintained in such relations that we may say quite significantly that it is the same person who appears on these different occasions and that he does the same work or undertakes the same activity on these different occasions (every occasion or activity being itself continuous and divisible).

> If we think of identity there can be no connection, but there can be if we speak of continuity.

Lecture 23

Heraclitus continued—personal identity—being activities not having activities

Heraclitus makes a definite comparison between the mind and the sun based on the astronomical error that the sun is extinguished at night. But in spite of this error Heraclitus provides the solution of the problem of identity in the case of cyclical things, which as he argues means all things whatever. In discussing personal identity, many modern theorists have got into difficulties, because they identify the person with an ultimate and elementary consciousness and then they have to recognise the fact that this consciousness is intermittent, that it is not present in sleep and consequently the supposed

---
[23] John Burnet, *op.cit.*, Fragment 32, p. 135.
[24] [JA] Leibnizian alternative: a thing is its whole history (concrete universal): is no real alternative.

permanent entity which constitutes the identity of the self is found not to be present, and the problem arises of showing how a person can be the same person from one day to another—how he can overcome the gap between the two periods of consciousness and take up his activities where he left off. What Heraclitus shows is that that is not a real problem: that we do not have any identical element persisting through a period of waking, disappearing in sleep, and then reappearing when the sleep terminates, that what we have is the continuity of a certain cycle, a continuous passage through various phases, the recurrence of which constitutes all that we mean and all that we can mean by personal identity.[25] In terms of an abstract consciousness it would be difficult to see how it came about that we were the same persons from one day to another, and why an individual upon waking should not find himself a different person from the one who went to sleep. From the point of view of the doctrine of simple entities, it would be impossible not merely to account for identity from one day to another but even to explain identity from one moment to another (within one day). If the self were something permanent and unchangeable, then the different activities of different periods, no matter how closely they came to one another in time, would be quite irrelevant to the person himself and could not in any intelligible sense be described as his. What we have to account for in personal identity is the fact that the being in question acts differently on different occasions and also acts similarly on similar occasions, though even these similar occasions are different from one another. Now these phenomena, these activities by means of which we pass judgment on personality, are quite explicable if we regard the person himself not as an abstract unit or ultimate essence but in the Heraclitean manner as being himself complex and active; not as *having* certain activities but as *being* those activities in a certain order and with certain interrelations. And on this basis we are able to account for the occurrence of different phases in the activity of the person without having to conclude that he is a different person.[26]

---

[25][JA] Bodily metabolism and, within that cycle, *mental* metabolism.
[26][JA] Cf., river: flood and shrinking; or moon! that is, that it is in a different state of tension (differently attuned) in the two cases.

Thus although Heraclitus is wrong in thinking that the sun changes its character and not merely its position at night, he is quite right in thinking that the mind or person loses certain of its activities during sleep and acquires them again on waking. And this means that certain of the activities and tendencies which constitute the self or the mind are more active in certain phases of the mind's life or history, and less active in other phases. During our waking life certain of our tendencies or activities (which we may unite under the general term of motives) are dominant: we are undertaking particular pursuits to the exclusion of others. But these pursuits don't constitute our entire make-up. There is always a certain opposition, a certain inward tension unconnected with any activity whatever. So that during our waking life certain motives, certain potential pursuits or *wishes* (as Freud calls them) are repressed, are prevented from finding outlet and these repressed motives which are never without some effect even on our waking activity become more active during sleep.[27] And as Freud maintains, it is these repressed wishes that find satisfaction in dreams. This is quite in accordance with the position of Heraclitus who refers definitely to dreams as typical of the domination of desire over understanding and of error in general.[28]

> Dualism involves the discovery of a world to satisfy our desires—opposition between opposite tendencies.

Lecture 24

Heraclitus continued—the ethical theory

We may sum up the doctrine of Heraclitus by referring to his ethical theory. As we have seen, the statements like "day and night are one" are not to be taken as a denial of the difference between the two but as implying that the two are parts of a single cycle and are to be described in relation to one another. So the particular statement that good and bad are one is not a denial of ethical distinctions but is an assertion that these distinctions are to be understood not in any abstract way but in terms of the cycle of human activities.

---
[27] [JA] Sleeper: world of his own.
[28] [JA] (*Cf.* "myths", mystery-mongers etc.) *What is common to all*, namely, strife: logic of events, as against myths, Utopias. (A *certain strife* and thus a certain *thing*—namely, property—disappears in classless society.)

The Pythagorean theory of goodness was simply that of a fixed standard to which individual things required to be adjusted, and having made an absolute disconnection between discord and harmony the Pythagoreans were unable to show how the discordant could become harmonious. This is connected with their general difficulty in finding any relation between being and becoming when the former is considered as absolutely fixed and the latter as simply transient and indefinite.[29] And when a position of this kind is adopted in relation to ethics we find a number of insoluble problems, corresponding to the discontinuity between one configuration and another, between discord and harmony; that is to say, we are brought face to face with the problem which has proved exceedingly troublesome to almost all moralists since that time—the problem of the inducement to goodness. That is, granted that an individual does not come up to the moral standard prescribed, the question is, how can he be induced to do so or to attempt to do so. If he is not already good, then goodness will make no appeal to him and the mere statement that some other way of living than that which he adopts would be *better*, will either simply be rejected by him or else will be accepted verbally but really make no difference to his conduct. Thus we have such ethical dualisms as that between virtue and happiness or pleasure. Certain persons appear to pursue pleasure and to be indifferent to virtue and therefore if any inducement is to be offered them to become virtuous, it must be in terms of pleasure, and so they are informed that happiness is the reward of virtue, that if they are good they will be happy. But what this means, if these individuals will accept this assurance, is that they will still be operating on the basis of the pleasure-principle: and that though their acts may outwardly conform to what is called virtue, their inner acts will be quite different from that of a person who follows these activities spontaneously or pursues them for their own sake. So that in spite of a certain resemblance of a particular act (to what would be done by a virtuous person), the cycle of activity will still be dominated by the motive of pleasure; and it will be impossible legitimately to say that he has now acquired goodness in any definite sense.

---

[29][JA] Processes as definite and distinguishable (propositions; events).

That is the type of ethics to which Heraclitus is opposed. From his point of view we can only arrive at a theory of goodness by considering the history of persons and not by setting up any arbitrary standard external to these activities.[30] Granted that there is a real distinction between good and bad activities it will still be the case that the only inducement to goodness will be those good motives already in existence. It won't be necessary to make any external appeal to them since of their own nature they proceed in a good way. On the other hand, it will not be possible to make an appeal to any other motives since from their own nature they are not concerned with goodness. This does not imply that the only way in which goodness is acquired is by the operation of those good things which already exist, even though they do greatly assist its development. It is possible that at a certain stage in the history of some being it will rise to a higher level and display characters which previously were absent. Thus we might say that in human beings there is a general tendency towards certain good activities even though we know that these are considerably assisted and reinforced by other activities of a similar character around them. But whether goodness comes into existence in the natural course of a creature's development or by the aid of the good activities among other creatures, in general of the same species, at least there is no significance in the conception of *inducement* to goodness, that is, of prevailing upon individuals to adopt an arbitrary standard of which they do not see the significance, on account of other ends which will incidentally be satisfied. The result of applying a theory of that kind will be not goodness by conformity. And in its application, the historical character of individuals, their peculiar problems and requirements, will be neglected and consequently those who do not respond to this particular kind of training will be blamed for their failure to do so, though in point of fact the blame rests on those who have improperly treated them.

The most important statement which Heraclitus makes in this connection is the statement that man's character

---
[30][JA] >< good *fixed* and evil diverse ("unlimited"), we have good becoming and ceasing (*striving*). This very opposite of Burnet's "beyond good and evil". cf. It is the *opposite* that is good for us etc. [Ed.] The handwritten symbol >< is a very common abbreviation in JA's notes.

is his fate. Now this statement can be understood in a negative way as involving the denial of fate or destiny as an agency supposed to watch over and control a person's history, a conception which we find strongly developed in Greek tragedy. And this would be rejected in the same way that all mythological explanation of events would be rejected. But what is particularly important about this rejection of mythology in the case of Heraclitus is that he not merely *desires* to do away with mythology but has found a method of doing so. In the treatment of things as events or processes, and as existing in relation to a cycle and selves having inner complexity and a rhythmic succession of phases, he has made it possible to give an account of events in terms of events and to do away with any conception of an agency presiding over events, because such a conception adds nothing to our knowledge of events themselves and enables us to make no predictions. Now this is not the case with the Pythagorean units which are of a totally different character from the events which occasion their taking up one position, or entering into one configuration rather than another, and in terms of which such processes are completely unintelligible. But what Heraclitus means positively by this statement is that when all allowance is made for the influence of environment, it will be found that certain individuals are naturally capable of certain activities, that we cannot accuse circumstances of causing all our deficiencies; since it depends very largely on a person's character what circumstances he will find himself in. That which would be a difficulty for one person will be an opportunity for another. And the importance of this view, which is still deterministic, is that it disposes of a false conception of determinism according to which the history of a thing is entirely determined by its surroundings, a theory which would lead to an infinite regress, since these circumstances would be determined by their circumstances and surroundings, and so on. But a true determinism recognises that a thing's history is determined partly by the circumstances and partly by its own character (that is, to those circumstances which happen to enter into the cycle in which it exists).[31]

Lecture 25

Heraclitus continued—determinism—misunderstandings of Heraclitus—Burnet's errors

This question of determinism and of the importance of individual character is connected with what have been called the "aristocratic" views of Heraclitus. It is a natural consequence of his theory that not all individuals are capable of the same activities; that some have better characters than others and accordingly live better lives; those, that is, who have a better understanding and are not so much under the control of desire. Now this in itself does not imply an aristocratic theory. The theory of equality which is taken to be fundamental to democracy is not that all men have precisely the same capacities, it is simply that no man should be granted absolute authority and power to determine the lives of others. For though it may actually be the case that one man has higher capacities than another, these special abilities have to be discovered in some way, that is, in the working out of social relations we have to take account of personal beliefs. And we cannot say that the man who is generally thought to have the greatest capacities really has them. Still less can we accept any individual's own word that his capacities are the greatest. And further, granted that a person has great capacities, this does not mean that he should apply these capacities in dominating others. What is required is a system in which valuable activities will have the greatest opportunity for operating, and as regards the different capacities of different individuals, this difference will be dealt with by these individuals undertaking different social functions. What we require is a specific correlation between definite capacities and definite functions. But it does not follow even from this that there should be an authority whose function it is to work out this correlation. Because this supposed authority would itself be fallible and it would only be either by his own judgment or by the judgment of persons who were admittedly less capable, that this function would be given to him. Thus the position of Heraclitus would be quite in accordance with democratic theory, if it is understood that there are different social functions and that

---

[31][JA] Even so, we cannot find out the boundaries of soul.

Heraclitus 85

in the course of a society's development (particular) persons will come to undertake these functions, but that in every case they will be responsible to society, that it will not be for themselves to say whether they are performing the functions successfully or not, and that they will not continue it as a matter of personal privilege. We may say that democracy, while it can recognise differences of capacity, is opposed to privilege. But this is equally so with Heraclitus who contends that it is necessary to hold fast to what is common to all (also that things *change* and there are no "higher" units or principles), that is, to the logic of events, and not to deviate into a world of our own, in which we suppose that events are entirely under our control and that we have authority over them. When Heraclitus says:

"One is ten thousand to me if he be the best" (Fragment 113).[32]

he is objecting to that false conception of social equality according to which all men have similar capacities. And when he advises the Ephesians to hang themselves because they have cast out their best man, he is simply showing the illogical character of this rejection of the best, since after the best had been cast out, it would be similarly necessary to cast out the best of the remaining men with the eventual result that the society would cease to exist.[33] Now, what Heraclitus desires is a city or society in which as good lives as possible are lived, and what he naturally contends in accordance with his theory is that the best life is kindled or supported by means of less good lives and that they in turn in the course of the social cycle derive some of their support from the best lives in it.[34] Though he seems to have accepted the Pythagorean theory of the three types of lives he does not put forward the view, as they appeared to do, that only the speculative life is valuable and that it would be advantageous to do away with the other types. What he would contend is that these lives have to be taken in relation to one another, so as to constitute the system of interrelated activities which we call society. He certainly believes that

---
[32] John Burnet, *op.cit.*, Fragment 113, p. 140.
[33] John Burnet, *op.cit.*, Fragment 114, p. 140. "The Ephesians would do well to hang themselves, every grown man of them, and leave the city to beardless lads; for they have cast out Hermodorus, the best man among them, saying, 'We will have none who is best among us; if there be any such, let him be so elsewhere and among others.'"
[34] [JA] With him also society is a thing—a cycle—just as much as persons are; they are not "*units*" of which society is a "harmony"—that is, *operating* harmony.

the value of a society is measured by the best life which is lived in it, but he does not consider that the other lives are unnecessary to the good of the whole or are valueless in themselves. The emphasis which he lays on the importance of laws in a city, apart from which laws it would not be a system but a mere aggregate of individuals—that emphasis shows that he had the true conception of equality as equality before the law, that he regarded the citizens as equal in the sense that the various functions which they performed were all equally necessary to the continuance of the city and to the living of good lives within it. This being the case, we can't accept Burnet's contention that Heraclitus despised the mass of mankind. What he certainly did contend against was the tendency which appears in the mass of mankind, and which no doubt he recognised in himself also—the tendency to be dominated by desire and to fall into error by turning aside into a world of our own in which all our expectations are fulfilled.

A further misunderstanding of Heraclitus (not by Burnet) is the view that he supported reason at the expense of sense. He certainly attacked the domination by desire which is commonly called sensuality, but his criticism of the dreamers, the sensual persons, was not that they used their senses, but that they did not know how to use them rightly. But as the fragments show, Heraclitus considered that unless we use our senses, we cannot find the common objective world. It is only necessary that we should use them with understanding, that is, in using them we should understand that we are capable of falling into error by expecting the satisfaction of our desires. The dreamer who expects all his desires to be satisfied[35] used neither his senses nor his understanding correctly. But in true theory, Heraclitus insists, understanding and sense cooperate. (Hence Pythagoreans were not *scientists*.)

A further point, on which Burnet misrepresents the theory, is that of the question of wisdom. Burnet says that according to Heraclitus wisdom is beyond good or bad, that it is

---

[35][JA] Or the Pythagoreans who expected things to be "rational": who tried to dictate to nature, instead of expecting the unexpected (and who thus purchased their heart's desire—the static, the abolition of time, the "eternal"—at the expense of soul, that is, who sold their understandings to get a "tidy", "natural" certainty; *measurers* cf., . . . [unclear]

the pure fire in which oppositions disappear as in their common ground. And Burnet says that this doctrine of the transcending of opposition is the *word* of Heraclitus.[36] Now if this were his word, then it would contradict his general theory and his main line of argument. It would contradict in particular his statement that the hidden attunement is better than the open, which implies that things have internal complexity and internal activity. And it is this theory of things as active complexes and the theory of exchange which is connected with it that is really the word ($\lambda o \gamma o \varsigma$) of Heraclitus, or alternatively it is the view that strife is harmony. When Heraclitus says that good and evil are one, he means that they belong to the same cycle. But if he meant that there was no difference between them, that their opposition could be overcome, then his whole theory of change and of cycles would fall to the ground.

---

[36][Ed.] *Logos*, speech, account, reason, definition, rational faculty.

VI
Parmenides

Lecture 26

Parmenides—beginnings in Pythagoreanism

Parmenides, who was 65 when he came to Athens with Zeno, was born in 515 B.C. Pythagoras was born in 570 B.C., Heraclitus in 540 B.C., and Zeno was born in 490 B.C.

Parmenides worked out an answer to the theories of the early Pythagoreans. From other evidence and also from the second part of his poem we can infer that he was originally a member of the Pythagorean society but that he had found Pythagorean views unsatisfactory and so had given them up. He puts forward a different answer to the Pythagoreans from that given by Heraclitus although we can see certain resemblances between the two lines of criticism. Both Heraclitus and Parmenides seem to have seen that we cannot, as the Pythagoreans tried to do, begin with identity, with the pure unit, and then bring in differences from the outside. Accordingly Heraclitus concludes that the so-called unit must already have *differences within it*, that it must be complex. But Parmenides with his denial of *not-being* maintains that the position of Heraclitus amounts to saying that a thing differs from itself and he regards that as an incoherent statement. Accordingly he retains the pure identity of the Pythagoreans and denies that any variety can be introduced from any source, so that having begun with simple identity we find that we can add nothing to it. Reality consists of this simple identity and nothing more.

Now this position was made possible by the way in which the previous theory had proceeded—by the fact that logical questions had not been thoroughly discussed. The Milesians take it for granted that we are presented with a variety of things each having various characters and the question is to determine what is their fundamental character—that character in virtue of which we call them things. Now the contention of Parmenides seems to have been that to know even this fundamental character is not the same as knowing the thing itself. Even if we call anything a thing, the question can be raised, *what is it* that we are calling a thing? According to the doctrine of Heraclitus to describe it as a thing means describing it as being active and complex, but, it may be argued, this does not settle the question of what it is that is being called active and complex.[1] If the theory of Heraclitus is to convey information, then we must know what is the subject that has these predicates, otherwise we do not have a definite assertion but we have a predicate without a subject. So that when Parmenides speaks of *It*, that, namely, of which it can be said that *It is*, he is speaking of a subject (which may have predicates) but which we are bound to know independently of the predicates in order to know what they apply to. Now when this position is pressed to its logical conclusion we can only say that *It* is completely indescribable because to give it any predicate whatever is to attach to it something which is known independently of it and therefore cannot belong to its essential nature. The ultimate subject is one which is apart from all predication and can only be known in itself.

Now if Parmenides had consistently adhered to that position, he would have been unable to expound his theory for he can only expound it by making statements, that is, by utilising certain propositions, by attaching certain predicates to certain subjects, and if because the predicate is different from the subject we had to conclude that it did not belong to the subject, then all theory would come to an end. It is therefore unavoidable that there should be inconsistencies in the doctrines of Parmenides. Consistently he could not even say that It *is*, since if this statement is to be intelligible, *is* must be different from *It* and therefore on Eleatic principles the statement must be false. He is still more inconsistent in likening *It* to a sphere, in saying that it extends equally in all directions, that it is continuous and full, and he is further guilty of inconsistency in attaching a number of negative predicates to it, such as immutability. Inevitably in order to present an argument he has to allow the presence of difference and plurality, and in order to understand his argument we should have to be able to distinguish between

---

[1] [JA] The point being, of course, that what it is is its *peculiar* character or quality: and in virtue of which we call it an *X* thing; variable, not pervasive, though *some* quality is required. But having "some" quality is being active and complex.

It and *its being* and *its being spherical* etc. But though these objections can be brought to the Eleatic position, it is nonetheless true that it raises difficulties of which previous philosophers had not taken sufficient account. Even the theory of Heraclitus suggests that active complexity is a character of things, and the question naturally arises—what are the things which have this character. The way in which these difficulties could be solved does not appear until Socrates and Plato, the solution being that things are not to be thought of as prior to propositions, but it is only in propositions that we know things at all, and only in that form that we can conceive them to occur. Now Socrates, though he introduced consideration of the proposition, did not arrive at a solution of the Eleatic problem because he was still too greatly influenced by Pythagoreanism. But in the *Sophist* Plato arrives at the method of solution and in particular by reference to the theory of propositions he solved the problem of not-being. The solution is that not-being is to be understood by reference to the negative proposition, that we do not speak of it as if it were something subsisting by itself, but only as existing in the relations among things. A proposition, A is not B, conveys all that is meant by not-being: it doesn't suggest, as Parmenides supposes, consideration of a particular object described as *that which is not*. Parmenides is certainly correct in holding that reality is not divided into two parts, the existent and the non-existent, but what the negative proposition shows is the way in which the not-being occurs among existents. (*Cf.*, the *Sophist*.)[2]

Lecture 27

Parmenides continued—the question of pure being

The consideration of the position of Parmenides can be divided into five parts: a consideration of (1) his fundamental postulation, the *assertion of pure being*; (2) his objections to the position of Heraclitus and the extent to which these were justified; (3) his relation to the Pythagoreans—what he derived from, and what he rejected in, their theories; (4) the detailed development of his positive theory as a result of these criticisms; and (5) the reaction to his theory, the lines along

---
[2][Ed.] 237b–.

which the attempt was made to find an answer to the Eleatic criticism.

As regards (1): the question which Parmenides is dealing with is substantially the same as that which was presented to the Milesians and which may be regarded as the fundamental question of philosophy, namely, what do we mean by saying of anything that *it is*? As regards things in general the Pythagoreans would have said that we mean that the thing is an arrangement of units against a background of emptiness. So that in describing what the thing is, we are introducing considerations of what it is not, namely, this reference to the background of emptiness. Exactly the same criticism applies to the contention of Heraclitus that we mean that the thing is an attunement of opposite tensions or that it exists by means of exchange.[3] Here again we are introducing consideration of what it is not when we are asked to give a positive description of the thing. These explanations might show how the thing is constructed or how it comes about, but the real question is—what *is* it? If we answer the question by referring to the thing's elements or to the parts which go to make it up, that merely brings us back to the question—in what way do *they* exist? So that from the point of view of Parmenides all these explanations in terms of complexity or composition lead nowhere. We are required to give an account of the thing solely in terms of what it is and not at all in terms of what it is not. We must, if we are to give an account of being at all, express it in terms of self-subsistence, of something which exists in its own right, quite independently of the existence of anything else. Because if we attribute dependent existence to anything, then our explanation will always remain incomplete unless we can arrive at something which exists independently. The question for Parmenides is—what is it that *is* absolutely or essentially? What is it that exists necessarily or which must exist by its own nature? Now this notion of the self-subsistent is really the same as the Pythagorean notion of the unit or element, namely, that which has its reality within itself and on which the reality of everything else depends. From the Pythagorean point of view it is only by getting down to the elements of

---

[3][JA] Note similarity to *Phaedo* (no extrinsic explanations). Fundamental Eleaticism of Socrates! (self-subsistence) (self-relation: or the self-explanatory: the Good).

things that we acquire a knowledge of them (and then it is the *elements* we know, not the "things"). According to Heraclitus the components of a complex thing are themselves complex and we cannot positively conceive anything which would be perfectly simple. Now Parmenides takes up the position of the Pythagoreans that there must be simplicity before there can be complexity, that there must be something self-subsistent or self-sustaining, in order that actual existence may be possible. And then he endeavours to work out this theory to its logical conclusion. He argues that we cannot conceive of the existence of *many* self-subsisting units, since, if there were many, they would have to exist in relation to one another and therefore would not be self-subsistent. It is by a peculiarly similar argument that Spinoza disposes of Descartes' theory of a number of different substances and points out that if substance be taken as that which is in itself, then there can only be one substance. And the similarity can be extended further, because, just as the atomists endeavoured to solve the Eleatic problem by means of their theory of many units, so Leibniz endeavoured to solve the difficulties of Spinoza's theory by means of a doctrine of spiritual atomism.[4] But he had precisely the same difficulty as Descartes had, in showing how the various spiritual units could differ from one another. Parmenides expresses the difficulty by saying that *difference* introduces not-being: that is, it introduces the conception of "that which is not in itself",[5] and which therefore from the point of view of self-subsistence has no reality at all. And the same applies to any attempt to exhibit relations between units, and similarly to any attempt to attribute a history to them. All these descriptions of things are described from the Eleatic standpoint as attempts to describe things in terms of what they are not. This type of argument is definitely exemplified in the fragments. Parmenides says that the way of truth is the inquiry according to the principle *that it is and that it is impossible for it not to be.* The false principle is that according to which it is not and must needs not be. He continues,

---

[4] [JA] Atomists really *early* that is, pre-dialectic non-propositional Pythagoreans.
[5] [JA] Ontological, again. "That which is not in itself" is the same as "That which in itself *is not*".

"For thou canst not know what is not—that is impossible—nor utter it, for it is the same thing that can be thought and that can be." (Fragments 4 and 5).[6]

Also,

"It needs must be that that which can be thought and spoken of *is*: for it is possible for it to be and it is not possible for what is nothing to be". (Fragment 6).[7]

Now one important consideration in connection with these fragments is that they show that Parmenides did not take thought as determining or limiting reality: he did not say that because a thing could not be thought, therefore it could not be. But his argument is really the opposite, that because a thing could not be, therefore it could not be thought. That this was Plato's understanding of the position is shown in the *Sophist* (also the *Parmenides*) in which an attempt was made to solve the difficulties raised in the *Parmenides* and in which the fundamental issue is how it is possible to think what is not—that is, to fall into error. What Parmenides is saying is that the view that though something is not, it might still be thought or believed, cannot be maintained, because, as he says, it is the same thing that can be thought and that can be. Of course if we say that what cannot be cannot be thought, it follows that what is thought is. And it is clearly what Parmenides himself argues in the beginning of Fragment 6, where he gives as the reason why what is thought must be that it is impossible for what is nothing to be. This shows that his fundamental contention is a logical one, that what he is doing is to deny negation, and the question of what we may say or think about the positive reality so postulated is a subsequent one.

Lecture 28

Parmenides continued—his criticisms of Heraclitus

(2) In criticism of Heraclitus, Parmenides speaks of that way of inquiry upon which mortals "wander two-faced", "undiscerning crowds" in whose eyes "it is and is not the same and not the same", and "all things travel in opposite directions".[8] And he adds,

---
[6] John Burnet, *op.cit.*, Fragments 4 and 5, p. 173.
[7] John Burnet, *op.cit.*, Fragment 6, p. 174.
[8] John Burnet, *op.cit.*, Fragment 6, p. 174.

"For this shall never be proved, that the things which are not are;" (Fragment 7.)[9]

Parmenides assumes that according to Heraclitus contradictions may both be true at the same time. And this was a view which appears to have been prevalent among the successors of Heraclitus. And it must be admitted that a certain justification for this criticism is given in some of the fragments. Actually, however, we find that these are merely forcible expressions of some fundamental tenets which do not involve contradiction unless, as Parmenides imagines, existence and change are themselves contradictory. When for example Heraclitus says,

> "Mortals are immortals and immortals are mortals, the one living the others' death and dying the others' life", (Fragment 67)[10]

what he means is really explained in the following fragment which indicates that when anything ceases to be it goes to form something else, which at the same time comes to be. So that though the thing, strictly speaking, has come to an end, its influence continues and so we can say in a loose and metaphorical way that the thing itself continues, that is, there is discontinuity in the sense that any particular thing that we care to name comes to an end at some time. But there is continuity in the sense that its cessation is the occasion of the origin of something else. And similarly, (81) "We step and do not step into the same rivers: we are and are not" is explained by (41,2) "You cannot step twice into the same rivers, for fresh waters are ever flowing in upon you",[11] that is, we simply have the treatment of things as in process and the recognition that what we call the same thing at a subsequent time is not absolutely identical with what it was at a previous time, and if considerations of time and process are applied to stepping, then we find that this process can be broken up into a series of processes which are successive, so that when one begins, another has ceased. In other words, the process contains differences within itself; and if this were to be denied, if it were to be maintained that stepping or any other process must occur either all at once or not at

---
[9] John Burnet, *op.cit.*, Fragment 7, p. 174.
[10] John Burnet, *op.cit.*, Fragment 7, p. 138.
[11] John Burnet, *op.cit.*, Fragment 81, p. 139, Fragments 41,42, p. 136.

Parmenides 95

all, then we should certainly have to admit that processes do not occur.[12] But the recognition of internal differences does not involve contradiction, because we are concerned not with instants but with durations. (That is, we step through a duration, and do not step, at an instant. And the processes of stepping may be broken up into a number of processes, number one of which can be called stepping.)[13]

Lecture 29

Parmenides continued—agreement with Pythagoreans on self-subsistence of what is—Eleatic paradoxes

The position of Heraclitus as against Parmenides is that anything which is real has duration, that having duration it can be exhibited as a number of distinct processes, and that it is incorrect to assume that there must be something which remains fixed and unchanged throughout all these changes. We saw, in connection with the theory of Heraclitus, the importance of this point in connection with personal identity. If the identity of a thing is something over and above its history or the various events which it passes through, then these events would be perfectly irrelevant to it and in no sense could they be held to constitute *its* history. So that in insisting on this point both Heraclitus and Parmenides are bringing out the weakness of Pythagoreanism. If what is is permanent, then that which we say is not permanent is really nothing at all. Now Parmenides accepts this conclusion, but his criticism of the Pythagoreans does not apply to Heraclitus, because Heraclitus has argued that what is is *not* permanent, that what we call a thing is as much a process as any event in its history, that in fact it is the process of which all these events are constituents. And the same applies to any one of these constituents: it likewise has constituents, that is, has phases, processes which fall within it, and so on. According to Heraclitus, complex activity is precisely what is meant by being anything, so that there is no distinction between being and becoming or between pure being and being something in particular.

We see that in rejecting the position of Heraclitus Parmenides retains one of the fundamental tenets of

---
[12][JA] *Cf.*, Bergson.
[13][JA] We *are* in process and we are not *fixed*. And "we" are on the same footing (!!) as "our stepping".

Pythagoreanism, namely, that what is is self-subsistent and does not in itself involve otherness or difference. Unless this assumption of fixed being is made the criticism directed against Heraclitus breaks down. But Parmenides rightly points out that *if* this assumption is made, then difference and multiplicity cannot be accounted for, that only that which is in itself can be, and consequently there are no differences. Or, putting it in Pythagorean terms, if the boundless has a different way of being from the unit, then the two cannot be spoken of together, and if there are units, there can be no boundless. But if there is no boundless, then all the units coalesce into one. Now the position of the Eleatics on this question introduces a real difficulty which is made still clearer by Zeno. If we say that things exist in space, then either space is not a thing or space exists in space. Now it seems impossible to think of space as a thing, to speak of the medium in which things exist as being itself a thing in the same sense; in that case, the Eleatics ask, how do we come to talk about it?[14] We make statements about space just as we do about matter, and that suggests that we recognise it in some way. Yet if all events are in space, we cannot regard space as being any particular event. Now this difficulty is sometimes met by saying that space and time are merely relations among things, a way of stating the case which suggests that things are in some way prior to space and time, as if they *themselves* were non-spatial and non-temporal but simply happened to enter into spatial relations. This position cannot be accepted because we have no notion of the things at all except as existing in space and time. Moreover, if we treat space and time as a mere name for temporal and spatial relations, we have to admit that these relations are related among themselves in a systematic way.[15] And the system of these relations is not something which we discover by adding together a number of distinct relations but is something which we seem to take for granted from the beginning. As far as ordinary experience is concerned, we never doubt that any time is continuously related to any other time and that any space is (likewise) continuously related to any other space; there is a space connecting any two spaces etc.[16] These facts

---
[14][JA] When does a thing "become"?
[15][JA] Kant.

are not learned by examining a number of individual cases and finding the connections, they are rather assumed. If we were capable of doubting the connection between one time and another and one space and another, then we should never be able to prove it. Even if we say, then, that we know space and time as constituting the medium in which things exist and are related, we cannot treat them as constituted by the relations between things. We have to treat them as in some way prior to things or as conditions of the existence of anything.[17] But even so this still leaves the difficulty that in speaking of them as conditions of the existence of things, we are taking them as particular objects of contemplation just as we might take any particular things. This is substantially the same problem as that which arises from saying that the being of things consists of complex activity, because there we seem to be applying distinctive predicates to things, and yet, if the theory is correct, the predicates cannot be distinctive because they must apply to all things alike. And similarly we would seem to require to distinguish the subject of the proposition from the predicate, that is, we would seem to require to know that which we call active and complex, independently of its being active and complex.

The problem may be partly solved by reference to the distinction between space and time, that is, taking it for granted that we have these two media of events or this complex medium, we can say that it involves this fundamental distinction between space and time. And that on account of the continuity of time we can recognise distinct spaces and also recognise their relation to one another, that is, we can use the term "space" in a generic way or as a classname for all the different spaces: and then go on to recognise that all the members of that class are continuously related to one another.[18] And similarly by means of spatial continuity we can recognise individual times and so be able to use the general term "time". And we can further recognise that these times are connected with one another. Now allowing for the difficulties of this fundamental problem which is in certain respects similar to the problem of determining how,

---
[16][JA] Whitehead.
[17][JA] Or as that which things are *in* when we say they are *in* existence.
[18][JA] Generic use shows how we can use *terms* (because spaces are in space etc.); space and time themselves have to do with the "form" of the proposition (copula and distinction between space and time.)

if in knowledge the knower and the known are two different things,[19] we are able to have information about ourselves; allowing for these difficulties we can at least recognise that the postulation of different ways of being leads to insoluble problems and that the statement that the only way of being is occurrence in space and time can at least be made to allow of the possibility of speaking of spaces and times, since there is no paradox in saying that any particular spatial region occurs in space as well as in time. On the other hand, the position of Parmenides which is an attempt to show that the only way of being is essential or necessary being—that position, while it does bring out the weakness of Pythagoreanism, inevitably leads on to a similar division in reality, when it is said that there are illusions or false beliefs. These illusions can't be treated as aspects of the One or as having the sort of being which it has, and so we have a duality of ways of being; and any criticism which the Eleatics have passed upon the Pythagoreans applies to their own position.

Lecture 30

Parmenides continued—the Way of Truth—change impossible

The method of Parmenides in dealing with the fundamental problems of existence is shown in "the way of Truth", that is, the way in which everything which introduces the suggestion of negation is rejected. On that basis, coming to be and ceasing to be are impossible and therefore according to Parmenides all his predecessors were mistaken. If anything could be said to come to be, that would imply that at some time the thing *was not*. But that is a meaningless statement and therefore there can be no such thing as coming to be. Similarly as regards ceasing to be, we should, if we accepted it, have to make the meaningless statement that something which is will *not be*. Now even if we find reason for rejecting this position and for maintaining that it is quite possible to say that something which is now was not at some previous time and will not be at some future time; even if all that is admissible, there is a fundamental difficulty in the notion of becoming, that is, if we say that at a certain time a given

---
[19][JA] Spatial-temporal problem to be solved by working out its analogy with knower-and-known problem? That is, similarity to way in which we *do* know ourselves, space and time are *in* space and time.

Parmenides

thing came to be, then the question is—what precisely did the thing *do* at that time? If the thing were not already in existence, how could it perform this act of coming to be. And if it were already in existence, would it have any need to come to be, that is, we should recognise that at any time a thing either is or is not, but the question remains, what is it when it is said to be coming to be? In order to solve this problem we have to recognise that the term "coming to be" is not a perfectly exact expression (as opposed to coming to be X); and we have further to recognise the distinction between instants and periods of time. Now this distinction was not recognised by the Pythagoreans according to whom time was composed of ultimate units and could only be measured in terms of these units. Now in the notion of the unit of time we have a confusion between instants and durations, and as Zeno shows, the attempt to treat the units as either instants or durations leads to insoluble problems. In other words, we cannot have a time which involves instants but not durations and similarly we cannot have a time which involves durations and not instants. Even if we reject the Pythagorean theory of discontinuity, we cannot correct the error by establishing a continuity without any distinction, which is what the Eleatics tried to do. If we recognise durations or periods of time, then we require to recognise instants, just as in regard to space recognition of distance implies recognition of points. Any measurable distance has a beginning and an end, and it is also divisible. In order to be divided, a distance must be divided at a point. The suggestion that we arrive at the notion of a point as the limit of division of a line or as a result of progressive reduction in the length of a line—that notion is incorrect, since the notion of points is already involved in the very first division that we perform, and even in the conception of the line as having a determinate length. Now when this is recognised, and when it is further recognised that any particular event has duration, then we should no longer speak of a thing's coming to be as if it were a specific and distinguishable event, because it would have to be an event which occurred instantaneously. But the point is that we can divide a certain period of time at an instant which is such that if we take a period ending in that instant, then at that time the thing was not; and if we take, within certain limits, any period beginning at that instant, then during that period the thing is. That is, there are (some) periods beginning at that instant during which the thing is. But there is no period when the thing is in a state of coming to be, conceived as some intermediate state between being and not being. At any period we like to take the thing either is or is not. So that the Eleatic criticism of becoming is important in that it necessarily leads on to a more exact description of time.

Lecture 31

Parmenides continued—Eleatic criticisms of Pythagorean units correct

We may say that as criticisms of the Pythagorean theory of units of being, the Eleatic arguments hold. If we had to think of absolute units of being, if we could not make the distinction between a thing and a particular state of that thing, or in Heraclitean terms between a cycle and a particular tension in that cycle, then it would be impossible to show that anything could come to be or could undergo alteration; and it would be equally impossible to show that there could be any difference in things, because we can only distinguish one thing from another by showing that the first has a character (position?) which the second has not. Now according to the Pythagoreans the units differed not in character but only in position. But how are we to make this distinction between the position and character of a thing. In order to have a position a thing must have some distinctive existence of its own, and it must have a certain character. When we have come to consider the varieties of things, we can then distinguish between these characters which they have simply in virtue of being in space and time—the "primary qualities" of things—and their other qualities. But without this general method of applying descriptions to things, we could not make that description. So that Parmenides is quite right to argue that if there is really no difference between two units, then they are in fact one unit. The Eleatic position can only be overthrown by an abandonment of the Pythagorean conception of being as the substance of particular things, and by asserting that the reality of things consists precisely in the various special characters which they possess; and from this point of view we can say that the atomists as well as the Pythagoreans cannot escape the Eleatic refutation. In the second place, so long as space is considered in Pythagorean fashion as something over and above the reality or being of things, something added to them from outside, and something irrational in character as compared with them—then the Eleatics are quite justified in saying that in terms of this position space does not possess being and therefore there is nothing whatever to be added to the units or to keep them apart from one another; and again, the supposed multiplicity of units combines in a single unit.

The argument may be put in the usual form of a dilemma. If two things have nothing between them, then they are in contact with one another, and if there is *something* between them, they are in contact with *it.* So that in either case separation (of units) is inconceivable. In other words, what is could only be separated from what is by something, but that something is. And therefore there is no separation. Now the same general difficulty presents itself here as in the argument on becoming, namely, that unless we understood what was meant by separation, unless we had something in mind when we used the term we could not appreciate the argument of Parmenides or see that he had reduced the Pythagorean theory to an absurdity. Accordingly there must be inconsistency in the Eleatic argument itself, since its conclusion is that separation means nothing at all, a conclusion arrived at by an argument in which separation means something. While we have to allow that space cannot be brought in subsequently to the existence of things so as to ensure that they will be related to one another in certain ways, we must assert that thinking of the existence of anything we are already thinking of space; except by reference to distances or directions we could not understand the complexity of a thing and except by taking it as complex we could not regard it as (definite) and distinctive.[20] When it is understood that there are distances within the least thing that we can consider, it can also be understood that there are

---

[20][JA] Things are *tensions*: tension implies space and time.

distances between any two things that we may consider. This is already involved in thinking of the particular parts of the original thing, because each of those parts is itself entitled to be called a thing. So that the general argument of Heraclitus that external differences and internal differences are to be understood in relation to one another has its equivalent in the particular cases of space and time, that is, the external spatial differences are to be understood in relation to the internal spatial differences. And, similarly in the case of time, the external temporal differences are to be understood in connection with the internal. In relation to any historical thing or event we can understand what is meant by past and future, what went before that thing and what will come after because already in considering the thing we have to make distinctions of past, present and future within it, or simply the general distinction of before and after. We recognise stages in a temporal process just as we recognise parts in a spatial thing. But the fact that the thing has parts is not in general considered a reason for saying that the thing as a whole does not exist. And similarly the fact that a process has stages is not a reason for saying that the process as a whole does not occur. The Eleatics argue that if a thing does not occur all at the same time, then we cannot regard that thing as one occurrence. But there is an ambiguity in meaning of "at the same time". The different stages of the process occur at different times, but each of these times is itself a duration; and accordingly we can understand what is meant by the whole process occurring within a similar but longer lapse of time. In this case as in the Eleatic argument in general, the argument employed to show that the whole process is not a lapse of time depends on assuming that the parts of a time (process?) occupy certain lapses or durations. So that the Eleatics assume, to make the argument significant at all, the very types of existence which they claim by means of their argument to disprove.

Lecture 32

Parmenides continued—criticisms

To consider then the picture of reality given by Parmenides on the basis of his denial of all relations and differences, and his assertion of substance or thinghood as the sole possible type of object of thought, we find that he arrives at the conclusion that what is is uncreated and indestructible, that it is complete, immovable and without end, that it has no past or future, but it now is, all at once, a continuous One. He also says it is the same and remains in the same place, abiding in itself. And for this reason he considers that it cannot be infinite, so that it is to be considered as complete on every side like a rounded sphere, equally poised from the centre in every direction. Now it may be suggested that Parmenides did not desire that the One should be thought of literally as a sphere, but if we consider the theory of his successors, particularly Empedocles, those successors who accept the Eleatic demonstration that there can be no such thing as becoming, we find that this notion of a sphere and the corresponding notion of a centre from which the sphere radiates is of great importance. So far as his successors are concerned, it seems to have been considered that Parmenides intends the One to be taken literally as a sphere. And if this were not so, the correction of Eleatic doctrine made by Melissus would not be intelligible. We cannot reasonably say therefore that the position of Parmenides was mystical, though some of the weakness of his arguments corresponded to difficulties in any mystical theorising, and though likewise in his doctrine the One if it is to be known at all must be known by a sort of intuition or revelation. We may take that as a reason why he brings forth a (sphere?)[21] as explaining the nature of the One. Whatever positive description we attempt to give of this ultimate entity, we fall into difficulties if we take the description literally, just as in this case, if we take the One to be literally a sphere, then we have the problem of determining what is at the surface of the sphere, and apart from what is outside it, we require to make a distinction between its centre and its circumference so that the absolute unity demanded is not attained. On the other hand, if the description is not to be taken literally, if we say that certain descriptions give an inadequate representation of the ultimate object that they symbolise, then we are committing ourselves to a comparison between the symbol and what is

---

[21] [Ed.] The student notes at this point have "brings forward a goddess".

symbolised, and unless we know the latter definitely and in terms of specific characters we cannot even say that the symbol is an approximately correct symbol, or that the One is capable of standing for the other, unless we have a knowledge of both. Strictly according to the Eleatic postulation of the non-existence of difference that difficulty would not arise; it would have to be admitted that we cannot give any particular description of the One, and accordingly cannot say that we are acquainted with any such thing. But while this may be advanced as a criticism of Eleaticism, it seems to be the case that Parmenides did regard his argument as valid and that he definitely thought of a solid continuous sphere without past or future as the sole reality.

The first point of criticism is that in describing *what is* Parmenides has introduced considerations of space. He has distinguished between the centre and the outer parts of his sphere, he has described it as finite, because self-contained. And these notions of a centre and of containing are spatial notions and imply *difference.* It may be said that in his criticism of the Pythagoreans, Parmenides did not wish to discredit space but only empty space; that he wished to do away with the distinction between space and what was in space, because it was impossible to consider the one apart from the other. Yet if we cannot distinguish space from what is in space, then we cannot use spatial conceptions at all. We cannot understand what is meant by containing or the notion "in". If we once distinguish space from the things that are in space, then we imply the possibility of empty space. We don't require to assert its actuality but we could understand what was meant by actual space without reference to its occupation by a particular thing. If we can think of one thing surrounding another, then we can equally think of the former as surrounding a certain space without determining whether or not there is anything in the space.

The second criticism is that he doesn't consistently abide by his rejection of not-being. Apart from the spatial predicates which he attributes to what is, we find that the other predicates are expressed negatively: uncreated, indestructible, immovable, without a past or future. Now if negation were a meaningless conception, then all these predicates would be meaningless; and further Parmenides' denial of negation, which is his fundamental postulation, would itself be meaningless. But more fundamental still is the difficulty of understanding how what is can have any predicates at all. If to say that it is continuous means the same as that it is, then the term "continuous" is entirely superfluous. If it means something different, then according to the Eleatic argument it must mean something that is not, and therefore cannot be asserted. Putting the matter generally, in saying that It is continuous and spherical etc., we are distinguishing its being continuous and its being spherical both from one another and from it. We are inevitably introducing difference and not-being. The result is that by pursuing (pressing?) the Eleatic method, we arrive at a rejection of Eleaticism itself, we arrive at the position of Gorgias that *nothing* is. If we say of anything that it is, then we are distinguishing the thing from its being or from the being that belongs to *it*, and if that distinction is possible, then we have committed ourselves to saying that the thing is not. Or as Gorgias puts it, nothing is. His position was avowedly sceptical, but just like the Eleatics, in the course of his argument he arrives at a useful result. He shows that if we persist in denying not-being, then we will have to say that there is no being either and so there is nothing at all. And the difficulty can only be resolved by going back on the Eleatic contention and asserting that there is such a thing as not-being, without implying that it is a distinct entity which can be known by itself (*per se*), on which assumption the Eleatic criticism would be quite justified. Plato's *Parmenides* shows that he had understood the importance of the argument of Gorgias, and his *Sophist* shows the method of overcoming the difficulty: by taking being and not-being not as subjects and predicates of propositions but as the forms of the copula of the proposition and as being intelligible only in (their function in) the proposition and performing that function for a particular predicate and a particular subject.

Lecture 33

Parmenides continued—criticisms continued

As a criticism of Pythagoreanism, the Eleatic doctrine may be said to be sound. We cannot significantly say, if we assume the notion of a unit of some primary substance, that there are many such units. Alternatively if, as the Pythagoreans suggest, being is to be treated as a certain substance, then not-being will have to be treated as a different kind of substance, and we will be unable either to show the connection between the two or to justify the distinction between them. At the same time it is impossible consistently to maintain that there is even one unit of this primary substance. And so Eleaticism itself breaks down. Now as we saw Parmenides has not scientifically considered the solution of these problems offered by Heraclitus, namely, that in considering things as processes we can see how they involve at one and the same time being and not-being, persistence and change. The theory of Heraclitus did require to be made more specific: his logic required development, but the position at which Plato arrived after the conflict between Pythagoreanism and Eleaticism had continued for more than a century, embodies many of the suggestions put forward by Heraclitus. What we have in Socrates is the introduction of the consideration of propositions; but he is still so far under the influence of Pythagoreanism that he practically reduces propositions to Pythagorean forms; that is, reduces the subject of a proposition to a complex of predicates, just as Parmenides had tried to reduce the variety of predicates to a simple subject. And the difficulty cannot be solved until we see that what is conveyed by the proposition is an event or process and that neither subjects nor predicates can be known except in propositions.

With a position like that of Parmenides no ethical doctrine could be reconciled. The only possible ethics that Parmenides could have had would have been the precept "Don't think of what is not". But this precept is itself stated negatively, and could not be consistently put forward by the Eleatics; and, secondly, according to Parmenides we *cannot* think of what is not, because we must always think of something. In this connection, then, we come upon the difficulty in the Eleatic theory of showing not merely that the opinions of mortals are wrong but even that there can be such opinions.

We may say that the most important question which Parmenides raised was the question of *time*, the question of the distinction between instants and durations, and again between past, present and future. If we say that a thing was, this can be interpreted as meaning that there was a time at which it could have been truly said "This thing is". But in giving that explanation we are re-introducing the term to be explained. It may be said, therefore, that if we take *is*, or the present, as perfectly simple, then we can give no account of the past or future. But if we consider what is meant by the present, what is meant by a present event, then we find that it itself includes an earlier and later stage. In other words, in conceiving the present we are already conceiving the past and future. Similarly in considering durations or lapses of time we are already conceiving divisions of time, that is, instants. We cannot if we begin with pure instants build up any duration, and similarly if we were asked to begin with pure durations, we couldn't arrive at the conception of an instant. But actually the two are given together and we cannot think of the one without thinking of the other. We have to reject the Pythagorean theory of units, but we have also to reject the Eleatic conception of continuity as something indivisible. That continuity, that supposed perfect continuity, was just what belonged to the units and again to the atoms in the atomic theory. And so in this connection Parmenides is again developing a particular side of Pythagorean doctrine and showing that it is inconsistent with another side of the doctrine. He is developing that part of the Pythagorean theory which was concerned with the rational and endeavouring entirely to dispense with what they considered to be irrational. The importance of his criticism therefore is that it shows that no such division of reality as that into the rational and the irrational can be made. But the very notion of rationality as Parmenides uses it depends upon the assumption of this division and therefore in undermining Pythagoreanism, he is at the same time undermining his own monism.

VII
Empedocles and Anaxagoras

Lecture 33 (continued)

The so-called Pluralists—Empedocles—Anaxagoras

The philosophers following Parmenides are: the Pluralists, Empedocles, 490 B.C., Anaxagoras, 500 B.C.; Leucippus, 490 B.C., the founder of atomism; Zeno, b. 490 B.C., who was contemporary with the chief Sophists, Protagoras, b. 500 B.C., and Gorgias, 480 B.C.; Socrates, b. 470 B.C.

We find among the immediate successors of Parmenides a tendency to admit that part of his criticism which referred to coming and ceasing to be. That is, we find an acceptance of the view that there can be no real or substantial change of things but there can only be redistribution, or mixture and separation as Empedocles says. At the same time, the Eleatic criticism of motion and multiplicity is not accepted and it is by means of movements among a number of different units that those processes are explained which make us imagine that there has been real change. So that essentially these philosophers give us a re-statement of Pythagoreanism, as is inevitable when the notion of units of substance is retained. But they do not seem to see that the Eleatic criticisms of multiplicity and motion are just as cogent as the criticism of becoming or change in general. Consequently we find Zeno employing the criticism of multiplicity and motion, *particularly* of motion, while Melissus emphasises the criticism of multiplicity and points out that if there were that kind of multiplicity which the opponents of Eleaticism allege, namely, the multiplicity of *different* units, we should be no nearer accounting for the appearance of change than before.[22] This argument of Melissus, the argument that if we do recognise a variety of substances, we are still not in a position to show how the particular variety that we have recognised can account for any new variety—that criticism is fatal to a position like that of Empedocles. According to Empedocles any particular substance that we like to take

---
[22][JA] Hence Melissus' criticisms apply just as much to atomists as to Pythagoreans.

is made up of units of each of the four elements in certain proportions. And by means of the mixture and separation of these units, new substances make their appearance and old ones disappear. But if all that is real about any given substance is so much fire, so much air, water, earth and if change is only redistribution or alterations of proportions in a given case, then we are as far as ever from accounting for qualitative change. We cannot show how it is possible to regard a number of units of the four elements in a fixed proportion as anything but these units: how it is possible to take them all together as constituting a *complex* substance. In fact, the most important result of Eleaticism is precisely that which was neglected by the successors of Parmenides, namely, that the complex cannot be built up out of the simple—a position which had already been put forward by Heraclitus.

Lecture 34

Pluralists' reactions to Parmenides

Considering the reaction of the so-called pluralists to the position of Parmenides we find that they are prepared to admit that nothing can come to be or cease to be, that there can be no substantial or qualitative change, but only re-arrangement; and in formulating theories of that kind, the pluralists are returning to the Pythagorean position which Parmenides had attacked. There are certain minor variations but the fundamental view is that what is called change is in reality only the substitution of one configuration for another, and that the substances involved in these operations remain unchanged. Now this is to neglect the importance of Eleatic criticisms not merely of change but of any sort of multiplicity or motion. To admit multiplicity or motion is to admit not-being and if the things which are said to be many or to be moving are taken to be elementary units of some ultimate substance, then their differences and their motions must be regarded as unsubstantial and unreal. We may recognise that while these pluralists did not meet the fundamental philosophical difficulties raised by Parmenides, they at least made the progress of science possible by recognising that, simply as a matter of fact, differences and movements appear to occur and that it is possible to speak intelligibly about those differences and movements.

But at the same time, in so far as these phenomena had to be explained in terms of the conception of substance, and, where this was insufficient, by the further conception of power or agency—and since there was no way of reconciling these metaphysical conceptions with one another or with the facts—the science which was based upon them was bound to lead to insoluble problems, just as Pythagorean science had done. In effect the successors of Parmenides accepted his criticism of Heraclitus and rejected his criticism of the Pythagoreans. They accepted what was weakest in his argument and rejected what is strongest; consequently their theories are under the same objections as could be brought to the Pythagorean position. If, with Empedocles, we assert that there are four different kinds of matter, we are no nearer being able to explain the infinite variety of qualities that confront us than if we said there was only one kind of matter.

Again in the philosophy of Anaxagoras we find a recognition of the infinite variety of kinds of things, but these "seeds" out of which things are built up are themselves regarded as static, and motion has to be added to them from without. So that even if we recognise an infinite variety of kinds of things, so long as we recognised these as reducible to so many ultimate units we are not in a position to explain complexity and the actual history of things. Now this view of the history of speculation after the time of Parmenides is different from that of Burnet. According to Burnet, the position of Parmenides is most exactly to be described as a corporeal monism, and it was the intellectual courage of Parmenides in working out this position to its logical conclusion that made progress possible. "Philosophy," says Burnet,

> "must now cease to be monistic or cease to be corporalist. It could not cease to be corporalist, for the incorporeal was still unknown; it therefore ceased to be monistic, and arrived at the atomic theory, which is the last word of the view that the world is matter in motion. [Having worked out its problem on these conditions, philosophy next attacked them on the other side. It ceased to be corporalist, and found it possible to be monistic

once more, at least for a time. This progress was due to the rejection by Parmenides of what was to him unintelligible.]"[23]

In criticism of Burnet's view we may say that the progress involved in this development is not apparent from his description. If recognition of the incorporeal made it possible for philosophy to be monistic, it would appear to be implied that the corporeal was found to be unreal; that is, we have a position similar to that of the Pythagoreans, in which we begin with a distinction between a higher and a lower reality or between the rational and the irrational, and find that we are logically committed to saying that the irrational or the lower simply doesn't exist. In that sense we have a monism in which the One may be said to be incorporeal, just as in the doctrine of Parmenides it was said to be corporeal. But whichever we call it, we arrive at the same difficulties: the One must be wrongly conceived if we take it to have any predicate at all, because then we are breaking it up, we are separating some particular aspect of it from its totality, which alone can be regarded as real. The difficulties of the Eleatic theories then are the difficulties of any monism: that anything less than the One is unreal, and so, that any description of the One is incorrect. So that as Gorgias points out, even if there were such a thing, we could say nothing about it. And in this connection it is worth noting that Empedocles and Anaxagoras, though they are commonly called pluralists, did endeavour to work out a *monistic* position. Empedocles recognised a sphere conformable to the sphere of Parmenides except that it was not homogeneous, and, similarly, Anaxagoras speaks of the motion which is responsible for the redistribution of things as beginning at the centre. So he also must recognise, however inconsistently with Ionian ideas of infinity, something similar to the sphere.[24]

As we have already seen, Burnet is incorrect in saying that Parmenides took what can be thought as a test of reality. And he is similarly incorrect in regarding the monism of Parmenides as fundamentally corporalist. It is an attempt to work out a logical theory of being when not-being is

---
[23] John Burnet, *op.cit.*, p. 180. [Ed.:] The last two sentences bracketed in the passage cited by Anderson do not appear in the cited passage by Burnet.
[24] [JA] *Cf.*, physical theories regarding "centre of gravity of Universe". If infinite, *no* centre of gravity.

denied, and its consequences must be similar to those of any theory which recognises a totality of being or some single object which we can describe as the world or the universe. As we saw in dealing with Heraclitus, though he appeared at times to be taking up a monistic position, the logical conclusion of his position is the plurality that any system whatever that we take is included in some wider system, just as any component of a system itself has components. This is real pluralism and is quite different from the position of Empedocles and Anaxagoras. It depends on the recognition that things themselves are active, that there is no division of reality into states and processes, whereas a division of this kind was precisely what Empedocles and Anaxagoras formulated and tried to give a logical account of.[25]

Lecture 35

Empedocles and Anaxagoras continued

We find that these two philosophers neglect that aspect of the position of Parmenides in which it constitutes a criticism of motion and of multiplicity but they accept his criticism of qualitative change. They accept the contention that nothing can come out of nothing, that whatever can be said to become must in some sense exist already. Now this line of argument neglects the very important distinction between the acquisition of a character by a thing and the appearance of a thing itself; it neglects the fact that whatever does come to be, does so within an already existing system. But while the system gives all the continuity that is required, the fact remains that the thing that appears within the system is quite new. Or, the occurrence of the thing in the system now is, but previously simply was not. Parmenides saw quite correctly that if there is to be any process whatever, if we are to be able to make any distinction between an earlier and a later state of affairs, then we must recognise that from a certain time a thing exists which previously was absolutely non-existent, and since he regarded non-existence as a perfectly meaningless expression, he was bound to come

---

[25][JA] Why Stranger is Eleatic. He is answering Eleatic question—how it is possible to *think* what is not. And in order to show that, he has to deal with still more fundamental question—which for Eleatics almost went without argument: though Parmenides has statements on it also—how it is possible for what is not *to be.*

to the conclusion that there was no distinction between one state of affairs and another, but that the universe consisted of a single fact. Accordingly, if any part of his criticism of becoming is accepted, it must be accepted entirely and the concepts of mixture and separation like the Pythagorean conceptions of arrangement and re-arrangement cannot be accepted. And similarly any other attempt to account for the appearance of change is bound to break down, and the conclusion is that there is no such thing even as the appearance of change. That assertion places the Eleatics in an obvious difficulty, but it is not sufficient for the opponents to point out that difficulty. In order to meet the Eleatic criticisms they require to assert not merely the appearance but the reality of qualitative change, and to admit the not-being which facts of this kind involve. The theory of Heraclitus that things must be treated as active and complex does make the necessary admissions, but the theory of compounds, that is, the theory of the variety of things being occasioned by the different ways in which certain kinds of simple units were put together or arranged—that theory does not meet the difficulty. Moreover a special agency or a number of special agencies are introduced so as to account for these arrangements. In order to pass from one structure to another (to have construction and destruction) Empedocles and Anaxagoras have to introduce something which has both structure and function, something which holds things together or keeps them apart. The agencies which Empedocles postulates are *love* and *strife*, and that of Anaxagoras he calls *mind*.[26] Now if these are actually found in things, then they should be treated as elements just like the others mentioned. And if they are not found in things, if they cannot be observed in the same way in which the elements themselves can be, then we have no means of affirming that these really are the agencies that move things about, or that there are any such agencies. If we consider, for example, the function of mind in the philosophy of Anaxagoras we find that it only represents a power of spontaneous motion.[27] We are not entitled to separate the elements, or structure, of things from their function, or powers, when as a matter of fact the

---

[26][Ed.] Socrates claimed that he became excited, then lost interest in Anaxagoras. See *Phaedo*, 96b-99d.
[27][JA] As also in the *Sophist*.

theory can only be applied by finding the two together; by finding, that is, that we do not begin with static things which afterwards are set in motion by some mysterious external agency, but that we begin with dynamic things, with things which as they stand are capable of acting as well as of being acted upon.

If an attempt is made to separate the passive from the active, to assert that there is one kind of thing which can be acted upon and a quite different kind of thing which can act, then we can arrive at no connection between these two classes of things. Because if a thing is to be acted upon, then it must change in some way, that is, it must pass from one condition to another. But we have no means of distinguishing this passage or change from an action of the thing itself. If a thing were absolutely passive, it would remain quite unchanged. On the other hand, if we attribute a particular change in a thing to the operation of some other thing, we can only establish this fact if we find that the other thing goes through some change at the same time. If it continued to exist unchanged, then we couldn't say that it had acted on the other thing at one time rather than another. Now if in influencing another thing, a thing itself undergoes change, then we are entitled to say that it not merely acts but is acted upon in the interrelation of the two things. So, in terms of the division of reality into agencies and things affected by agencies (active and passive), we could never be certain what was the particular cause of any particular change. (Or, between two given things, which was the agent and which the patient.)

VIII
Melissus and Zeno

Lecture 36

Later Eleatic responses to Pluralists—Melissus

The main line of Eleatic criticism of pluralism is found in the arguments of Melissus. He points out that if we take things to have a certain definite nature, then no matter how many of these kinds we specify, we are still unable to give an account of process and change, and of the manifold variations that in ordinary thinking we consider we find among things. If we lay down *a certain number* of qualities of things, then no amount of mixture of the things having these qualities can increase the number of apparent qualities, but the constituents remain exactly as they were before. So mere composition, putting of things together, even if there were no difficulties about motion required to enable this composition to take place, would not actually explain qualitative change. That is brought out in Fragment 8 of Melissus.

> "This argument then is the greatest proof that it is one alone; but the following are proofs of it also. If there were a many, they would have to be of the same kind as I say the one is. For if there is earth, water, air, iron, gold, and fire, and if one thing is living and another dead, and if things are black and white, and all that men say they really are—if this is so, and if we see and hear aright, each one of these must be such as we first decided, and they cannot be changed or altered, but each must be just as it is. But as it is, we say that we see and hear and understand aright, and yet we believe that what is warm becomes cold and what is cold warm; that what is hard turns soft, and what is soft hard; that what is living dies and things are born from what lives not; and that all those things are changed, and that what they were and what they are now are in no way alike. We think that iron which is hard is rubbed away by contact with the finger; and so with gold and stone and everything that we fancy to be strong, and that earth and stone are made out of water; so that it turns out that we never see nor know realities. Now these things do not agree with one another. We said that there were many things that were eternal and had forms and strength of their own, and yet we fancy that they all suffer alteration, and that they change from what we see each

time. It is clear, then, that we did not see aright after all, nor are we right in believing that all these things are many. They would not change if they were real, but each thing would be just what we believe it to be; for nothing is stronger than true reality. But if it has changed, what was has passed away, and what was not is come into being. So then, if there were many things, they would have to be just of the same nature as the one."[1]

The assumption of this argument of Melissus is that when we give a certain description of a thing, we mean that description to sum up all that there can be said about it, to be a statement of the thing's substance or essence. If that were so, we could not go on to give another description of the thing or to say, for example at a later time, it had a new character, because we should be dealing with a different substance, that is, with a different thing. Undoubtedly so long as we maintain the doctrine of substance, we must continue, as Empedocles does, to say that the real nature of a certain thing is to be earth or water, and that that is all that can be said about the thing itself; and though it may take up different positions in relation to other things, we cannot speak of change. Empedocles arbitrarily selects the four qualities to be the fundamental ones, but if we take any particular substance such as iron, then, to be able to describe it in that way implies that it is as much entitled to be called a quality or substance as any of the four elements. We have no criterion to tell us when a quality is fundamental and when it is not, and as far as our *statements* are concerned, we have to express the nature of what is said not to be fundamental in precisely the same way as when dealing with what is supposed to be fundamental. Accordingly if it is denied that earth can ever become not-earth, it must equally be denied that any substance whatever can change and become different from what it was before. Now the solution of this problem may be said to consist in treating things as complex; that is, as not having their character completely described by any single term whatsoever. In that way we are able to say that the thing has changed and still call it the same thing, because we recognise that while it has lost certain characters and acquired opposite characters, there are other characters which it retains throughout the whole process.

---
[1] John Burnet, *op.cit.*, pp. 323–24.

Thus we can speak of a particular thing changing its colour (for example turning from green to yellow) and we call it the same thing, because we observe that it does not change in other respects and retains its relations to its surroundings which remain fairly constant; in saying that a green thing becomes yellow, we are not saying that green becomes yellow, but that *would* be implied if there were anything of which the term "green" expressed the whole nature. The fact is that we can make no ultimate distinction between substance and qualities, because if we separate the two, we can never show how the qualities adhere to the substances so as to be called *their* qualities. That was precisely the difficulty that confronted Parmenides in attempting to apply predicates to his single ultimate reality. If it (the One) is treated as that which is always subject and never predicate, then it will be found never to *have* any predicates. The solution of these difficulties is to be found in recognition of the fact that we do not first know subjects and then attach predicates to them, nor begin by knowing predicates in isolation and then attaching them to subjects, but we know the two in connection with one another. We know green by knowing green things, and similarly we know and recognise things by the qualities they have. We begin in fact with *propositions*, in which subject and predicate or thing and quality are related, and in the development of our propositional knowledge we find that any term can either be subject or be predicate. Now the same fact is put in other words by saying that we know things as complex, as having a variety of interrelated characters; and the argument further depends on the fact that we know things as occupying space and time, that is, Empedocles and Anaxagoras and the atomists were quite correct in maintaining that in accounting for changes, we have to take into account change of position. (But change of position alone, that is, re-arrangement of units, doesn't account for change of quality, and Eleatic objections to the latter weigh equally against the former.)

Lecture 37

Later Eleatic responses to Pluralists—Zeno

It is to be remembered that the Eleatics were primarily critics of Pythagoreanism and the view of motion which Zeno rejected was fundamentally the Pythagorean view. No doubt he thought that at the same time he was refuting any other possible view of motion, but even if we deny that he showed motion not to be possible, we can at least assert that he showed the Pythagorean view to be incorrect. The same applies to Eleatic criticism of multiplicity. If to say that there are many things implies that there are so many units, then the contradictions which the Eleatics dwell upon are bound to arise. Similarly, in the cases of space, time and motion, if we regard these as made up of units as the Pythagoreans did, then we fall into the same sort of contradiction, that is, the unit, if it is to be properly so-called, must be indivisible, but if it is indivisible then no number of units can make up anything which is divisible.

Now what is required if we are to get out of these difficulties is recognition of the fact that we can choose units wherewith to measure space, time and motion without implying that these units are in any way ultimate; that they could not themselves be measured in terms of other units. All that is required for the purposes of measurement is that while dealing with a given problem we should continue throughout to use the same units, but should where necessary be able to express the one in terms of the other. The question of measurement is of particular importance at this stage in the history of Greek philosophy—the most acute problem was the problem of *incommensurability*. The Pythagoreans had divided the world into the realms of being and becoming, since they were unable to find terms which were applicable to both, that is, to find a common measure of things. There could be, on their theory, no common measure of being and becoming because they regarded being as something static, something from which all becoming or change had been excluded. If that were not so, they considered we could not say that the same thing continued to exist. That is the point against which Heraclitus had argued when he contended that internal differences and succession of phases did not prevent us from recognising things and describing them as the same. But if that view is taken of the nature of being, then we are bound to conclude that becoming is excluded from the realm of being, and consistently with this exclusion we ought to say with the Eleatics that becoming is not, that is, that there is no such thing. The Pythagoreans were unwilling to adopt this view, but instead of revising their conception of being they compromised by treating becoming as having an indefinite kind of reality, intermediate between being and not-being. And accordingly, with the later Pythagoreans, reality was definitely divided into two realms—of being and of becoming; *or* the sphere of reality was distinguished from that of appearance.[2] This division, far from solving the problem, merely increases the difficulties. If the appearances are not real, how can we say they *are* appearances? And if becoming is not, how can we use the term? It was along these lines that the sophistic criticisms of pre-Socratic philosophy developed. According to the sophists, certain things do appear to us and to say that these are not real is to fall into a contradiction. The same may be said of the attempt to find a reality behind the appearances, since, unless this reality appears to us, we do not know anything about it. Accordingly, the sophist Protagoras solves the difficulty of commensurability by saying that "Man is the measure of all things": that we are bound to accept things as they appear to us since we know nothing else. Gorgias carries the argument further by pointing out that any attempt to describe the underlying reality leads to contradictions. If we take any number of units of this reality we find that they are incommensurable with one another and so cannot all be described as real; and if we take a single unit, then we are bound to admit that any description of it, not being the unit itself, is similarly incommensurable with the unit, so that the unit is quite indescribable. But if so we cannot even call it a unit.

Pythagoreans themselves had been led into difficulties in connection with the relation between arithmetic and geometry. And they had discovered the existence of certain incommensurables ($\sqrt{2}$, $\sqrt{5}$). Burnet suggests that it was as a result of such discoveries that they were led to make

---

[2][JA] Note that *divisions* always have a psychological basis: "ideals".

the absolute division between appearance and reality, and also that they considered that by doing so, they could evade the criticisms of the Eleatics. But actually these criticisms apply even more strongly against the later theory than against the earlier. Likewise they apply to the atomic theory. The only way of rebutting Parmenides and Zeno is to drop the distinction between reality and appearance, though the sophistic method of doing so, by dropping reality and retaining only appearance, is defective.[3]

Lecture 38

Zeno continued—the paradoxes

We find that Zeno is primarily concerned to show that it is impossible to measure motion, that is, to have any rational standard to which motion can be referred and which will explain how motion is possible. Even if that position were accepted, even if it were agreed that motion cannot be explained in terms of what is not motion, that does not show that there is *nothing but motion*. It does show that the theory of rational standards and explanations is illogical. As Parmenides has indicated, when we put forward what we take to be a true explanation we find that that which was to be explained has really been explained away, that it was to be considered as a mere illusion. But if in a similar way we ask for an explanation of a standard, then either we enter upon an endless series of explanations such that nothing is ever explained, or else we must come to something which explains itself—the Eleatic One.

The issue between Pythagoreans and Eleatics is whether or not there can be many things which explain themselves or which are *rational* forms or standards. And the Eleatics show clearly enough that there cannot be many self-explanatory things; just as Spinoza shows in criticism of Descartes, that there cannot be many substances, where substance is defined as that which is in itself and is conceived through itself. But this does not settle the question whether there can be even *one*, and if we choose to apply Eleatic methods to the Eleatic position, as Gorgias did, then we find that the single self-explanatory thing is really unexplained. For if we say

---
[3][JA] *Cf.*, modern "positivism", theories of "pure experience" etc.

that a thing explains itself, then we are asserting a *relation*, that is, we must assume some difference between that which explains and that which is explained, even if we say that they are two aspects of the same thing. And once we have recognised a plurality of aspects, then the same question can be raised—whether or not they explain themselves; and so we either arrive back at the Pythagorean plurality, or else we have to say that the One has no aspects and consequently that it is really nothing at all.

Now turning to the actual paradoxes of Zeno we find that in the Achilles paradox he is concerned with the problem of how one motion can be compared with another. If we are going to measure motion we must have some standard motion and we must be able to show how other motions differ from the standard. But if we take any two motions whatever, even one which is said to be very slow and another said to be very fast, we cannot show how they differ. In order to make a comparison between them we must be able to say that every point on the one corresponds to a point on the other; if when one motion was somewhere, the other was nowhere, then we did not compare the two. So in making the comparison between the two motions, in trying to show that one is different from the other, we cannot find any difference in the number of points passed through. But if we do not find that difference then, Zeno argues, we cannot find any difference between the motions at all. We can only show them to be different if one passes through points that the other does not pass through, but if there is a point to point correspondence, then that demonstration is impossible. Zeno concludes that there can be no difference among rates of motion and that overtaking, which is a type of occurrence which we imagine we see every day, is actually impossible. Now the form of this argument is the deduction of the same conclusion from contradictory premises, or of contradictory conclusions from the same premise. In the former case the conclusion is considered to be certain, in the latter the premise is considered to be absurd. Now this type of argument is what is known as the *simple dilemma*:

If A, then B; if not-A, then B: ∴ B.
If not-B, then not-A; If not-B, then A: ∴ not-not-B.

Now if we consider any argument of that type we find that it cannot possibly be valid: that is, that it must contain some fallacy or ambiguity. If the one part of the argument is valid, if the absence of A really follows from the absence of B, then the other part must be invalid, the presence of A cannot follow from the same premise. That being so, we must expect to find that Zeno's arguments, though they are plausible, really contain ambiguities on which their plausibility depends. If we take the Achilles paradox we find that the underlying argument is this: if the number of points which two motions pass through is the same in either case, we cannot find any difference between the two motions. And so we cannot prove that overtaking is possible. In the second place if the number of points passed through is not the same in either case, then to some points in the one series there will be nothing corresponding in the other series; that is, the one motion will be in existence at a different time from the other, and so again it will be impossible for the one to overlap the other.

Now to say that if we have an equal number of points overtaking is impossible and also to say that if we have an unequal number of points overtaking is impossible cannot both be correct statements, and in point of fact the former statement is incorrect. In order that overtaking should be possible, one of the bodies must pass through a greater *distance* than the other in a given time. But it will follow that it must pass through a greater number of points only if the distance consists of a number of points. Now the theory that distance, and space, time and motion in general, were made up of units was the theory of the Pythagoreans, and Zeno may claim to have shown that according to their theory the comparison of motions and in fact any sort of motion are impossible. But he has not shown that the comparison of motions is impossible according to a theory which does not assume that space and time are composed of units. *Unless it was possible for Zeno to take a different view of motion from that taken by the Pythagoreans, then he could not demonstrate the other part of his paradox.* It is quite correct to say that if there were not a point to point correspondence between one motion and another, the two could not be compared, that they would really be in different spheres of existence. But in order to determine that this is so, Zeno has actually to refer to two different motions which we are setting out to compare. And that means that for the purpose of the second part of his dilemma he has to take a commonsense view of motion, according to which it is not made up of units or of jumps with intervals of rest between, but is continuous. And if it were not possible to take some such view his whole argument would be unintelligible. We find that what is demonstrated is not that overtaking is impossible but that the Pythagorean view of its nature contradicts the commonsense view and cannot be worked out consistently with our ordinary experience. But this contradiction between Pythagorean views and the findings of experience does not show, as Zeno *appears to think*, that they are *both* to be rejected; on the contrary, we can only reject one by adhering to the other, and it is by adhering to the commonsense view, by utilising the findings of experience, that Zeno is able to refute the Pythagoreans. But this is not consistent with Eleaticism, according to which the deliverances of experience are untrustworthy.

Lecture 39

Zeno continued—the simple dilemma—against Pythagoreanism—influenced later sophists

The simple dilemma is an argument in which the same conclusion is drawn from contradictory premises and is therefore held to be necessarily true; and it has as its equivalent an argument in which contradictory conclusions are drawn from the same premise, which is therefore considered to be absurd.

Now taking the two parts of any such argument, we can say that if one of them is valid, then the other must be invalid and therefore they cannot be used together to establish any conclusion. In regard to Zeno's arguments in particular, we find that he opposes the Pythagorean position to what we may call the position of commonsense, and considers that they cancel one another out. But actually if there is this contradiction between them, it only shows that one of them must be false, not both of them. In the case of the comparison of two different rates of motion, we find that by reference to unit positions, no distinction can be made. But we only find this because we have considered the actual motions in relation to one another. And if Zeno's conclusion that no such comparison can be made were correct, then his whole argument from the beginning would have been unintelligible. What he does then is to show by reference to the actual character of motion that Pythagoreanism is a false theory. He does not show, as he imagines he does, that any theory of motion must be false—for if this were so, he couldn't even state his examples.

His dilemma in fact depends upon his at one time making the assumption that distance consists of a number of points and at another time assuming that it does not—that it consists of a continuous stretch. (For example, how do we know that Achilles is *behind* the tortoise when he *reaches* the point where it was?) And it is only this ambiguity that makes it plausible to maintain the two parts of the argument at one and the same time. When the ambiguity is removed, we see that the view of distance as a number of points has really been disproved by reference to the actual facts of motion.

Now, the same sort of criticism applies to any of Zeno's paradoxes. In the example of the flying arrow instead of measuring one motion in relation to another, the question is of measuring it in relation to the space which it has passed through (or to *rest*, to show by how much it exceeds zero); and Zeno considers that this cannot be done, because in order to do it, we would have to see the arrow going from one space to another, whereas at any time we can only see the arrow *occupying* a space. As far as that occupancy is concerned there is nothing to show that the arrow previously was in any one different space rather than another. Or, to put it another way, if we are to see the arrow going from point A to point B, where AB is greater than its own length, then we must say that we have seen the arrow occupying the whole of that distance. But, Zeno says, it cannot occupy the whole of that distance because its length is less than that distance. Here the ambiguity is that it cannot occupy the whole of the distance at any one *moment* but it may pass through the whole of the distance in a certain period of time. When Zeno says that the arrow is always at rest, because it always occupies a space of its own length, by "always" he means at all *instants*. But when we speak of a thing as at rest we really mean that it occupies the same place throughout a *period* of time. The question is whether or not motions are to be represented as series of positions. The fact that that is not so does not prevent us from recognising both motion and position, and correspondingly both motion and rest. But we can distinguish between the two when we consider the connections and distinctions which any knowledge either of space or of time involves.[4]

We find then that the real effect of Zeno's paradoxes is to show the untenability of the Pythagorean theory of units of time, space and motion. But the way in which he formulates his arguments, the method of dilemma, caused him to have an influence on the subsequent theory in regard to other questions besides the mathematical ones. His method resting on ambiguity was developed by the sophists into a method of criticising any theory whatever that could be put forward. It was always possible by means of some ambiguity to make out a plausible case for assuming that a certain theory was self-contradictory. This fact led to the concentration of Socrates on *definitions*, because it is only by definitions that ambiguity can be removed. This concern with definitions was also influenced by the Pythagorean theory of forms, which Socrates considerably developed.

---

[4][JA] Multiplicity. "Infinity" not a (definite) number any more than "the infinitesimal" is a (definite) quantity. So "space" not a (definite) thing. Not that space *is* but that "being" is "spatial".

Part II
Socrates, Plato and Aristotle

I
Introductory Lectures

Lecture 40

Socratics—introductory—inflence of Pythagoreans and Eleatics on Socrates

The theories of the later Pythagoreans are of importance not merely as indicating the effects of Eleaticism but also because of the influence that they had on Socrates. We find, as Burnet points out, that later Pythagoreans adopted a number of suggestions from the philosophy of Empedocles. They tried to work out his theory of elements in terms of their own conceptions of geometry. Now though this particular part of their theory is of importance in a complete account of the development of Greek philosophy, it does not indicate the main line of development so well as their reaction to Eleaticism. The difference between early and later Pythagorean theory can be summed up by saying that for the doctrine that things are numbers there was substituted the doctrine that things are like numbers. The former view had taken reality as One in nature, even though they (sic) were many different units of reality. But in the later development, reality is divided into two parts, the world of forms or of being and the world of appearances or becoming. Now this division was a natural result of the earlier doctrine of the limit and the unlimited. If becoming cannot be expressed in terms of being—if it cannot be represented by means of fixed figures, then it cannot really be taken to belong to the world of figures. Now what the Eleatics have shown is that this leaves the so-called sensible world in an ambiguous position. We cannot say that it *is*, because it has not the pure being of the units, and yet we cannot say that it *is not*, unless we are going to allow that it cannot be spoken of at all. (That is, we *perceive* arrangements and rearrangements: and if we do away with one, we do away with the other.) Accordingly the later Pythagorean theory of the two realms of being and becoming does not meet the difficulties which the Eleatics had raised. In fact it is even more open to objection from the Eleatic point of view, than the previous theory. For, on the one hand, we have the conception of sensible things which neither are nor are not. But even if we were to neglect them entirely there still remain problems connected with the world of being or of the figures. Because if we are to give any account of that world, we must be able to show how the forms or figures are related to one another; that is, we have the two problems of the relation of forms to sensible things and of the relation of forms to forms. Both these difficulties are pointed out by Parmenides in Plato's dialogue of that name. When we think of forms and distinguish one from another, it is because we think of them as the forms which sensible things take. And if we cannot show how something which is *merely* becoming can take one form rather than another, then the very expression "form" (or becoming?) becomes obscure. But in the second place, in asserting the existence of a world of forms we do imply that there are relations among the forms; and then the question arises—are the various relations and distinctions between forms to be regarded as themselves forms. If they are not, they cannot be said to occur in the world of forms, but if they are, then the world of forms becomes just as complex as the sensible world was found to be, and the affirmation of their existence does not really solve any of our problems. Recognising that these difficulties remain on the side of what the Pythagoreans regard as *being*, we must also recognise that their original account of the relation between the two worlds is defective. On account of the facts of becoming and of the various incommensurabilities that they had discovered, as well as those which had been pointed out by Zeno, the Pythagoreans could no longer say that the forms or numbers inhere, in their own character, in the things that we contemplate. Accordingly they said that the objects of observation resemble the forms to a greater or less extent and that the world of becoming as a whole is an inadequate representation of the world of being. The dominant conception is that of likeness or imitation. Thus, in the case of the relation between the hypotenuse and the side of an isosceles right-angled triangle, we cannot say that this ratio really is a number in the arithmetical sense in which the Pythagoreans used the term. But we can say that it is like a number, that is, we can establish a series of numbers, in the strict sense of rational numbers, that is, of integers and relations between integers, which give a closer and closer approximation to the value required. (For example $\sqrt{2}$: 1/1, 3/2, 7/5, 17/12, 41/29, 99/70 etc.)

According to Burnet, the Pythagoreans understood the possibility of working out this series as meaning that while $\sqrt{2}$ was not a number it was very like a number or was tending in the direction of being a number. In the same way, especially in the form of the theory given by Socrates, sensible things, or things which become, were represented as trying to be real things or forms. In the world of becoming it was possible to find closer and closer approximations to any particular form. For example it is not possible, Pythagoreans and Socrates consider, to find two physical things which are exactly equal. But we can find by examination pairs of things which approximate more and more closely to equality. This position is expressed by saying that perfect equality is a form which is not found in the world of sense; which is not subject to becoming, but which remains absolutely constant in the world of forms. The difficulties of this position appear to some extent in the working out of the argument of the *Phaedo* itself. But even as regards the original example (the example of the "*irrational*" numbers) we can see the defects of the system. It is not correct to say that a series of approximations to $\sqrt{2}$ represents a tendency on the part of $\sqrt{2}$ towards being a number. Unless we had a definite conception of the ratio itself, we could not say that the series was getting nearer and nearer to it, and the actual position is that we are finding numbers which differ in a continually less degree from $\sqrt{2}$.[1] That would be impossible unless the two numbers were of the same order. The same applies to forms and sensible things. Unless we could recognise that sensible things actually possess definite characters, we could not observe any likeness between them and characters which they *don't* possess.

---

[1] [JA] Or, rather, whose *squares* (do so) from 2 *squared*. Consider.

Lecture 41

Pythagorean doctrine of imitation—reality and appearance—being and becoming

The later Pythagorean theory of imitation or approximation was simply their way of expressing the relation between the two different spheres, that of reality and that of appearance, being and becoming, thought and sense. Among other philosophical schools of the same period, a similar distinction was made, even though a similar account of the relation was not given. The Eleatics maintained that there is no relation, that if we recognise being itself, we cannot recognise appearance but are bound to say that it is not.[2] The atomists simply dismissed the appearances as illusory and did not attempt to show in what precise way they depended upon or were related to the realities. But unlike the Eleatics they acknowledged quite definitely the existence of these illusions. (Also of different *states* of reality at different times: real *occurrences*.)So that their position is intermediate(?) between that of the Eleatics and that of the Pythagoreans, but in each case it is assumed that the objects of true knowledge are quite different from the objects of ordinary belief, and it was on this question that the sophists took up their position of opposition to all current philosophical views. We can see that whatever were the defects of the sophistic position, they at least recognised certain important facts. When the attempt is made to separate the world of reality from the objects of opinion, this can only be done by neglecting the fact that in order to know reality, we must have opinions about it. We must be able to make statements about it in the very same form as statements we make about what we believe. (We must know a particular fact at a particular time.) If we are to know reality it must appear to us and therefore the realm of appearance must include everything that we know. That is one way of removing the separation which had been set up in the later pre-Socratic theories, especially in the Pythagorean. But the sophists continued to speak of appearances in the sense in which they are distinguished from reality, even though they had maintained that there are no realities distinct from appearances. They took up the

---

[2] [JA] Parmenides' "way of opinion" is a failure to be thorough enough: conformable to Socrates' denial of a form of mud.

position that everything is a matter of opinion. This seems a natural consequence of the view that we can only know by having opinions. But the phrase "a matter of opinion" is intended to convey something more than the mere fact that we are aware of the object; it is intended to convey that the object is in some way dependent on our awareness of it, and would not exist if we did not know it. But in order to make even this position intelligible, it has to be allowed that existence has a definite meaning and consequently cannot be identified with being known. It must be possible for a thing to exist without being known (or else there would be nothing to know) and equally possible for something to be supposed or imagined to exist without actually existing. That is, any analysis of opinion is defective which does not recognise that the meaning of opinion depends upon the possibility of things existing by themselves, that is, of scientific truth, and also on the possibility of our making mistakes about these things.

In the conflict between Socrates and the sophists it was the aim of Socrates to show that opinion had these implications, namely, that there was some objective issue, in regard to which opinions could be expressed, and that the mere having of an opinion was not sufficient for the determination of the issue. There must be a distinction between true opinion and false opinion. As far as that part of his argument is concerned, we can say that Socrates supplies a complete answer to the sophists and that he even demonstrates as against the Eleatics that we must acknowledge opinions to exist and to have meaning. But his further distinction between true opinion and knowledge indicates that he had not completely realised the consequences of the insistence on objective truth and that he still to some extent left himself open to Eleatic criticism. The distinction between knowledge and true opinion corresponds to the later Pythagorean distinction between reality and appearance. We can have correct opinions about appearances—that necessarily follows from the fact that there are appearances, but we do not have knowledge, Socrates considers, if we have not *connected these appearances with the corresponding reality.*[3] In taking up that position Socrates shows that he has not got over

---
[3][JA] Or reduced to *elements*. *Cf.*, *Theaetetus*.

the separation (between reality and appearance) which the Pythagoreans had maintained. In fact we may say that it is the importance of Eleaticism that it shows that this separation cannot be got over, if once it has been definitely made. And the only way of meeting the Eleatic arguments is to show that the separation need not have been made, and that it cannot logically be made, that any attempt to make it involves us in inconsistencies. In fact we can represent the position of the sophists by constructing paradoxes, analogous to Zeno's, relating to forms and particulars, and to knowledge and opinion.

We can say:

"If forms are to be known, they must be known in particulars, since there cannot be a form which isn't a form *of* something. On the other hand, if forms are to be known, they must be known apart from particulars, otherwise there will be no distinction between forms and particulars, and we will be left only with particulars. The assumption of a knowledge of forms leads to contradictory conclusions: namely, that these must be known both in and apart from particulars; and consequently there can be no knowledge of forms."

Now that argument, like Zeno's paradoxes, can be seen to be fallacious from the form it takes. Only if there is some ambiguity in our notion of the forms, or of the way in which they are known, can it be possible to draw these contradictory conclusions with any plausibility. But the importance of the paradox is that it shows the necessity of making our conception of forms (as of space, motion etc.,) more precise. If we think of the forms as characters of things, then we will agree to the conclusion that they have to be known in things; but we will not admit that they require to be known, or can be known, apart from things. At the same time, if there is to be a distinction between a thing and a character it would appear necessary that we should be able to know them separately. The solution of the difficulty is suggested by Socrates himself in the *Phaedo* when he points to the desirability of conducting our investigations in terms of propositions. In the proposition we have a certain subject with a certain predicate which can be said to characterise the subject. What we know, when we know a proposition, may be described as *a thing having a character*. And though the subject and predicate are distinguished, the proposition itself shows that they are not separate. It is possible to distinguish the thing and the character because the same thing has other characters and the same character may belong to other things. But even so we cannot make an absolute distinction between things and characters or between a class of subjects and a class of predicates without coming to the same sort of difficulties as the Eleatics and sophists had pointed out. What we require to complete the theory is the recognition of the fact that any term whatever can be either a subject or a predicate: it can have either of the two functions of characterising or being characterised, though in a given proposition it has only one of these.

Lecture 42

Socrates continued—knowledge and opinion

The two possible arguments in the case of knowledge and opinion are as follows. If we are to have knowledge, it must be something above and beyond opinion, since otherwise it may not be true and so would not be entitled to be called knowledge. The second argument is: If we are to have knowledge, we must have it by means of opinion, that is, by believing something, since otherwise we would not know it. Taking these two arguments together in the manner of Zeno, it would be said to follow that we cannot have knowledge, since to assume that we have leads to contradictions. But in terms of the criticism of the form of argument which the Eleatics adopt, it would have to be said that if one of these consequences followed from the possibility of knowledge, the other did not. That is, we must say either that knowledge is or that it is not above opinion, but we cannot say both. The position of the sophists is that knowledge is impossible and that the only sort of truth we can arrive at is that which is involved in having an opinion. In other words, whatever we hold as our personal opinion or belief is true for us, but there is no question of its being true in any other sense. In this part of the sophistic position, just as in the rejection of the notion of an underlying reality, the sophists are really adopting certain of the assumptions of the Pythagoreans, while professing to overthrow the Pythagorean position. They are, that is, assuming that if there is to be true knowledge, knowledge of objects or independent reality, then it must be the result of the operation of some mental faculty which is infallible. And finding that there is no infallible faculty, they draw the conclusion that there is no knowledge of objective truth. It may be said in support of their position that they at least bring out inconsistencies in the Pythagorean doctrine and that some of these inconsistencies are still to be found in the position of Socrates. Socrates, that is, recognises both a faculty of knowledge, one which cannot possibly be deceived, and a faculty of opinion, which may or may not be deceived. Accordingly, he is committed to drawing a distinction between *knowledge* and *right opinion*. But when it comes to working out this distinction in detail, we find that it is reducible to having a single right opinion and having a number of right opinions. That is, in the case of what is called knowledge, we are supposed to have a true belief, not only in a particular proposition, but in another proposition from which it follows, and also, of course, in the fact it does follow. But to have a number of right opinions does not take us beyond the realm of opinion, and even if a single opinion is right, then what is believed must be absolutely true—even though a person who believes it may be capable of losing this particular belief and falling into error again. If opinions were really concerned with an intermediate realm between being and not-being, then it could never be right, because we can only call an opinion right, if what is believed actually *is*. The objection to the position of Socrates is that he tries to find a place for both knowledge and opinion, and thus opens the way for Eleatic or sophistic criticism. But in allowing that there can be right opinion he indicates the way in which sophists can be criticised. If opinion can be right, then there is the possibility of knowing the truth, that is, having knowledge in the fullest sense by means of opinion. But the mere fact that there are opinions is sufficient to show that right opinion is possible. In saying we have a belief, we imply that we believe something to be the case, that is, to be true objectively or independently of us, and any attempt to work out a theory of subjective truth inevitably leads to inconsistencies. If Protagoras says that a certain opinion is true for him even though it need not be true for anyone else, he is putting forward a proposition which must be taken to be either true or false in the absolute sense—a proposition with which he would expect other people to agree. That is, Protagoras' own theory of subjective truth is either objectively true or objectively false. As is pointed out in *Theaetetus*, unless Protagoras thinks his own theories are true for everyone and not merely for himself, then his claim to be a teacher can have no foundation. What is indicated then is that apart from the notion of truth, it would be impossible to explain opinions and also the clash of opinions or discussion. When two persons disagree as Socrates and Protagoras do, for example, then there must be something about which they are disagreeing. That is, there must be some issue of fact and even if it were agreed that we could never be quite sure of the facts, it would still be the case that believing anything and believing it to be a fact are the same thing.

We saw that every opinion which has not been certified in any way implies a reference to absolute truth and not merely to personal supposition. Now similar concerns apply in the case of arguments and definitions. A person who held that there was no absolute truth, would likewise hold that there was no absolute standard of valid argument, and there was no absolutely correct definition of any term. Accordingly, the sophists considered that they were entitled to make any statement they pleased and use terms in any sense they liked, for the purpose of persuading people to adopt their own opinions. Following out the arguments of Zeno to their logical conclusion,[4] Protagoras declared that on any subject, it was possible to make two opposite statements, neither of which was any truer than the other, but one of which might be stronger than the other, in the sense that it applied more to a particular audience—that they found it to be plausible—and it was the business of a sophist to show how to make the weaker argument stronger, that is to say, how to make an audience change its opinion and consider plausible and worthy of acceptance the position they had previously

---

[4] [JA] That is, the One is the *unambiguous*: that which has no aspects, and must either be known wholly or not at all.

rejected. Now the objection to all this, which was worked out by Socrates, is that it implies those very standards of truth, validity and accuracy, which it was supposed to dispense with. Unless we have a conception of truth, we cannot understand what is meant by saying two statements are opposed, or that a man has changed his opinion. Unless we have a conception of valid argument, we cannot understand how any particular argument could be regarded as plausible. For to say we find an argument plausible or persuasive is to say that we *think* that the conclusion *follows* from the premises, even if this isn't so as a matter of fact. That is, the mere offering of, or listening to, an argument implies the belief that one proposition implies another, and so indicates acceptance (in accepting the implication) of a distinction between validity and fallacy.[5] In exactly the same way, to profess to *understand* a statement, whether or not we really understand it, implies the possibility of correct definition of the terms employed. (Explication.) So that even if Socrates is wrong in thinking that we can discover these standards in any other way than in having beliefs and acting on them, he at least shows that the sophists are wrong in thinking we can have beliefs without accepting some standard and implying there is a correct standard.

Lecture 43

Socrates continued—influence of the physicists

Socrates says in the *Phaedo* that he was dissatisfied with the methods of the physicists and that he substituted for them a new method of his own. He represents the latter as a second best but actually he considers that it is the only one that we can employ under present circumstances at least,[6] and criticism of his position might take the form of asserting that this propositional method is the only one under *any* conditions. So that Socrates when he speaks of contemplating the forms in their purity is really making the same mistakes as the physicists when they claim to deal with substances in their particularity and in isolation from one another. We may take the valuable feature of the

---
[5][JA] *Euthyphro*
[6][JA] That is, best would be to have *no* method at all, but direct *revelation*. Socrates' fundamental scepticism.

sophistic attitude and of the attitude which Socrates adopts in his (anti-physical) position—though he doesn't consistently adhere to it—to be recognition of the fact that there is no other way of obtaining truth than by having opinions, that is, we recognise that opinions may be true or false. So that the issue is really something over and above our having opinions, but still it is only by having opinions that we can have any information on the subject. We cannot identify ourselves with the objects of our knowledge, and when we distinguish these objects from ourselves we have to admit that we may be wrong about them. The pre-Socratics had proceeded as if there were no question of such error—as if it were quite sufficient that the mind should be confronted with things, for it to know all about them. But while it is important to recognise this possibility of error, it is illogical to try to solve the difficulty by making a distinction among faculties, one of which is taken to be infallible; because in the case of the operation of that faculty we again have the conception of the mind's being merely confronted with certain objects in such a way that it must necessarily know them. And if that assumption is made, the fallible faculties will remain unrelated to that which is supposed to be infallible. So that the most important implication of the recognition of the possibility of error is that all that we know must be considered as taking the propositional form: that the proposition must not be regarded as our peculiar way of dealing with things which are not in the propositional form, but as the way in which these things actually occur. For if we assume that things occur in a different form, then we cannot solve the problem of showing how the propositions we formulate apply to these things. If we take a particular substance and describe it in certain ways, our statements will really be meaningless unless we can find these characters actually belonging to the substances. So that what we have before our mind is not a simple substance which we can afterwards go on to deal with in various ways, but it is a substance having some particular character—in other words, it is a proposition. And when it is recognised that we do not have indivisible objects of knowledge but that whatever we take as the unit for the time being has internal differences (subject, predicate and copula)—when that is recognised, then there does not seem to be the same difficulty about finding the relation between one proposition and another.

Continuity is introduced into knowledge by a recognition of the proposition, and of definition as applied to its terms and implication as relating it to other propositions. From the sophistic point of view, each opinion, however it might be expressed, would have to be taken as an absolute unit, conformable to the Pythagorean units, and thus each opinion would be unrelated to every other, since a consideration of any such relation would introduce entities of a different order similar to the Pythagorean unlimited. So that at best it could be said that it was a mere matter of chance what opinion followed from any other opinion, and that what the sophists claimed to teach—special rules and methods of persuasion—would not be possible or intelligible. The fact that the sophists did propose (profess?) to teach methods of discussion shows that they implicitly recognised relations among propositions, forms of arguments, and therefore that they couldn't consistently maintain their treatment of opinions as units. One of the most important features of the work of Socrates is that he attempted to determine the forms of argument and of discussion in general and that in so doing he introduced the consideration of logical questions—the forms of our speech indicating what we consider to be the nature of things.

Lecture 44

Socrates continued—attitude of criticism in the Dialogues—philosophy as free thought

We might express the attitude of Socrates as indicated in the Platonic dialogues most accurately by saying that it is an attitude of criticism, that is, Socrates is unwilling to accept any statement for which no ground of belief can be given or of which we cannot give an account. And even if we do not accept his distinction between knowledge and right opinion we can recognise that there is some value in his critical attitude, because even a right opinion must be one that can be subjected to the closest possible scrutiny. It is of course to be remembered that in stating the reason or ground for any belief we have to make another statement (of belief), and if a reason were demanded for all beliefs we should be committed to an infinite series of arguments, without any possibility of arriving at a final justification for the belief in question. In fact we see in the *Phaedo* the two complete tendencies in the thought of Socrates, when it is taken to be sufficient in order that argument should proceed that the parties to the discussion should agree upon some particular proposition, while at the same time it is suggested both in the *Phaedo* and in the *Republic* that there might be ultimate premises which were agreed upon simply because they were self-evident—which could be taken as in some sense proving themselves, or which were such that anyone who understands them was bound to believe them. In respect of the latter tendency Socrates is merely substituting other dogmas for those which he had rejected when they appeared in popular thought, and if his critical method is to present a real alternative to dogmatism, then it must be allowed that there are no propositions which cannot be criticised or which are their own ground; but that it is sufficient and indeed necessary for investigation that the investigator should have certain definite beliefs, or should observe a particular set of objects, with the purpose of solving some problem, that is, of coming to a conclusion on a matter about which he had been previously doubtful. Or again, in the case of a number of investigators, that they should have determined certain points of agreement or certain propositions which for the purpose of the argument they had agreed not to question, with the object of determining the truth or falsity of some other proposition about which they were doubtful or in disagreement, or of making a discovery in some realm of fact which they had not previously investigated. In so far then as it involves this latter tendency, the attitude of Socrates is valuable and it is valuable also in that it raises the question whether or not there are propositions not requiring proof, distinct from those propositions which people think may be taken for granted simply because they have not realised that there is fundamental disagreement on these questions. Now it is particularly in connection with *ethical* (in reality, *social*, not necessarily ethical at all) questions that the determination to abide by received beliefs and not to recognise that there can be genuine difference of opinion on the subject, that that tendency appears. The sophists had been occupied in pointing out that on ethical matters there are different opinions in different communities, but instead of concluding that there were certain objective issues which required thorough discussion, the sophists concluded that no certainty could be reached on the subject and that each man should hold to his own opinions and make them prevail as much as he could. But in order to take up a practical attitude to those questions, the sophists had like Xenophanesto distinguish between controversial and non-controversial matters, that is, between those opinions which are generally received in a given community and those about which there are disagreements even among the people of the community (let alone with outsiders).

In regard to this attitude of the sophists, just as in regard to that of Xenophanes, it has to be pointed out that it is impossible to draw a line between opinions which can be disputed and opinions which cannot be disputed or which there is no point in disputing. For it is obvious that the laws of a country at any time differ not merely from the laws of other countries but also from the laws of the same country at a different time. And this development of laws indicates that policy does affect the matters which were supposed to be above party and to be agreed upon by everyone. Further, if it is said that certain opinions are held throughout a community, the fact remains that for this to be so each member of the community must hold these opinions, that is, he must have gone through some process whereby he came to believe that certain kinds of action were right and proper, and that certain others were not. He could not simply have accepted them on being told that they were true, since before he could accept them, he would require to be capable of understanding them. (Of course, we often suddenly awake to the fact that we *don't* understand something we have been repeating all our lives; that it is "cant". The value of the study of philosophy is to "clear our minds of cant", remove hypothesis, and make us unwilling to believe everything we hear—that is, it is opposed to all *authority* in thinking;[7] philosophy as "free thought".)

As Socrates would argue, he would require to have some notion of what "right" and "proper" meant and here, in the development of the individual mind, in the fact that no one is born with the knowledge of the laws of his own community, we have a further proof of the fact that these laws cannot be taken as above argument, since some sort of argument, some sort of *presentation* of the issues, must have taken place before anyone could learn what the laws of his community were, and decide to uphold them. The consideration of change and development, so far from upholding the sophistic view that in these matters each man must abide by his own opinion, shows, on the contrary, that there are definite methods of examining these opinions; since unless it were possible to criticise an opinion, to bring forward tests of its value, it would not be possible to attempt to persuade people to adopt that opinion—there would be no such thing as education. It is implied then, even in saying that there are current opinions, that there are also ways of examining these opinions, and Socrates considers that it is an absolute requirement of education that these methods of testing opinions should be presented to the learner, and not that he should be simply told what to believe without knowing how his belief could be defended. It is that sort of belief—the belief which has been adopted because it is the right thing to believe—that is not held fast by the mind because no basis for it has even been stated (*and* because the mind has not found it out for itself). But what requires to be emphasised in the development of the position of Socrates on this point is that a person who accepts an opinion merely because he has been told to believe it, cannot properly be said to believe it at all and so to have right opinion even if the belief happens to be true. For he is not in a position to understand the proposition in question. He has accepted it merely verbally and accordingly what he takes it to mean may be something quite different from what it is intended to mean by those who have an understanding of the subject. It is for this among other reasons that Socrates considers definition to be of such

---
[7][Ed.] "Clear your *mind* of cant" was the celebrated advice of Samuel Johnson in an exchanged recorded in Boswell's *Life of Johnson*, as recorded in Boswell's diary for May 15th 1783.

great importance, though even then it has to be pointed out that the definition of a term has to be expressed in other terms, and that these might be the subject of the same sort of misunderstanding. If we attempt to define our terms, we may expect to come nearer to thinking consistently (at any rate, to raise *problems*, though we cannot *always* be defining).

II
The Euthyphro and The Apology

Lecture 45

The Dialogues—Euthyphro on piety

The theme which is discussed in *Euthyphro* is piety or holiness, and it is important in connection with the fact that the main charge against Socrates in his trial was one of impiety. And what the argument as a whole is intended to bring out is that those who accused him of impiety had in reality no clear conception of what piety was. Socrates approaches Euthyphro as one who claims to have a special knowledge of these matters—to be an expert in matters of holiness, and accordingly to be able to instruct Socrates and explain to him where he had gone wrong. And the suggestion is that if Euthyphro who had made a special study of these matters, had really no settled convictions which could stand criticism, still less could the accusers of Socrates, and the Athenian public generally, who admittedly had made no special study of the questions, have such knowledge as would justify them in condemning the errors of Socrates.

There is also a comparison between Euthyphro and the sophists. Euthyphro himself is not a sophist: he is an Athenian citizen, whereas they were all foreigners, and this, as Burnet points out, was one of the reasons why the Athenians objected to them. But he is a person who claims to be able to give instruction in a certain important part of conduct, namely, the part which relates to the gods, and it is the aim of Socrates to show that those who try to develop codes of morality on the basis of common opinions and common practices, fall into confusions, since there is really no coherence among the common and accepted views; but on the contrary many contradictions, which can be brought out when an attempt is made to apply precepts in an exact manner to particular situations. And secondly, Euthyphro shows that misconception of which the sophists are guilty—that misconception of morality as divided into parts (moral units), the notion that one can separately consider what are a man's duties to the gods and what are his duties to his fellow-citizens, what are his duties to his family and even to himself.[1] As A. E. Taylor points out, the profession in the Socratic discourses of the unity of virtue really implies that we cannot in this way divide our lives into separate parts and set up special rules for each special activity, so as to suggest that a man might fulfil his duties to the gods without fulfilling his duties to men, and *vice versa*; because in each case there must be some settled criterion whereby we determine what is right and what is wrong, and the notions of right and wrong cannot vary in different cases. What ethics has to consider is the nature of the good life, and even if it is possible to carry out certain good activities and not others, still their goodness is the same, and the one will prove of assistance to the others.[2]

On the logical side, the *Euthyphro* is specially concerned with the question of definition—a question which as we have seen is important in connection with the distinction between knowledge and right opinion. Even admitting the difficulties of making this distinction, we must allow that Socrates has drawn attention to an important point—namely, that if our reason for adopting any belief is simply that we have been told so, and that it is current in the society in which we live, we cannot be certain that we really have the required belief and that each of us understands by the formula employed, the same as any other. In order to be able to accept that information, we must understand something about the subject on which the information is given, and in order to have that understanding we must have done a certain amount of investigation for ourselves. But if we have done that investigation and have become acquainted with the subject, then it is quite possible that we may not accept the formulae, however generally received they may be. So that for an individual person to accept a belief on authority or because other people accept it, is really an illogical procedure, and we may expect that in the case of those beliefs which are said to be generally accepted, different persons understand them in different ways, so that the supposed general agreement is merely apparent. And

---
[1] [JA] *Cf.*, the *Sophist* "goodness"—the power of directing states and families aright.
[2] A. E. Taylor, *Plato: The Man and His Work*, London: Methuen 1926.

this type of misunderstanding is most likely to occur in connection with moral questions on which each person, no matter how uninstructed he may be, is ready to express opinions, and, in particular, in connection with the *terms* which are employed in moral propositions. Such a term is *piety*—a term which was current among the Athenians and which they considered to mean something so important that they were prepared to try Socrates for his supposed violation of it.

Now the first difficulty in connection with getting an exact definition of piety is that we learn to apply this term to particular kinds of action and we are apt then to distinguish the pious from the impious simply in this nominal way. Certain kinds of action are said to be pious and so ought to be commended, certain other sorts of action are said to be impious and so ought to be condemned. But if we ask why these judgments of approval and disapproval should be passed, we are brought back to asking what in particular is praiseworthy about piety. And it is impossible to give an answer in terms of the particular rules or precepts which have been laid down. Now this in itself raises a difficulty in regard to the understanding of terms. We cannot begin by defining all our terms because in order to define any term we must use other terms which we suppose ourselves to understand.[3] We must have begun by simply being told that certain terms apply to certain things, and it is only after that that we can proceed to find out what there is about these things that distinguishes them from other things, and so understand in what way the term is to be applied. It is possible for us to do so only because the things in question really have characters which enable us to find what is common and peculiar to a particular group. Now unless we do this, unless we decide not merely what things are pious but what piety means, we will never be able to think for ourselves and to discover whether a particular situation of a different type from any we have hitherto encountered is to be put in one class or another. If we have simply been told that a certain number of things are pious and if that is all we know about piety, then we are bound to consider any

---
[3][JA] *Names*.

other action not to fall within that class. And so, as Socrates points out, if justice is different from piety, then certain just acts will be impious. In the second place those particular things to which we apply this common predicate can only be recognised by means of certain general features that they possess. That is, we do not believe that any particular act in its pure particularity, that is, simply as an individual and isolated occurrence, is to be described as pious, and that that is all the information that the statement gives. If that were so, we should have no rules whatever, and we should be able to make no statements about any other particular act. But actually, in applying the word *piety* to a particular thing, we consider it in terms of the characters that we recognise, and since it is possible that these characters should be found also in another thing, we are in a position to say that this later and similar situation is also characterised by being pious. So that we have in reality formulated a universal proposition, namely, that any act of a certain sort is a pious one.[4] But if we do not pursue our inquiries further, if we simply assume that we have now learned one of the rules of piety and can apply it to subsequent situations, then there is an immediate danger of error and contradiction. Because the characters which one person recognises in the particular thing that was called pious may be different from those which another person recognises, since the characters of any particular thing are not limited, and since even from a limited set of characters, different selections can be made (LMNP, LMN*P*, *L*MNP etc.,—and since, in addition, people can mistakenly attribute any one of these characters to any particular thing, or fail to notice a character a thing has). Accordingly while the formula remains the same, quite different rules may be recognised under the head of the formula by different persons and so we will have a conflict of opinions, which for a time may pass unnoticed, but which if it comes to be noticed can only express itself in a wrangle, one person saying this is pious and another this is not, and the settlement of the question being quite impossible, unless we go back on our initial assumptions and try to find out what piety means. And we may have the particular case which appears

---

[4][JA] Singular propositions as universal.

at the beginning of the *Euthyphro*, namely, that of an action which according to one rule would be classed as pious and according to a different view (rule) would be classed as impious.[5]

Lecture 46

The Dialogues—Euthyphro continued

Starting from the statements that we make or the opinions that we say we have, we find that they require for their proper understanding the possibility of definition and of hypothesis, that is, the possibility of finding propositions from which a particular statement follows and which may be regarded as proving the latter statement; and also the possibility of finding for any sort of event *a condition which is both name and statement, that is, a definition or a cause.*

Now in the case of the discussion on piety we find Euthyphro putting forward a certain opinion which was simply accepted because it was traditional but which was opposed to another traditional opinion. The opinion by which Euthyphro chose to abide was that it is always pious to prosecute a murderer, the opposed opinion is that it is always impious to prosecute one's father. Now, in terms of these opinions, we have a particular act which would be judged to be both pious and impious. And this is a contradiction of which there must be some solution. We cannot solve it in the popular or sophistic manner by simply choosing to abide by one of the opinions and relying on its plausibility to secure the acceptance of a particular view. If the one type of action is really pious, and the other is really impious, then it becomes necessary to show what makes the difference between the two and if we cannot show that, then we are not entitled to make the distinction. We cannot be satisfied by saying that piety is recognised immediately, because it is just two of these immediate recognitions that are in conflict. It should be noticed that in both cases we are dealing with conceptions of a primitive character, that the notion of blood guiltiness enters into both. Euthyphro is anxious to prosecute the murderer because he is afraid

---
[5][JA] Correct use of names verified by our ability (a) to deal with things, (b) to cooperate with other people (by means of the things) Get what we want or get work done, that is, names are *tools*.

that otherwise he will share in the guilt. On the other hand, family relations are one of the most important spheres to which this conception applies, and so in terms of primitive thought with its fundamental notion of contamination we have an absolute conflict of duties. (What Euthyphro is finding is "pleasure without guilt" that is, a way of *justifying* an act which would otherwise be guilty: by showing that it is his duty (*cf.*, totem feast). A *rationalisation* or dream: an "ideal", which permits him to do what he *likes*; but fears.)[6] And in regard to this and kindred problems we may say that the *Euthyphro* like many other Socratic dialogues is concerned to show that the conception of duty cannot rigidly be maintained, that the ultimate conception of ethics is that of *goodness*, and when we have taken account of this, we can avoid the multiplicity of duties and precepts, and the conflicts to which that multiplication inevitably leads.

That is the ethical import of the dialogue (removing hypotheses), and Socrates points out that it is chiefly in regard to ethical questions (questions of *conduct*) that these conflicts and apparently insoluble problems appear. But at the same time in endeavouring to establish a method of solving ethical problems, Socrates is laying down the principles of all scientific discussion. Unless we define as ethical any subject which gives rise to disagreement, then we are bound to recognise that there is no subject about which there cannot be disagreement. If there were, it would be a subject on which investigation was impossible, since the need for investigation implies the possibility of error and hence of disagreement.

In any actual case of persons disagreeing, we can consider the matter from the ethical point of view. We can consider the actions of the persons as moral or immoral. And it seems to be on this account that Socrates tends to think of all science as subordinate to ethical science, and all forms to the *form of the good*. But even if a person in making a particular scientific inquiry is acting morally, it does not follow that the subject into which he is inquiring is a moral subject or that moral considerations can in any way assist us to settle the problems. Similarly, though in investigating

---

[6][JA] Stekel. Freud. [Ed.:] Wilhelm Stekel (1868–1940), physicist and psychologist, among the earliest followers of Sigmund Freud (1856–1939).

we are exercising our cognitive faculties, it does not follow that the consideration of the nature of our knowledge is necessary for the elucidation of the subject. In the end it is possible to investigate any subject only because its nature is independent of our investigation (for example our investigation itself is independent of our investigating *it*). And even if some inquiry into the condition of our minds may be necessary to remove particular errors or to show why we have made them, this question would never arise unless we could treat the subject objectively, that is, we could never settle any question if we thought that our opinions could alter the facts. And in the second place it is possible to find the psychological basis of our errors only if we can investigate the conditions of our minds objectively and find that certain propositions are, as a matter of fact, true statements of the condition of our minds.

Now this objective consideration of things and this recognition of the fact that questions of knowledge and conduct do not affect the subject-matter of the various sciences, apart from the particular sciences of human life—all this is implied in the rejection of the sophistic theories of opinion. But it is not fully worked out by Socrates because he still retains to some extent the Pythagorean conception of higher and lower orders of reality. In other words, he is still partly committed to an ethical treatment of all science and all things. But as far as his direct criticism of the sophists and similar thinkers goes, we find that he is setting forth the logical conditions of investigations and in doing so, supporting an objective treatment of things.

In this particular dialogue having come to a conflict of opinions Socrates demands a definition, that is, he wishes to know how we can distinguish what is pious from what is not pious, and Euthyphro in reply offers his own action as an example of what is pious. Socrates then points out that this cannot be accepted as a definition, that it does not enable us to make the necessary differentiation in critical cases and in particular in the case which is being considered. We require a universal definition, that which merely consists in giving an example is not a definition at all. Or, putting the matter in Socratic language, we desire to know the *form* of piety and not any particular, which is merely an *imitation* of the form. The definition which Euthyphro proceeds to give appears to conform to the requirements of definition in that it gives a basis for differentiation. That is pious which is pleasing to the gods and that is impious which is not so pleasing. This would make a satisfactory distinction if it were possible for us to know exactly what is pleasing to the gods and what is not. But, as Socrates proceeds to point out, it is not possible to make a clear line of division in this way, fundamentally because it is only when (because) we have already concluded that certain things are pious, that we come to believe that they will be pleasing to the gods. But the point which Socrates immediately takes up is important because it raises the whole question of opinion. Instead of defining piety by reference to the opinions of men, Euthyphro has simply pushed the difficulty further back by referring to the opinions of the gods, and Socrates points out that in the case of the gods, just as in the case of men, there is a possibility of disagreement, and even if there is agreement, it must be agreement about something.

Lecture 47

The Dialogues—Euthyphro continued—stages in the argument

The stages of the argument in the *Euthyphro* are as follows. First, we have the conflict of opinions: that conflict indicates a problem for those who are scientifically-minded, the problem of determining within what limits certain lines of action are allowable, since if we set no limits to them we arrive at a contradiction. Now the fact of this contradiction and the fact that even Euthyphro is constrained to admit that there is a contradiction shows that we cannot reconcile ourselves to the theory of opinion as our only guide and as justifying ourselves (itself?) (our actions?). Since opinions conflict and since in conflicting they indicate that there is a real issue and a real logic independent of them.

Now the desire to solve the problem brings us to the second stage of the argument which is the demand for a definition, the demand, that is, for a criterion whereby we can distinguish anything which is pious from anything which is not pious. If we can secure a criterion of that kind, a necessary and sufficient condition of piety, then we will be able to determine in any particular case whatever whether piety is present or not.

We then pass on to (thirdly) the different attempts made by Euthyphro to find a definition, that is, to explain what is the difference between piety and impiety. And he begins by attempting to define piety by giving a particular example. Now apart from the fact that the example which he chooses is his own particular action which was the very matter in dispute, we can see that any attempt to define by giving examples involves our falling back upon opinion, that is, on *denying the problem*. If we could solve the difficulty in this way, the problem would never have arisen. Socrates expresses this fact in his own way by saying that what we require is the *form* of piety, and that any particular example is only an imitation of the form and depends for its recognition on a previous recognition of the form. And even if we reject the Socratic theory that forms can be known apart from particulars, we must still insist that since the same character can be found in many particulars, we cannot take any one particular as our criterion because in that case we may confuse between what is peculiar to the thing and what is common to it along with other members of the class.

In the fourth stage of the argument, Euthyphro offers a definition which has the appearance of satisfying the requirements, namely, that the pious is that which is pleasing to the gods. That, he suggests, is a criterion whereby we may distinguish it from anything which is not pious. Now the objection of Socrates to this definition, expressed in terms of "the rules of definition", is that it is *obscure*. It does not solve the problem which it professes to solve. If we had any difficulty in discovering what is pious, we should have still greater difficulty in determining what was pleasing to the gods.[7] As Socrates proceeds to point out, we have simply arrived back at definition by opinion, only we are now taking the opinions of the gods instead of our own. Now where there is opinion, there is the possibility of disagreement and

---
[7][JA] *Cf.*, Milesians and mythology. (Praying for rain: if it comes, gods have attended to our prayer; if not, gods are angry at us and require to be *propitiated*; *cf.*, later part of *Euthyphro* on "traffic" between gods and men.)

according to the stories that we hear, there are disagreements among the gods, and therefore the same thing will be pleasing to some gods and displeasing to others. In other words, the same thing will be both pious and impious, which is precisely the contradiction which prompted the whole inquiry. (What is pleasing to Euthyphro is unpleasing to other Athenians.) Then Euthyphro, recognising that his definition is not satisfactory, modifies it by saying that what is pious is that which is pleasing to *all* the gods. Now in the first place this will leave a number of actions about which we will be unable to determine whether they are pious or not—those which are pleasing to some and displeasing to others of the gods. And the mere existence of this class would show that the gods are capable of being wrong in their opinions and consequently that we cannot rely on their opinions, even when they are agreed. But Socrates doesn't insist on that defect. What he points out is that even in cases where the gods are agreed, they are agreed about something, that is, they agree in recognising that something is the case, is true, and accordingly it will be this truth which enables us to make the distinction between piety and impiety and not the fact that the gods all recognise this truth.

We can in fact say that this attempt at definition is a *circular* one, that is, it implicitly uses the term to be defined in the definition. Euthyphro wishes to say that that is pious which the gods love, but when we inquire what sort of things are loved by the gods, we find that it is precisely those things which are pious. The definition then involves circularity and it is defective also in this way, that it is not an account of the "essential features" of piety; that piety is supposed to be defined by the relation which certain beings have to piety, but that relation cannot belong to the nature of piety itself.[8] It is only if it has a character of its own that the gods or anyone else will be able to take up an attitude to it, and it is that character which we have to try to discover.[9]

As A. E. Taylor points out, this problem is similar to the general problem in ethics of whether ethical rules can or cannot be regarded as commands issued by some authority, that is, whether things are good because they are

---

[8][JA] Contamination, infection; *magic* as basis of all rationalism and as what philosophy has to remove.
[9][JA] That which "makes a thing what it is"; powers (authority) (Psycho-Analysis and Philosophy).

commanded or are commanded because they are good.[10] As regards the former view (that things are good because they are commanded) the command must be regarded as perfectly arbitrary. If there is nothing in the character of the things themselves to indicate that they ought to be commanded, if the mere command is the only possible authority, then anything whatever might be commanded and there would be no question of criticising it or even of calling it good. Or, in theological terms, if good merely meant what God commands, then we could not intelligibly use the word in any wider sense or say that God himself was good.[11]

The criticism of these attempts of Euthyphro's at defining piety is connected with the general criticism of the attempt to define anything or to arrive at positive conclusions, in terms of mere opinion. In the first place, wherever we have opinion, we have disagreement, and that implies that truth is not determined by opinion but is independent of it. Not only does having an opinion imply taking something to be true, but if opinion determined truth, then there could be no such thing as a conflict of opinions—each opinion would be its own guarantee and every other opinion would be irrelevant to it. The sophists may be said to have believed in a position similar to that of the Pythagoreans, except that their units were opinions, and they found themselves in similar difficulties, difficulties of finding connections or in general of establishing continuity. According to the Pythagorean theory, all the relations between self-contained or self-subsisting units had to be referred to the unlimited, and so, as the Eleatics showed, no account could be given of continuous motion or of any other connection among things. So that even the plurality or multiplicity among units became unintelligible. Similarly, if opinions are taken as units, then arguments or investigations which depend upon passing from one opinion to another, will be unintelligible. For reasons of that kind, opinion cannot be taken as our guide in any matter so long as we regard the opinion as something arbitrary, something capable of guaranteeing itself and not implying any reference to objective things. Now the point which Socrates makes as regards Euthyphro's amended definition is that opinion

---
[10] A. E. Taylor, *op. cit.*, p. 151.
[11] [JA] *Cf.*, Hume's *Dialogues Concerning Natural Religion*.

does imply a reference to objective things; that taking the particular instance of acts which the gods love, the gods cannot be said to love it simply because of their own attitude to it, they must love it on account of some property it possesses (though it is possible to love something *magically* or by projection or infection—extension of ego, for example). In the same way a proposition is not true because we believe it, but we believe it because we take it to be true. Accordingly, all definition by reference to opinion must be rejected, and we pass to a formal method of definition: definition by genus and difference.

Lecture 48

The Dialogues—Euthyphro continued

Having rejected any attempt at definition by means of what a thing is related to, or something that happens to it from without, Socrates is concerned to find a method of definition which will show what a thing is in itself. And in order to do so, he suggests, we have to state within what class the particular thing to be defined falls. Already in the dialogue it has been presumed that the distinction between what is pious and what is impious falls within the sphere of human acts: and that particular assumption is not called in question in the further course of the dialogue. But merely to say that piety is a species or mode of human behaviour does not take us very far towards determining what piety is (seeing that the same may be said of *impiety*). We have to find some more restricted class of human acts within which piety falls. And it is suggested that this is the class of just or right acts, that is, that piety is a species of justice. Then the question arises: what species of justice is piety? What distinguishes pious acts from other acts which are also just? Euthyphro proposes as the basis of distinction to take pious acts as those which are done in the service of the gods, and other just acts as those which are done in the service of men. Now in putting the matter thus, Euthyphro has formulated what is certainly the conventional understanding of the meaning of piety—the service of the gods (which is again a *relation.*) But in order that the distinction should be a clear one, it is necessary that we should understand precisely in what the service of the gods consists. In the case of the services that we render to men, the natural assumption is that we *benefit* the men in some way. But, Socrates asks, can we imagine that by pious acts we are benefiting the gods?—that we are capable of making the gods better, or again that they are in need of anything from us? If we make the service of the gods analogous to the service of men, then we are representing piety as a sort of traffic between gods and men, in which men offer prayers and sacrifices to the gods, and receive in return certain advantages. Now this, Socrates suggests, and Euthyphro is unable to contest it, is a quite inadequate representation of the divine nature, namely, as engaging in traffic or commercial transactions with men, and so Euthyphro is reduced to saying that pious acts are not those which benefit the gods in any way but are simply those which are pleasing to the gods. In other words, he has simply come back to his original definition and opened the way for the same criticisms as Socrates had previously put forward, the only difference being that piety has now been recognised to be a species of justice. But again it may be said that even this was taken for granted from the beginning, that piety was at least represented as something praiseworthy; so that, in effect, Euthyphro can offer no better definition than that which has already been shown to be defective.[12]

Now this fact and similar conclusions in other dialogues have led to the suggestion that the dialectic of Socrates is useless, that it leads to no practical advantage but leaves us just where we were. But before accepting that conclusion, we have to remember that it is admitted that the value of such discussion depends upon the attitude that we take up towards it. If Euthyphro had really desired to clear up his ideas, then he would not have remained satisfied with any such ending, but would have sought some new hypothesis or fresh definition which would have met the difficulty. So that what the ending of the dialogue actually shows is that Euthyphro and all others with a sophistic outlook prefer to abide by certain fixed opinions or prejudices and have no desire to subject them to critical examination. They think that their views are good enough for practical purposes and

---

[12][JA] Unscientific misology; cannot all agree. Truth lies between the two. No exact formulation possible, etc. (Scientific Scepticism: Relativism.) Getting a "broad" view.

on that account they are prepared to reject logic itself or to close their eyes to any contradiction.

Now, although as far as Euthyphro is concerned the dialogue has served no useful purpose, it has certain quite important implications for those who wish to learn from it, that is, it has indicated the weakness of uncriticised opinion, it has indicated the need for exact definition and a number of the rules which have to be adopted in obtaining that definition, and finally it has demonstrated the ethical inadequacy of any view which attempts to divide life into water-tight compartments. If we make an absolute separation between piety and other kinds of goodness, then we are suggesting that justice among men, for example, is impious. Or, if we are going to think of the gods being pleased with particular acts of men, then we are not entitled to say that there is any good act whatever at which the gods would not be pleased. So that we would have to say that the service of men is at the same time service of the gods, and we might presume that service of the gods would also be advantageous to men. Ethics then if it is to be a science, must be a coherent whole and we must not make a sharp division between different kinds of duty.

But in the second place even the conception of duty is not wholly satisfactory from the ethical point of view, since it merely indicates under what conditions good acts are to be done and what effects they may have when they are done. But the primary object of study in ethics is the nature of good acts themselves without any consideration in the first instance of their conditions and consequences. Until we have determined what acts are good, the consideration of conditions and consequences is irrelevant to ethics.

The way in which Socrates criticises conventional religious views shows how it was possible for him to rouse a great deal of opposition and how the accusation of impiety according to Athenian standards would at least be plausible whether or not it was the real ground on which Socrates was attacked. And when we consider what Socrates says in the *Apology* we find that he makes no direct reply to the accusation of religious innovation, that, in fact, his defence on this point really consists of an accusation against his accusers and the

Athenians. It is the Athenians who are impious because they refuse to inquire into the most important matters, because they accept the views which have been handed down to them and overlook, as far as possible, any difficulty to which these views may lead. And in doing so and in handing to their own descendants the views which they have received from their ancestors, it is the Athenians and not Socrates who are guilty of corrupting the youth. They care so little for the welfare of the youth that they do not take the trouble to find out whether the things that they teach them are true or false. Socrates is saying, in effect, that since he has *attempted* to discover the nature of piety and of education, he is much less worthy of accusation than are the bulk of Athenians who have made no such attempt. In fact while they are proposing to condemn him for impiety and corruption, he condemns them on the same account. Even if we take the religious charge to have been a mere cloak for a political charge, we can still find a close connection between the two. That is, Socrates in his discussion and inquiries demanded of the Athenians that they should give an account not merely of their worship of the gods but of their worship of themselves, of the assumption of their political system that there was some special virtue in being an Athenian. We see in the *Meno* that this line of criticism was particularly infuriating to the people, because there Anytus warns Socrates to be careful how he expresses himself and to avoid those general criticisms of the Athenian people (and their democratic leaders).

Lecture 49

The Dialogues—Apology

The general line of the argument of Socrates in the *Apology* as well as in some other dialogues is that anyone who proposes to take part in politics ought to have a thorough training in the theory of the subject and to have carefully investigated what was good for the people and what was bad. But he contended that the politicians of his time had taken up politics without any theoretical preparation whatever. And he considered their inability to meet the difficulties in political theory that he raised as showing that they had no knowledge of the meaning of politics or of showing what had to be done in guiding the state. Socrates does not represent himself as expert in these matters. He is particularly concerned to rebut the accusation of being a wise man. He points out that the references in the works of the comic poets to his concern with natural science and sophistry are inaccurate. The wisdom which he claims is negative rather than positive. *Or*, all that he knows is that he has no certain knowledge. Now this view, while it brings up some of the difficulties connected with the Socratic theory of forms and their relation to sensible things, is in the main an ironical way of expressing the Socratic method—that of critical examination of beliefs in contrast with the acceptance of beliefs simply because they are current. The latter, Socrates maintains, is not knowledge, a man cannot be said to have knowledge unless he can give an account of his beliefs, unless he can defend them by argument and show how they apply to different situations. And Socrates considers that the person who represents himself as practical and not requiring to indulge in any speculative theory is not really distinguished from other men by not having a theory. He actually has, or acts upon, a theory—namely, that what has been accepted should continue to be accepted, but he has not *examined* this theory and couldn't give a reasonable defence of it if required to. The politicians have incompletely worked out theories, they make many references to justice and virtue but they never attempt to explain what justice is. Accordingly, Socrates considers that, being ignorant of the true nature of justice, they are quite incapable of directing the state in a proper way. Similarly Socrates objects to the assumption of the ordinary citizen that without any training at all, merely by being a citizen, he knows what is right and what is wrong in political affairs. Such knowledge, Socrates contends, does not come by nature, nor by mere habituation, such as continued residence in a particular city might give, but only by a rigorous course of training, by a careful examination of the characteristics of justice itself and by the removal of common misconceptions. Such a misconception is indicated in the closing part of the *Apology* where Socrates implicitly attacks the ordinary view that it is better to do injustice than to suffer injustice. The position of Socrates, on the contrary, amounts to this, that it is impossible for a man to suffer injustice, that injustice is something that a person does, that whatever is evil in an unjust act attaches to the doer of it, and that if a man follows justice in his own actions, then the actions of others (or again any of the changes of fate) can never affect him adversely.[13] It is for a reason of this kind that Socrates refuses after the trial to make his escape from prison. To do so would be to admit that the Athenians could really injure him, whereas he maintains that in acting unjustly towards him they are injuring themselves. In the second place, it follows from this Socratic contention that death is not really to be feared, since nothing that can happen to a just man is to be feared. The only thing that a man ought to fear is that he might act unjustly. It is even possible that death is to be welcomed in that after his death a man may be able to contemplate justice itself, whereas in this life he could only find approximations to it or likenesses of it. And that sums up the typical "wisdom" of Socrates, namely, that in this life we only have approximations to the truth, but in another life we may be set free from particulars and find truth itself.

---

[13][Ed.] *Apology*, 41d: "know of a certainty that no evil can happen to a good man, either in life or after death"

III
The Phaedo and The Parmenides

Lecture 50

The Dialogues—Phaedo—on soul and body

In connection with the distinction between this life and another life, and between truth itself and approximation to truth, Socrates emphasises the distinction between soul and body. It is the body which is concerned with particular objects of desire, while the soul is concerned with things themselves; not with mere appearances and temporary acquisitions but with what is eternal. The soul finds these things or approaches more nearly to knowledge of them as it succeeds in dissociating itself from the body. And it is in that attitude of dissociation, in the separation of the soul from bodily concerns, and its attention to those things which are out of relation to the body, that the philosophic life consists.

Accordingly we find Socrates at the beginning of the *Phaedo* declaring that the philosopher more than any other man should not be afraid of death, since he has spent his life in detaching the soul from the body to the greatest possible extent. In fact from the point of view of the distinction of soul from body with the implication that death is their separation, it may even be said that it is the present life which is death, because in it our souls have been separated from knowledge of *things in themselves*—a knowledge which they had in another life.[1] In arguments of this kind, *immortality* is taken for granted, or at least it is assumed that the soul is capable of existing by itself, which is the main assumption necessary for belief in immortality. In this part of his theory Socrates is following the early Pythagoreans who consider that the body is the tomb of the soul. While in the *doctrine of reminiscence*, he follows the later Pythagorean theory of imitation or likeness, and connects it with the early Pythagorean doctrine to which later Pythagoreans had ceased to adhere. We have then in the *Phaedo* elements of early

---
[1] [JA] Socrates wants definition by what a thing *is*: yet he himself defines it by what it aims at (or partakes of).

Pythagorean theory, of later Pythagorean theory, and finally, in the *doctrine of participation*, the contribution of Socrates himself. So that in this dialogue we actually have different stages in the development of the theory of forms, and the final suggestion of Socrates is made for the purpose of avoiding the difficulties which had arisen on the earlier view. But the fact that all these theories are presented in the same argument suggests that Plato had recognised the failure of Socrates completely to overcome these difficulties, though he had suggested the method by which, if it were consistently pursued, the difficulties could be solved, that is, the method of considering things in propositions.[2]

There is at least a superficial difference between saying that the particulars are likenesses or imitations of the forms, and that the particulars participate in the forms, or that the forms are actually in them. If the latter view were consistently maintained, the doctrine of recollection would have to be abandoned, because if the forms are actually there in the particulars, then we do not require any previous experience in order to find them there. But in spite of his adherence to propositions which appear to assert that a certain predicate or character is actually to be found in a particular subject, Socrates continued to think that the form appeared only imperfectly in the particular, that it was something which the particular was aiming at, an ideal to which it could approximate but to which it could never quite attain. That is, he retains the distinction between being and becoming which had led to the difficulties in the Pythagorean theory pointed out by the Eleatics, that is, if what becomes cannot be said to be, then we cannot even say that it *is* becoming; but if we consistently adhere to the view that forms or characters are in things, then we don't require to separate them from the world of becoming, but we can say, on the contrary, that they are actually forms of becoming or ways of acting. Unless that view is taken then the difficulties pointed out by the Eleatics remain and Plato's later dialogues, particularly the *Theaetetus* and the *Parmenides*, show that Socrates had not succeeded in finding an answer to the Eleatics.

---

[2][JA] Derived from Eleatics. The *Parmenides* to show that Socratism and Eleaticism were fundamentally akin in the theory of *being* and open to the same objections; the *Theaetetus* to show the same about Socrates, sophists and theory of *knowledge*.

In so far as the method of Socrates was a method of dialectic, in so far as he depended upon the statements which people actually make, he would have been committed to the view that it is possible for things actually to have the characters we attribute to them. Otherwise the statements would be meaningless. For if the proposition as we employ it requires interpretation, then that interpretation will have to be made by means of propositions; these propositions in turn would have to be interpreted, and so we should never arrive at understanding what any statement at all really meant. We can say that it was his insistence on the forms of discussion which led Socrates to diverge from Pythagoreanism, but that it was his failure completely to dissociate himself from Pythagoreanism—a failure due in part to his absorption in the religious views of the Pythagoreans—that led to the inconsistencies which still remained in the Socratic system.

There are in the *Phaedo* three main arguments regarding immortality, each of which involves some reference to the forms.

The *first proof* is made up of two parts, that which introduces the theory of generation from opposites, and that which introduces the doctrine of recollection. These two together and not either separately are put forward as implying immortality.

The *second proof* is a proof by analogy and accordingly cannot be regarded as a satisfactory proof on any view. It can only be regarded as giving presumptive evidence and not any demonstration. It depends on the likeness of the soul to the forms in certain particular respects, and leads to the presumption that the soul may resemble forms in other respects, particularly in being eternal.

These two proofs are not regarded as satisfactory by Socrates himself. He is prepared by the objections which are made to him by the Theban Pythagoreans and then gives an account of his own intellectual development, leading up to a statement of his own conception of the forms and of their relation to scientific method, by means of which he gives the *third* and what he considers the most conclusive argument. But the myth at the end indicates that none of these arguments was the actual reason which led Socrates to believe in immortality; and that even if they were all shown to be fallacious, he would still believe in it.

Lecture 51

The Dialogues—Phaedo continued—the proofs of immortality—forms as eternal

Three main proofs of immortality are offered in *Phaedo*. In the first proof, and in the second part of it, the character of forms which is emphasised is that they are *perfect*. In the second proof, proof by *analogy*, the important point is that they are *unchanging* (eternal), and in the third proof we have introduced the peculiar theory of Socrates that the forms are predicates or characters. It is to be remembered in connection with this last point that Socrates did not think of the subjects to which these predicates were attributed as having independent reality, but, as Burnet puts it, he regarded each subject as merely a meeting-place or point of intersection of a number of predicates. But if there is nothing of an independent sort for the forms to characterise then they cannot properly be described as characters. That is, if we can say of the predicates that they *are*, but cannot say of the subjects that they are, then the proposition would seem to disappear leaving only what we had previously called the predicate but which couldn't now be called by that name. Though Socrates retains the conviction that the forms alone really are and thus can have no consistent view of the nature of the proposition, the fact remains that he does introduce the proposition and so makes possible a modification of the theory that the forms alone really are. And this is necessary because the insistence on their perfect and unchanging character and so on the unreality of the imperfect and changing has led to difficulties, not merely as regards immortality but as regards the possibility of knowledge in general. Because if, as we must admit, the soul has a history, then it would seem to belong to the realm of becoming and so to be unreal. (If it is suggested that the soul learned the forms *at no time*, so that they are "innate" or "transcendental", the answer is (a) that Socrates does not say so; (b) that the soul which is at no time is quite a different thing from our soul and has no connection with it.) And if the soul is unreal, then it is impossible for it to have real knowledge. That fact, and not any implication that it has as regards immortality, is the important point emerging from the argument in the first part of *Phaedo*.

Taking the first argument, then, we find that it follows upon a description of the philosophic life. According to that theory, the philosophic life consists in withdrawing the soul from the contemplation of particulars to the contemplation of universals, and according as in this life it has approached true knowledge the soul may hope in a future life to contemplate things themselves. But, as Simmias points out, even if the soul by perfecting itself as much as possible makes itself worthy of immortality, it may still as a matter of fact perish when that occurrence takes place which we call death. This introduces at once the question of generation and decay which had been one of the most important questions for the pre-Socratics. Accordingly Socrates introduces the theory of generation from opposites. In regard to this theory it has to be noted that it is concerned only with things that become. As Socrates points out in a later part of the dialogue, we do not mean that a *form* is generated from its own opposite but we mean that a particular thing comes to have a certain form after having had the opposite form. When we express the matter in relation to becoming we find that the argument is really a commonplace. If it is true that a thing has become greater, then it must obviously be true that the thing has been less; if a thing becomes hot, it must have been cold, and if it becomes cold, it must have been hot. The only difficulty here is whether or not the terms employed are precise opposites. That is, the argument will be absolutely sound in the case of heat and cold, if it is true that a thing must either be hot or cold. Now if there are intermediate regions (conditions), then it will not be correct to say that that which becomes hot has been cold. We can only say that it must have been other than hot, but that may mean that it was in the intermediate region and not that it fell within the region of cold things. In the same way in the particular case in which Socrates is interested, his argument will be quite sound if alive and dead are correct opposites: if the term *dead* covers everything which is not alive. In that case if a thing becomes alive, it must have been dead, and *vice versa*. But in any case, whatever becomes alive must certainly have been not-alive, and whatever ceases to be alive must have been alive. As regards our ordinary judgments of things, we find many things which are not alive and which we should regard as falling in the realm of becoming, and yet we should not consider that these things had ever been alive. Again we should certainly say that what is dead has been alive, because we mean by dead precisely that which has ceased to live. We may agree with Socrates as regards that particular case, that is, the transition from being alive to being dead. But we need not agree with him with regard to the other transition. If anything comes alive, we can certainly say that at a previous time it was not alive, but we cannot say that it was dead, because of the special way in which that term is used. Socrates, however, takes it as a consequence of the theory of generation from opposites that living things are generated from the dead and that the dead is that which has been alive. And from these admissions he draws the further conclusions that that which was alive and is now dead will again be alive later, because it is only from those things that are dead that future life can be generated. If then we agree that from the living comes the dead and *vice versa*, then, Socrates considers, we can think of any living thing as having a series of lives with intervening periods of death. And therefore, he considers, the soul which appears again in a later life cannot have perished at the end of the previous life, so that it must have existed in some form in the intervening period. That is, the body *sleeps*: the soul leaves it and comes back to it.[3] And, that being taken to be the consequence of the doctrine of generation from opposites, the doctrine of recollection is introduced to show that in these intervening periods the soul was not merely existent but also conscious; because only if it had been conscious could it have learned anything in these intervals, and only in these intervals could it have learned to know the forms, since it could never have found the forms in this life (or while in the body).

---

[3][JA] animism and dreams. Dreams as basis of transmigration.

Lecture 52

The Dialogues—Phaedo continued—the soul—arguments from analogy—the treatment of forms as predicates

Assuming that the soul has been shown to have a series of bodily existences, the question is—what sort of existence does it have in the intervals between these bodily lives. Socrates argues that it must have a conscious existence because we find it to possess knowledge which it could not have acquired in any of its bodily lives and which therefore it must have acquired at another time. Socrates contends that in order to recollect or remember anything, we must have known it previously. He also points out that when a presented thing brings to our minds the idea of something which is not presented at the moment, then the latter thing is said to be remembered, that is, Socrates is laying the foundation of later theories of association of ideas and of recall by means of association, and he points out that there are the two types of association which we now know as association by *contiguity* and association by *similarity*. As an example of the former, he refers to Simmias and Cebes and says that since they are generally found together, when we see one we think of the other. In the second case, that of resemblance, a good example is that of a picture which reminds us of the thing which it represents. Now in this case we can also raise the question whether it is a good likeness or not, and this can only be determined if we know both the picture and the thing itself. Now taking the case of our knowledge of the things that are presented to us in ordinary experience, we find that we speak of some of these as equal, but at the same time we recognise that they do not exhibit perfect equality: that they are not equal in all respects but only up to a point. And again even if in a particular case equality were exhibited, that particular would not be precisely what we mean by equality, since otherwise no other particular could be an example of equality. Socrates is a particular man, and in saying so we are attributing humanity to him, but we can think about humanity without thinking about Socrates. So that in saying that he is a man we are saying that he, as a particular object, reminds us of another particular object, humanity, which he does not completely embody. The argument then is from the recognition of imperfection to a previous recognition of the perfect standards which enable us to make the formal judgments. And since there is this imperfection in particulars, since no particular can be exactly what we mean by the universal, we cannot have come to know the universal in the realm of particulars, any more than we come to know men by means of portraits of them. In this argument then, what is insisted on is that the forms really exist and they have the character of perfection. In terms of which view we must regard particulars, or the objects of sense, as imperfect imitations.

In the second argument, the emphasis is on the conception of the forms as eternal. It is pointed out that the soul has a number of important resemblances to these indestructible forms and accordingly it is suggested that the soul itself is indestructible. The forms are unchanging but particulars are always changing; the latter are known by sense, the forms by intellect. And whereas the objects of sense are visible, the objects of intellect are invisible. Now the soul resembles the forms in being invisible, just as the body resembles the particulars in being visible. It is further pointed out that the soul when it conducts investigations by means of the body becomes confused, whereas when it inquires into things by itself, it arrives at a clear conception of what is pure and unchanging. It is further argued that that which naturally rules is more akin to the divine than that which naturally is ruled. Now it is natural for the soul to rule the body[4] and consequently we can regard it as more divine and more likely to be immortal than the body. Even the body can be made to last a long time after death, and so we can expect the soul to last still longer, especially if it has during life avoided as much as possible interest in the changing and mortal things which affect the body.[5]

Now these arguments depend entirely on the use of *analogy*: the soul resembles forms in being invisible, it resembles them in dominating particulars and therefore it may possibly resemble them in being eternal, especially if it has kept itself in relation to what is eternal.

---
[4][JA] Though it becomes *confused* when it acts by means of the body!!
[5][JA] That is, avoided *ruling* and so being akin to the divine!

At this point Simmias brings forward his objections to the argument. He takes the example of the harmony produced by a lyre. The lyre, he says, is visible and the harmony is not, and yet we cannot say that the harmony can continue to exist after the lyre has ceased to exist. Now if, as certain Pythagoreans have thought, the soul is a harmony of the body, a certain figure or arrangement of bodily elements, then it will not exist after the body has ceased to exist. In answer to this suggestion Socrates points out that neither could the soul have existed before the body according to this assumption, and yet if the doctrine of recollection is true, the soul has existed before. Secondly, if the soul is a harmony, then virtue will be a harmony of a harmony and vice a discord of a harmony; or, alternatively, vice will be impossible. In the third place, it has been admitted that the soul is capable of guiding or ruling the body, but the existence of a harmony is determined by the elements harmonised. Any one of these objections is considered sufficient to show that the soul is not a harmony of the body. It should be noted that if we do not accept the doctrine of recollection, then one of these arguments breaks down, and it may be possible to find objections to the others. We find that Socrates does not regard the objections of Simmias as having any great weight. He attaches much more importance to the objections of Cebes. The latter argues that even though the soul is more lasting than the body, this does not prove it to be immortal. It might be possible for the soul to go through a great many lives and yet in the end not to survive one of them. In fact we may say that even in a single life, the soul outlasts many bodies because the elements which make up the body are being continuously destroyed and renewed as the life goes on. The position then is that in either case the soul outlasts many of its bodies, but this does not prove that it will outlast all of them and that it does not at some point in the course of its tenure of bodies, come to an end. This is not inconsistent with the doctrine of recollection because it would allow for the existence of the soul prior to its being in a particular body, but it would not in any way imply its existence after being in that body. And again it does not imply a rejection of the view that the soul is more powerful than the body—it may in fact control a great number of bodies and yet be outlasted by one, just as a weaver may have made many cloaks for himself and may have worn them out one by one, but still one may be left not worn out at his death. What this implies is that arguments based on analogy or likelihood are insufficient and that if we are to give a proof of immortality we must show that it belongs to the very nature of the soul to have eternal existence. It is for this reason that Socrates here points out the dangers of misology. If our arguments break down, then the fault is our own; it cannot be the fault of the nature of things, and what we have to do is to try to find a better argument, one which will be entirely conclusive. In fact, if there could not be conclusive arguments, then it would be impossible to *show* that any particular argument was ineffective. The questions that have to be dealt with in order to meet with this objection involve the whole distinction between being and becoming, and make it necessary for Socrates to outline his philosophical method and to bring forward his own particular way of treating forms, namely, as *predicates*.

Lecture 53

The Dialogues—Phaedo continued—the Socratic method as considering propositions

In formulating his method Socrates contrasts it with that of the physicists (that is, of those who are commonly known as the pre-Socratics) in that instead of trying to define things by their own nature, they defined them by the way in which they happen. For example, an attempt is made to define the number 2 by saying that it is the result of the addition of 1 and 1, or that it is the result of a single division of one thing. What Socrates insists on is that we are not concerned in the first instance with how 2 comes to be, whether by addition or division. What we need to know is the nature of 2, what is really meant by 2. As Socrates says, there is a common confusion in all these questions between the cause and the condition. The occasion upon which a thing comes about or the circumstances which accompany it, are properly to be called conditions of the thing, but they are not causes in the sense in which he uses the word *cause*, that is, they do not explain what the thing is (give an *account* of it). Now Socrates considers this an inadequate type of explanation. That is, the explanation of one thing by referring to another, is inevitable so long as we confine ourselves to separate things or particulars, that is, if we take each thing as simple and indivisible, then in order to give an explanation of it we are bound to refer to some other thing. But this other thing is equally simple and we have no way of understanding the relation of one simple thing to another. Consequently we really have no explanation. A new method therefore is required which would naturally be the method of considering things in their complexity and interrelation, but Socrates formulates this method as that of considering things in propositions, or in terms of what we say about them. It is only by reference to speech or discussion that we can understand the raising of any problem whatever, and therefore the solution of any problem must be equally expressible in terms of ordinary speech. In other words, the question of the conditions of existence can only be approached by a consideration of the conditions of intelligible discussion or of significant speech, since in any investigation and in any expression of things we require to use speech not merely to convey our view to others, but even to enable ourselves to understand at what point exactly we have arrived, and whether we have solved the problem or not. It is natural that a method of this kind should have commended itself to Socrates considering that his whole life was spent in examining arguments and considering under what conditions they might be sound. This being the case, the reference to dialectic or dialogue being explicit in what Socrates says, we cannot accept the description of his method as the use of "conceptions" (Church's translation) or the reference to the "mind" (Jowett's rendering), because neither conceptions nor mind can of themselves explain the persistent use of dialogue and the constant reference to the conditions under which it is to be employed.[6] When therefore Socrates goes on to describe his method as that of the formulation of hypotheses and the testing of them by their consequences, we can be quite

---

[6] *The Trial and Death of Socrates, Being the Euthyphron, Apology, Crito and Phaedo of Plato* translated by F. J. Church. London: Macmillan, 1891. *The Dialogues of Plato*, translated into English with analyses and introductions by B. Jowett In 5 volumes. Oxford: Clarendon Press 1892.

certain that he does refer to propositions and that the term λογοι is not to be translated *conceptions* and has no particular reference to the *mind*, except in so far as it is persons who do undertake investigations and discussions. But even so, the rules of discussion require to be determined objectively, that is, what requires to be considered is what are the particular forms of truth, and what are the forms of valid argument, questions which cannot be answered by any special reference to mentality.

Lecture 54

The Dialogues—Phaedo continued—the testing of hypotheses

The method suggested by Socrates is that of setting up some hypotheses from which inferences may be made and examining the conclusions arrived at to see whether or not they are in accordance with the facts. Now if we come to a false conclusion, if something follows from the hypothesis but is actually opposed to fact, then the hypothesis is shown to be false. On the other hand, if as far as we have gone, the consequences are found to be true, then the hypothesis is verified. This does not mean that the hypothesis is proved. It merely means that as far as our investigation has gone the hypothesis is not disproved and the question then arises (it *can* be proved, that is) whether it can be inferred as a conclusion from certain premises which are accepted. As Burnet points out, the necessary condition of an investigation of this kind is that there should be certain propositions upon which the participants in the discussion are agreed.[7] Or, if it is a single person investigating, that there should be propositions of which he is perfectly certain. The question is then, by bringing together the propositions agreed upon, and working out their implications, to see whether they will cast any light on the propositions regarding which there is doubt or disagreement. In the case of a dialogue, then, the method is that one of the participants should put forward a hypothesis or a theory which the other should endeavour to criticise. *Now Socrates proceeds to exemplify this method in the particular case of causes or explanations.* That is the problem in regard to which a hypothesis is required. For

---

[7] John Burnet, *Greek Philosophy Thales to Plato*, London: Macmillan, 1955, p. 163.

example, Socrates asks, what is the cause of a particular thing's being beautiful? And the answer he gives, the hypothesis which he proposes, is that it is beauty itself, or, more exactly, the thing's participation in beauty.

This is the first hypothesis of Socrates. It is what he calls a *simple-minded theory*. And the main point that Socrates wishes to make is that in explaining things, we must be careful to give a real explanation and not to explain them away. If when we ask, why is this thing beautiful, the answer is, because it is coloured in a certain way, that still leaves the unanswered question: why should being coloured in a certain way make a thing beautiful? Or again, if with the atomists, we say that the cause of all phenomena consists of atoms and the void, then we are not explaining the various phenomena which exist, because we cannot show in what way atoms with empty space between them can take the forms which we find things to have, so that this is in reality no explanation of the actual phenomena. Then again, Socrates takes the example of the difference between the two numbers 10 and 8, and of the cause of 10's being greater than 8. Some would answer by saying that the cause of this difference is the 2 by which 10 exceeds 8, but Socrates says that the cause is not this 2 (this difference) but is the number itself—that it lies in the nature of the numbers 10 and 8, and not in the excess which the one has over the other. That is, we still have to distinguish between questions of becoming and questions of being or nature. Granted that we can obtain 10 by adding 2 to 8, this is really beside the point, for we are not asking how 10 can come into existence in place of 8, or in any other way, but how 10 and 8 differ just as they stand. And the answer is that they differ by number. What Socrates is really doing in this argument is to distinguish cardinal from ordinal number. We learn numbers by taking them in series, that is, ordinally, each member of the series being greater by 1 than its predecessor. But the adding of ones is not what is meant by number. Granted that we can arrive at the number 8 or the number 10 by working out this series to a definite number of places (*what* number, being just the question), the fact remains that 8 and 10 have a meaning of their own, that in themselves they characterise certain aggregates or collections (though only of *units*) independently of the way in which we come to know them.

In order to give an explanation or a scientific account of things it is absolutely necessary to determine what predicates the things actually have, and this is quite a different question from the question of what things *cause* them to have these predicates or are the occasion upon which the acquisition of the predicates takes place. This "simple-minded" theory is not all that Socrates has to say on the subject. As we will see, he himself gives explanations in the form referred to, in terms of the conditions under which a certain character is acquired or lost by a particular thing. But what he insists upon is that this latter type of explanation can be given only subsequently to the type which he has described, namely, the correct determination of the actual characters of things. That is, if we cannot first correctly determine that a thing has a certain character, then obviously we are unable to determine under what conditions it might acquire or lose that character.[8]

Lecture 55

The Dialogues—Phaedo continued—explanation as stating what predicates things have

Having determined that explanation consists in stating what predicates things actually have and not primarily under what conditions, or by means of the action of what other things they come to have those predicates, Socrates goes on to consider what relation these predicates have to one another: their characters are "explained". (Socrates really deviates here from his own theory.) He has contended that if anything is great, it is so by participating in greatness, and if anything becomes great, it becomes so by coming to participate in greatness, and similarly ceases to be great by ceasing to participate in that form. He goes on to consider in what various forms a thing may participate, and how its possession of a particular form at a particular time affects its other characters and its subsequent history. Now it is pointed out, in the first place, that the same thing can be described both as great and as small. Simmias for example is great

---
[8][JA] Sufficient verifications. *Cf.*, view that it is by participation that things have characters. [unclear]

in comparison with Socrates but small in comparison with Phaedo, just as 8 is small in comparison with 10 but great in comparison with 4 or 6. Though in this way the same thing may be said to be great or small, this is due to the fact that greatness is a relative term, and if we confine ourselves to the same relation we do not find greatness and smallness at the same time. For example, Simmias cannot at one and the same time be greater and smaller than Socrates. In relation to Socrates he must have either greatness or smallness but not both. And this position Socrates expresses by saying that greatness (the form) does not admit of smallness. Or, putting it generally, that every form has an opposite and at the approach of its opposite, the form must either disappear or withdraw to another place—it ceases to be in that particular place. It is suggested in the argument that this theory of the exclusion of opposites contradicts the previous theory of generation from opposites. But as Socrates points out, the fact that a thing in order to become greater must have been smaller does not imply that it is greater and smaller at the same time, and the fact that the same thing can be at one time greater and at another smaller shows that the thing does not by its nature exclude either greatness or smallness. But that does not prove that greatness and smallness don't exclude one another.

The position that we have now arrived at is that there are two types of consideration that can be used in explanation, namely, the attribution of a specific character to a thing, and the exclusion of characters by one another or their opposition to one another. And by way of leading up to a discussion of the soul on this basis Socrates introduces another example of the way in which this type of explanation works—an example which shows that his method is really *syllogism.* What Socrates desires to show is that becoming, the history of a particular thing, can be explained in terms of the possession of forms and the interrelation of forms. Thus we say that snow is cold, that is, it participates in the form cold. Now cold itself excludes heat itself. We infer therefore that snow does not admit of heat. But this again can be carried still further: if we take, on the other hand, fire, we find that it partakes of heat. And now having the two things, snow and fire, one of which partakes of heat while the other does not admit of heat, we conclude that fire and snow cannot exist together—we cannot have fiery snow or snowy fire. Since then these two things cannot exist in the same place (or in the same subject), then if one of them is brought to the place where the other has been, either the other must be removed from that place, or one of the two must perish. Thus if fire is brought to a place where snow has been, then there are three possibilities—the snow may continue to exist by being removed to another place, or secondly the snow may melt, or thirdly it may put out the fire. In terms of this argument Socrates thinks he has explained the process of the melting of snow and the putting out of fire in terms of their characters hot and cold and of the opposition between these characters, the characters and their opposition being recognised in ordinary language, being established by reference to $\lambda \acute{o} \gamma o \iota$, propositions. Socrates would say that the cause of the melting of snow on the approach of fire is the opposition between the characters hot and cold. In exactly the same way, the same collection cannot have both the number 4 and the number 3, since 3 is odd and 4 is even, and the odd and the even exclude one another. And so again, Socrates says, 3 is odd and therefore cannot be even: the Graces are three. And therefore the Graces cannot be even.[9] Here we have syllogism in its simplest form, that is, the form in which we have a universal major premise, a minor premise referring to a particular instance of a class, and the consequent attribution to the instance of the properties of the class.

Socrates points out that in view of this development of his theory, he is no longer concerned with the simple explanations with which he began but with more detailed and precise explanations. According to the first type of explanation, if we are asked why a body is hot we should reply, because it has heat in it. But that answer, while it is necessary, is not sufficient for a truly scientific explanation. We should be giving a truly scientific explanation if we replied: the body is hot because it has fire in it and fire participates in heat. Now if in the same way we ask why a body is alive,

---
[9][JA]
 No 3s are even
 The Graces are a 3
 ∴ the Graces are not even.

we will not be content with the answer, because there is life in it; we will require to know what there is in it that gives it life, just as fire in a body would give it heat. And the answer that Socrates now elicits is that a body is alive because it has a soul in it. And in order that this should be a correct answer, it must be understood that a soul partakes in life, or is *essentially* alive, just as fire is essentially hot. But if a soul is essentially alive, then it cannot admit of death. If we consider the case in which death approaches a body which has a soul in it on the analogy of the case in which cold comes to a body which has fire in it, then just as we should say that the fire must either withdraw or perish, so we can say that the soul must either withdraw or perish on the approach of death, the reason being that, being essentially alive, it cannot admit of death. But if it cannot admit of death, this proves that it does not perish but, when the body dies, withdraws to another place. The conclusion is that the soul is immortal, and this conclusion is really based on the hypothesis which is accepted by the participants in the discussion that a body is alive because it has a soul in it, or that the soul is, so to speak, the principle of life. The conclusion depends upon the acceptance of the hypothesis. If the hypothesis were rejected, then the immortality of the soul would still be unproved. But this hypothesis as to the soul, which is introduced in terms of the Socratic method, is to be distinguished from the hypothesis on which the method itself is based, and which is considered to have been tested by means of the various examples, chiefly mathematical, which were previously put forward; the hypothesis, namely, that explanation is given by means of the proposition or the attribution of a character to a thing, and the further hypothesis that explanation can be carried further in terms of the exclusion of characters by one another. The fact that on these assumptions conclusions are obtained which seem natural and acceptable to those taking part in the discussion is held to be a proof, as far as the argument has gone, that the method is sound. (A fuller proof might show that any *other* method really comes down, at certain points, to the propositional, though it has also implications that contradict the propositional, that is, is at certain points, contrary to discussion—unspeakable or incoherent. The same applies to Socrates' method considered as a method of *forms*: what he says about forms is really opposed to his method as it is actually employed so as to give definite results or conclusions.)

Lecture 56

The Dialogues—Phaedo—Socratic theory of approximations

The first argument is divided into the two parts in which the doctrine of generation from opposites and the doctrine of recollection are respectively expounded. Taking the latter first we find that it depends on a certain theory of the nature of forms, the theory that forms are ideals to which particular things can approximate but which they can never quite reach. Now this at first sight seems to contradict that conception of forms which underlies the final argument for immortality and the propositional method. If the meaning of the proposition is that a certain form is present in a particular thing, then there would seem to be no need to speak of approximation, or to assume that any previous knowledge is required in order that that form should be known. That is, if the form is really present with the thing, then our present experience is quite enough to give us knowledge of the form as well as knowledge of the thing. If for example a thing really is beautiful, if it has beauty in it, then it is possible that when we contemplate the thing we are at the same time directly contemplating beauty. Now this seems to be what is really implied if we take the proposition seriously, and Socrates in insisting on the propositional method indicates the way in which the theory of forms as ideals can be criticised. But at the same time it appears that he does not fully realise the consequences of the use of the propositional method, that he thinks it possible to combine this method with a belief in a theory of approximation, that in fact he takes his method as a means of making the theory of approximation precise, of showing exactly how the approximation is to be understood. It is still admitted that though a particular form may be present to a thing, the thing does not embody the form completely but only to a greater or less extent. And it is this position which is criticised in Plato's *Parmenides*.

If we consider, from the point of view of the propositional method, the theory of approximations, then we find that it does not bear out the conception of forms as ideals. If we can say of the two sticks that they are not perfectly equal, but are only approximately equal, then from this proposition as it stands we should infer that the form in question is not the form of equality but the form of approximate equality, and this approximate equality is not something to which the particular things tend or approximate but is actually embodied in the things. If that is admitted, then we have a predicate which belongs to precisely the same realm as the subject to which it is attributed. So that no proposition that we can significantly affirm enables us to draw a distinction between the world of being and that of becoming. As far as the proposition that the two sticks are approximately equal is concerned, the approximate equality and the two sticks themselves occur in precisely the same place, are part of a single order of experience. Again if two particular things are not precisely equal, then they are unequal, and so the form of inequality occurs not approximately but completely in this particular instance. And further, if two things are unequal, this means that a part of one is precisely equal to the other, however difficult it may be to mark out that part, and consequently we have between two things just as particular as the sticks themselves, a relation of perfect equality. And further, we have the example of perfect equality whenever two surfaces are in contact, the part of surface A which is touching B becoming precisely equal to the part of B which touches A. All this indicates that in terms of what we say about things, of propositions, the forms that we speak about including the form of equality are found completely in particular cases and that no reference to a different kind of experience is required.[10] If that view is rejected, then we should have to reject the whole propositional method, since it would be no more possible to say that two particular things possess perfectly the character of approximate equality than that they possess perfectly the character of equality. We should be committed to an infinite series of approximations

---

[10][JA] That is, to *revelation*. Socrates, again, as Eleatic. And Eleaticism as showing how to destroy Socratism along with Eleaticism.

The Phaedo and The Parmenides 181

without ever arriving at a proposition which we could state with certainty.

The particular arguments dealing with the case of *beauty* indicate the reasons which Socrates had for not regarding predicates as perfectly embodied in their subjects. In the first place Socrates points out that when we say a particular thing is beautiful, we don't mean to deny that anything else is beautiful. And in the second place when we say that it is beautiful, we do not mean to assert that it has always been beautiful, or that it always will be beautiful. These two points imply that knowledge of this particular by itself is not necessary nor sufficient for a knowledge of beauty. If we took a particular thing for our standard (that is, if we identified it with beauty itself) then we would have to deny that anything else could possibly be beautiful, and also, since the thing belongs to the realm of becoming, we should have a fluctuating standard.

These arguments are based on the assumption that there is a particular object *beauty* which can be known separately from everything else, and consequently even to take an example of beauty is not to have true knowledge but only an imitation of true knowledge. The difficulty which this assumption meets with is that in that case it would be impossible to have even an imitation, that either we should have direct knowledge of beauty itself or we should not know it at all. But actually there is nothing in the proposition which says "X is beautiful" to show that there is such an object as this beauty itself;[11] that is, to show that beauty exists in any other way than as a character of existing things. And if we do not postulate this ultimate object, then there is no difficulty in recognising that a number of different things may one and all be beautiful, or that one particular thing may acquire the character beauty at one time and lose it at another time. The very facts with which we begin, the facts of variation and change, could not be stated without a recognition of an embodiment of characters in things, since, if at no time in the history of a thing was beauty really in it, then in that respect the thing has not changed at all. The point about the many members of a class simply amounts to [the

---
[11][JA] As above, revelation—why Socrates *does*, however illogically, think propositional knowledge a second best.

fact] that it is possible to know a character or predicate apart from a particular instance or subject, but this is possible only because we can know it in other instances. It does not follow that the character can be known apart from any instance whatever. We say for example that Socrates is a man and in saying so we recognise that it is possible to know what is meant by being a man without knowing Socrates. But it is quite another thing to say that it is possible to know what is meant by being a man without knowing any particular man. The propositional method indicates that we always find forms as forms of something, that we can always distinguish a particular character of a thing from other characters of the same thing; and a thing of a particular character from other things of the same character. But all this does not show that we can know subjects and predicates by separate acts of thought or otherwise than in a proposition.

Lecture 57

The Dialogues—Phaedo continued

The other part of the first argument is that which deals with *generation from opposites* and which purports to show that the soul exists when it is not in the body—the *doctrine of recollection* being required to show that in this non-bodily existence the soul is conscious. Actually, the doctrine of generation from opposites does not prove any such separate existence. If what is alive is generated from what is not alive, then it would not appear necessary to affirm the existence of a soul prior to the existence of a living body, but only the existence of a non-living body which at a particular time comes alive. If, on the other hand, we think of the coming alive of the body as an entry into it of a principle of life, which has previously existed elsewhere, then generation from opposites is quite irrelevant to this case. We are then saying not that what is alive arises from what is not alive but that it arises from the combination of something which was not alive with something which was alive; and since the latter has not changed, since the life of the soul is a reality both before and after the soul's entry into the body, we cannot say that life has been generated or that anything at all has happened except that a particular living thing, the soul, has taken up a new position. Now this theory is really opposed to the doctrine of generation. It practically amounts to saying that there can be no generation, no qualitative change, but only change of position, and in this respect it resembles the theories of the Pythagoreans and the atomists, and not the doctrines of Heraclitus on which it was supposed to be based.

In this particular argument and also in the final argument for immortality there is a confusion between two ways of regarding the life of the body—namely, in the one case, as being alive, acquiring the character *life* under particular conditions, and in the other sense, *containing* life, that is, containing the soul which is an essentially living thing. So in the theory of soul and body as constituting a living being, we are left in doubt as to whether it is the soul or the body which is really alive. Again there is a failure to distinguish between life in general and what we call consciousness. We should speak of plants as alive, but we should not call them conscious, we should not speak of them as having souls. But we find, particularly in Aristotle, that they are said to have souls; we have different types such as the vegetative soul and the sensitive soul. And this is connected with the animistic theory that whatever is capable of spontaneous development must have something of the nature of mind, directing that development. If we took the question as one strictly of consciousness, and if we considered that the doctrine of generation from opposites could be applied to this case, we would have to say that the conscious is generated from the unconscious. And there would be no difficulty in admitting that it could again become unconscious, that is, that the soul could perish. We can say that the doctrine of generation gives us no assistance in attempting to prove immortality, since immortality involves the notion of something that is ingenerable and indestructible; and that the doctrine of recollection also fails, because it depends on a separation of forms from things, in spite of their conjunction in the proposition, just as the whole argument implies a separation of soul from body in spite of their conjunction in human life. And it is on this difficulty that the objections of Simmias are based.

Second argument. It is pointed out that while the body in all respects resembles what we call particular things, things subject to becoming, the soul in many ways resembles the forms which are not subject to becoming, and as these forms are eternal, it is possible that the soul resembles them in this respect also, that the soul is also eternal. There can be no force in an argument of this kind unless what it is intended to convey is that the soul itself is a form. If it is not a form, then there must be certain respects in which it differs from a form, and we could as easily infer from these differences that the soul is not eternal as infer from the resemblances that it is eternal. The fact that the soul has a history, that it can enter into a body and have its experiences modified on account of the fact that it is in a body, that fact shows that the soul is not a form. But if the soul is subject to these conditions, if it is affected in these ways by the surroundings, then there is nothing to show that it cannot be at some particular time destroyed by them. Socrates maintains in the course of this argument that the soul controls the body, that it rules and guides it, and therefore may have a higher reality than the body. But he has admitted that the soul is obstructed in its search for truth by the tendencies of the body, and that implies that the body influences the soul and may even be said to control it to the extent of that influence. We cannot have one-sided influence, if the soul acts on the body, the body must equally act on the soul. When we have a particular state of the body, then the soul is moved to act in a particular way. Unless it responded to specific situations in that way, it could not be said to exercise control. But if it does so respond, that proves that its action is conditioned by states of the body and therefore we cannot attribute complete control either to the one or to the other. All this implies that the soul is a particular thing undergoing various processes of becoming. The conclusion would seem to be that it is of the same order of reality as the body, even though they differ in certain particular respects.

These difficulties also are brought out by the objections of Simmias which, though they are very quickly disposed of by Socrates, are not in reality fairly refuted. Their refutation partly depends on the doctrine of recollection which Simmias admits to be true, but if the objections to that doctrine are sound, then the view put forward by Simmias has still to be disproved. The same applies to that part of the refutation which depends on the conception of the ruling function of the soul, since as we have seen the influence must be mutual. Accordingly, the real force of the criticisms brought by Socrates is to be sought in the arguments concerning the term "harmony" itself, the argument that if the soul is a harmony, then all souls must be equally harmonious, and therefore we would be unable to make any distinction between a good and a bad soul. Or, if the soul is a harmony, then the existence of good and bad souls implies harmonies of harmonies and discords of harmonies. What really underlies the theory of Simmias is the conception of the soul as a form or as a particular kind of body. That is, when we speak about the existence of a mind or a soul, we are really speaking about a particular kind of body, differing in certain respects from other bodies which do not exhibit mentality. And this view can be worked *out* (in) with the theory that any predicate can be a subject, so that the fact that the soul is a harmony or *predicate* of certain bodies does not prove that it in turn cannot have predicates or harmonies. That is, a particular soul (that is, a body arranged in a certain way) admits of further arrangements which will justify us in calling it good or bad, just as a triangle is a certain arrangement of lines, and yet there can be further arrangements enabling us to distinguish one kind of triangle from another.

Lecture 58

The Dialogues—Phaedo continued

Final proof. The theory advanced by Socrates of the nature of forms is important, but it requires further working out in such a way as to make it clear that we do not have two separate sets of beings, subjects and predicates. And even if the general theory is accepted, we cannot say that on that account the proof of immortality must be accepted. We find in the examples offered by Socrates, that he admits the possibility of the same term being subject and predicate, and if this is not to be taken to imply that there is no ultimate distinction between subject and predicate but merely a different function in different cases (that is, the difference between characterising and being characterised) then we are committed to the view that there are ultimate kinds of propositions with different kinds of meaning. As Socrates suggests, we have the type of proposition in which a thing is said to participate in a form and we have the further type of proposition which states a relation between forms, as in the case of *exclusion of opposites*. Now if this relation is not a relation of participation, or, in the negative case, of non-participation which would be equally possible as between a form and a thing, then the different propositions refer to different regions of reality; and there will be no possibility of bringing them together in a syllogism, as Socrates professes to do. And if we take his positive examples, we find that the difficulty of making the required distinction becomes even clearer. We have the argument—The Graces are 3, 3 is odd, therefore the Graces are odd. In one of the premises of this syllogism the term 3 is the predicate, in the other it is the subject. And it would appear from ordinary inspection that the two propositions state exactly the same kind of relation, that is, that 3 is an instance of oddness or that oddness is a character of 3; just as the group which we know as the Graces is an instance of being 3 or has that character. If 3 can participate in oddness, then it is a particular. But the other proposition shows that it is also a form or character of certain groups.[12] If the same thing can be both a form and a particular, then there is no reason for saying of any term whatever that it can be particular but not universal, or universal but not particular. In order to say so, we would have to make a distinction between types of proposition, though they are both expressed in the same form of language; and so we could say that Socrates did not consistently adhere to his method of appealing to language or λογοι, but endeavoured to go beyond language in affirming his theory of forms. The consequence of this criticism would be that we would have to regard the term *forms* as a misnomer, since it implied that predicates belonged to a different region of reality from that of subjects—a suggestion which the proposition, in which subject and

---

[12][JA] Are not numbers really *ratios*?

predicate are brought together, conflicts with. This same difficulty arose in connection with the doctrine of recollection which depended on the belief that while particular things could not be absolutely and unconditionally said to have equality, they could absolutely be said to have approximate equality. In order therefore to be consistent in applying the propositional method, we would have to regard the distinction between particulars and universals as signifying a difference of function and not of kind. Only in that way is it possible to avoid criticism of the Eleatic or Sophistic type, according to which there can be no connection whatever between particulars and universals. Language suggests that anything whatever is capable both of characterising and being characterised, that is, has both universality and particularity.

Now the method of Socrates was introduced so as to make it possible to explain becoming in terms of being, and participation was supposed to be the link whereby changing particulars were connected with unchanging forms. But in order to explain things in this way, Socrates has to introduce the very terms to be explained. A thing comes to be beautiful and ceases to be beautiful by coming to participate in beauty or ceasing to participate in beauty, that is, terms signifying *becoming* are still employed in the explanation, and participation does not help us to understand what they mean. It could only help us to understand what is meant by *being* beautiful, and that would be participation in beauty. But even so, the term participation doesn't add anything to the proposition. It is only by means of propositions that we can state this theory, and if we could not understand directly what was meant by having beauty we should equally be unable to understand what was meant by having participation in beauty. Accordingly the appeal of Socrates to propositions is misdirected into an attempt to get behind the proposition, and it fails to explain becoming as it professed to do. The only way in which we can reconcile being and becoming by means of the proposition is by maintaining that the proposition itself signifies being and also signifies becoming, that is, that what we mean by being is being a state of affairs or situation, the sort of thing which is signified by a proposition; and that what we mean by becoming is also represented by the proposition in this way, that the predicate stands for a certain process or activity and the subject represents a region within which the process takes place. Now if that view were adopted it would imply the rejection of the conceptions of a higher or a lower reality, and therefore the loss of what Socrates considers to be the moral or ethical character of his teaching.[13]

Socrates thinks of particulars not as simply having or not having certain characters, but as striving to attain to certain forms, striving to arrive at certain ideals which can never completely be attained by particulars. From that point of view, the form of a thing is the ideal at which it is aiming, and the realm of becoming is just the realm of such striving against the obstacles which are implied by the very existence of things as particulars. But to describe the world of becoming in this way is not to account for it in terms of being, since no amount of contemplation of pure forms could tell us that there would be things striving towards these forms. On the contrary, that striving or becoming has simply to be accepted as a given fact, and thus as being of a different order from pure being, if pure being implies the absence of change. In the second place, it is possible to describe that world of becoming only by saying that it actually possesses certain definite characters, that is, only by setting up a class of characters which can really be attained to as contrasted with those which are merely ideals. These logical difficulties not only indicate defects in the conception of science which is adopted by Socrates but also indicate that his view of morality is not a strictly correct one; since ethical science must be subject to logic just as much as any other science.

Lecture 59

The Dialogues—Phaedo continued—forms as predicates conflicts with doctrine of approximations

The treatment of forms as predicates really conflicts with the treatment of them as standards towards which things could move but to which they could never thoroughly attain. The

---

[13][JA] N.B. Higher and lower has to do not simply with classes, but with domination or repression in general—for example in the family: as Engels crudely realises: and also in each person.

proposition really indicates that the particular has attained to the *state of being* represented by the predicate: or that the predicate is really in the subject. Now if the other view is taken a difficulty at once arises in connection with the various forms. These forms are distinguished from one another and thus when we refer to any one we are referring to a particular one. So that the forms in order to be spoken of must be in some sense particulars. But if that is so, then the treatment of them as eternal, as incapable of change, conflicts with their capacity for being represented as subjects. If they are subjects, then they are capable of coming under, or being described by, different predicates, that is, they are capable of becoming. While this is so as regards the forms, so that doubt is cast on the validity of the general position of Socrates, there is for similar reasons a dubiety about his particular theory of the soul. The soul is regarded as a thing, as a subject capable of having predicates, and not only so but as actually having a history, so that it *assumes* particular predicates at particular times. It would appear therefore that logically speaking the soul is in the same position as the body, that it is a thing which becomes, and consequently that it is possible for it to be created and to be destroyed. Now in the final argument for immortality in the *Phaedo* the soul, while it is represented as a particular thing, has attributed to it certain functions which it could only have if it were a form. The body is alive, it is said, because it has the soul in it. Now if this merely meant that it contained the soul, that the soul was inside the body, then that would be no reason for saying that the body itself is alive. In order to make the argument a valid one, we would have to express all the relations as relations of predication. We would have to be able to say *Souls are alive, Bodies are souls, therefore Bodies are alive.* That must be the argument if the life of the soul is to be a real proof of the life of the body. But in the first place, the statement that bodies are souls embodies the treatment of the soul as a predicate, that is, according to Socratic theory as a form, which in itself has no history. (In general, if a thing *comes under* a form, a form *comes over* a thing: so that the one "becomes", just as much as the other.) But, on the other hand, taking the proposition as it stands without any reference to a special theory of forms, the separation between body and soul can no longer be kept up. Putting the matter syllogistically, if bodies are souls, and if it be granted that bodies are mortal, then it follows that some souls at least are mortal. It appears therefore that this argument is not capable of proving what Socrates wishes it to prove.

Now in fact the real argument of Socrates is dependent on a particular treatment of the major premise in the former syllogism—that *souls are alive.* Socrates treats this as meaning that souls are essentially alive, that is, that there can be no question of the soul *coming under* the form of life at a particular point in its history, or similarly ceasing to be under the form of life. So long as there is a soul, throughout its whole history, we must think of it as alive. But even that contention is not sufficient to prove that the soul is immortal. To say that the soul is alive so long as there is a soul does not imply that there may not be a time at which neither the life of the soul nor the soul itself (*cf.,* the fire and the heat of the fire) is in existence. In other words we don't speak of dead souls, but that only goes to show that, throughout what we call the existence of a soul, life is present. In the same way it might be considered incorrect to speak about a dead man, since after death has occurred, we should no longer consider that the body was strictly speaking a human body. But that would not prove that men cannot die. It would only indicate that in ceasing to be alive, they cease to exist as men. An exactly similar argument has been employed in modern philosophy to prove that the mind always thinks—to show that the term "unconscious mind" is just as meaningless as "dead soul". If we care to maintain that only when there is consciousness of something is there what can properly be called mind (mentality), then we will find it incorrect to speak about unconscious mind; but at the same time we will not infer that the mind thinks all the time. What we will say is that it is possible for consciousness to be intermittent and in terms of the original assumption this will mean that the mind itself is intermittent. Throughout its periods of existence the mind will always be thinking, but those periods need not be continuous.

Lecture 60

The two conceptions of the form continued

We have the *two conceptions of the form*, according to the first of which it is an ideal standard to which things can conform to a greater or less degree but never completely, which things are capable of striving after (their reality in fact consisting in this striving) but never of reaching. In the second place, we have the form as predicate appearing in the same place as the subject, a theory which does not permit of a distinction being made between the realm of particulars and the realm of universals. Considering these conceptions in relation to the statement that the soul is essentially alive, if this really means that the soul is striving towards life, then there can be nothing in this statement to show that the soul is immortal; since, according to this theory, the subject *soul* can never completely embody the form *life*; that if we say the soul completely embodies the form *life*, then we will either have to say that the form also belongs to the world of particulars or that the soul belongs to the world of universals and therefore that it can have no history and no bodily existence. These are the difficulties which arise on account of the failure of Socrates to say precisely what the reality of the forms is, and what is the nature of their relation to the particulars. Judging from other dialogues, however, as well as from the general trend of the *Phaedo*, we can say that the earlier conception of the forms remains the more important one for Socrates: that he thought of the forms as ideals (propositions being *reflections*, and therefore second-best) and considered things as having their reality in the struggle to realise these ideals. This appears, as Burnet points out, in the *Phaedrus* where the emphasis is on the struggle to pass from particulars to universals, a position which is quite in accordance with the later Pythagorean theory in which the whole world of appearances is supposed to be striving to represent the world of reality. But the difference between the Pythagoreans and Socrates seems to have been that Socrates was not content to regard the world of becoming as mere appearance, since that allowed of both the Eleatic and the sophistic criticisms. He desired to show that the world of becoming has some reality of its own, even if it is not the complete reality which belongs to the forms. But even on this view, so long as the world of particular things is regarded as real only in so far as it comes under the forms and reflects their reality, we are driven to the conclusion that it has no reality of its own and that, as the Eleatics contended, the intelligible world is the only real one and there is nothing else besides. Socrates did not wish to accept this theory of the Eleatics because once it is accepted, we are driven to accept the further Eleatic contention that there is only one undifferentiated intelligible being. In order to maintain plurality even in the intelligible world, we have to recognise appearances, we have to admit not only complexity but historical considerations, we have to make the separation between what is and what appears, and then we are left with the problem of connecting the two. The position is that it was for the sake of finding an answer to the Eleatics as well as to the sophists who were so greatly dependent on Eleatic thought that Socrates formulated his new philosophical theory. And what Plato indicates, in the *Parmenides*, is that Socrates had not succeeded in answering the Eleatics; that a much more definite break with Pythagoreanism was required before the answer could be given. In accordance with that criticism, we find that in Plato's later dialogues there is no longer any question of separate worlds, but all things which are real are real in precisely the same sense.

The Socratic theory then emphasises the struggle to overcome the separation between appearance and reality, or, in his formula, between the particular and the universal. And this is represented as the struggle of the particular itself to come more and more thoroughly under the universal, to be a better representation of it. Now this struggle is identified with moral effort or endeavour. At the end of the *Republic I* Socrates contends that every particular thing has a function, that is, has something which it is fitted to do or intended for and that its good consists in carrying out this function as far as possible. Thus, in this theory, as far as particular things are concerned, their goodness and their reality are identical, the goodness or reality of a thing is what *it* aims at. As we have already seen, one of the chief difficulties of this theory is that we can speak of the progress of a particular thing towards an ideal character only if we can recognise it to have real characters, and to have different characters at different times. It appears therefore that while we are saying that there is one supreme predicate which the thing is trying to acquire and *coming under which* constitutes the thing's reality (or, to put it otherwise, one supreme predicate which presides over and directs one particular thing), there must be at the same time a number of predicates which the thing does acquire in its history as a particular. It seems absurd to suggest that the various characters which a thing actually possesses do not constitute its reality, while a character which it can never possess does. Putting it in the other way, we cannot accept as a general principle the statement that a thing is what it aims at, because already in making the statement we are *distinguishing* between the thing and its end or aim.[14] In order to say that it is *its* aim, to attribute the aim to *it*, we require to know it in distinction from the aim or purpose. That, then, is the difficulty which appears in all theories of a teleological character. But there are further objections to accepting this conception of things. Thus one of the reasons given in the *Phaedo* for not regarding a particular as having a peculiar reality of its own and as completely embodying any form is that the thing can be described in a number of different ways at the same time. Now if having a predicate means having an ideal in the direction of which to advance, then the particular things that Socrates speaks of must be "advancing in all directions". In order to make the theory intelligible we require to assume that there is one special character which applies more than any other to any given particular thing. This is the doctrine which has come to be known as the *Doctrine of Natural Kinds*, that is, that there is some kind to which each individual belongs and that the various other characters which he has are, in relation to this fundamental character, merely accidental. For example, if we take an individual man, it is contended that what is most important about him is his mankind, and consequently that any characters whereby he could be differentiated from any other man have a less degree of reality. If we accept that view it will mean that in the last resort or as far as true reality

---
[14][JA] Opening part of *Parmenides*.

is concerned, no man is different from any other, and the consequence will be that we will have to treat the peculiarities of individuals as scientifically of no account. Now this means that among all the characters that we recognise in ordinary life, some are essential, ultimately real, while others are accidental, and not ultimately of any importance; and the question is how we are to obtain a criterion whereby essential and accidental characters may be distinguished. As far as forms of statement are concerned no distinction can be made. We say *this is a man* and we use exactly the same form of statement in saying *this is an athlete* (of course Bosanquet would say his athleticism is really an element in, a component of, his manhood, but then the question arises, what are *components*? They are predicated in the same way as "complete" characters.) So that there is nothing to tell us that this latter quality is on a different footing from that of the former, and having a less degree of reality. Here again Socrates, who professed to uphold the proposition, has to go behind the proposition in order to support his views; the fact being, as is pointed out at the beginning of the *Parmenides*, that it is possible to make out a case for regarding certain characters as ideals—like *equality*, for example, which we have difficulty in determining precisely in our actual dealings with things—but it is quite impossible to make out such a case for all qualities. And therefore the theory inevitably leads to inconsistencies.

Lecture 61

The Dialogues—the Parmenides—the division of reality into higher and lower

The *Parmenides*. We find that the question which arises between Socrates and the Eleatics is that of the forms considered as providing a solution of the Eleatic paradoxes. This shows us that the real question before Plato's mind was just whether or not the Socratic theory did supply an answer to the Eleatic difficulties. Now at the very beginning of the discussion we find a point raised by Parmenides which indicates the weakness of the Socratic theory, namely, that if we make a division of reality into higher and lower spheres, then we are unable to account for the facts in the lower sphere. Having taken them to be comparatively unreal, we are driven to the conclusion that they are absolutely unreal, that as the Eleatics maintained, the supposed inferior and relative reality has no existence. Socrates had taken as his fundamental forms the conceptions of mathematics and also such ethical and aesthetic conceptions as the just, the beautiful and the good. As far as these are concerned, it seems possible to regard them as standards or ideals at which things might aim, and thus we might consider, though the theory has difficulties, that the reality of these things consists in their striving towards the ideal. It may be suggested that in the case of the mathematical forms, the striving is on our part, that is, that *we* have difficulty in deciding what is exactly equal or exactly circular etc., and that we can, in the course of our investigations, make more or less accurate approximations to equality or circularity, but this doesn't imply any striving on the part of the figures themselves. A figure which, for example, fails to be circular has just as definite a mathematical character as a figure which really is circular, and the reason for the circle and such figures being taken as ideals, as standards to which other figures should conform, is that it is particularly useful to us to know what is circular or to have a figure which comes very near to being circular, since circular motion is one of the most important kinds of motion in practical work and theoretical measurement.

That being so, it is possible to hold the theory that these are the supremely important figures and that all other figures are relative and subordinate to them, as particulars in general are supposed to be subordinate to the forms. But this way of looking at the matter in terms of standards becomes rather more difficult in the case of man or fire or water. Socrates says he is uncertain whether or not there are forms of man, fire and water; the reason being, Burnet suggests, that attempts have been made to represent these forms by means of figures which could not possibly convey the peculiar qualitative character of the things in question. At the same time it may be said that it may be of just as much practical importance to us to get pure water as to describe a perfect circle and so it would seem that in these cases also it is possible to have approximations and to have practical standards. But it would be more difficult to maintain that these practical standards imply some fundamental theoretical standard—to maintain for example that impure water was any less real than pure water. When we come to still more commonplace things like mud, for example, we find Socrates maintaining that there can be no form here. Yet if we consider what we say about things, then it would seem natural to maintain that the same kind of being and the same kind of forms, if there are forms, should be found in each case. If we use a descriptive term like *mud*, we must mean that that term applies to some things and not to others, that it is possible to predicate it correctly and incorrectly; and that it is possible to convey definite information by using this description about some particular thing. The term *mud* therefore must convey some general nature or character, just as the term circle does, and so it ought to be said, if there is a form of circularity, that there is also a form of muddiness. But we could hardly call this an ideal towards which things strive. And yet, if the term has any real significance, it must be possible to find things to which it applies, and other things which are more or less like these things. If Socrates continues to maintain that there are no forms in these cases, then he must deny that the terms have any meaning at all—he must declare that what he had taken to be lower and inadequate reality was simply non-existent. It is because Socrates does not draw this conclusion, because he wishes to maintain that these things are real in one and not in another sense, that Parmenides says that he has not yet become thoroughly philosophic (that is, he should follow out the consequences of speaking about *mud* and say that mud *is*, whatever being may imply). To be thoroughly philosophic one must accept all the consequences of any view which one holds.

After this preliminary criticism of the Socratic theory on account of its division of things into higher and lower, Parmenides proceeds to inquire into the meaning of the theory as Socrates states it, in particular into the meaning of *participation*. The question is, how is it possible to say, as Socrates says, that one form may be present to many things? If the form is present to all these things, then it must be either wholly or partly present to each of them. Now if the whole of the form is present to each of the particulars, then the form is in many different places at the same time. And yet it is supposed to be one and indivisible. On the other hand, if only a part of the form is present to each of the particulars, then we cannot say that the *same* part is present to all (without falling into the former difficulty) and consequently we are not in a position to say that these particular things have anything in common. If the particular thing possesses a part of the form of greatness and another particular thing possesses another part of it, then we cannot on that account say they have a common predicate, greatness or anything else. In fact, Parmenides maintains, we cannot say of any one such thing that it is great, since a part of greatness is not sufficient to confer greatness on it. In regard to this criticism, it may be said that it implies that Socrates means by participation the actual presence of the form within the thing, instead of the thing's coming under the form, or the form's presiding over the thing, which we would find to be more nearly what Socrates maintained. But the point is that Parmenides is concerned for the moment only with one particular interpretation of participation and that in a later part of the argument he goes on to criticise the conception of forms as standards. If, then, we say that the form is really *in* the particulars, as the proposition seems to imply, we are faced with this dilemma, and since it is impossible to take the second alternative (to say that different parts of the same form are in different things, which would not imply anything in common) we have to say that the whole of the form is in each thing, which implies that the whole occurs just as often as there are things to partake of it. But this is not a solution of the difficulty, because we cannot see how all these separate occurrences justify us in using a common predicate of the various particulars. (*Cf.,* Ramsey on Stout.) We should really require another form under which the form of each of the particulars would come, and so on indefinitely.[15]

---

[15][JA] *Cf.,* Stout's theory. Each thing has *its* particularity. (Particular character of particular thing.) Compare and contrast Berkeley. [Ed.:] F. P. Ramsey considered G. F. Stout's view "sufficiently answered" by G. E. Moore's contribution to the symposium for the Aristotelian Society of 1923 "Are the characteristics of particular things universal or particular?". Nonetheless, Stout's account is considered the classic expression of more recent views of universals as tropes or abstract particulars. Ramsey

Now this is a difficulty for the theory of predication only if we assume that there are special objects called forms. If we do not make that assumption then we can quite understand how it is possible that many things can have a common predicate; we can still say that the quality of A and the quality of B are not the same. But when we say so, we don't mean that X is different from X; what we mean is that A's being X and B's being X are different, that is, that *A is X* and *B is X* are different propositions, though they have the same predicate.

Lecture 62

The Dialogues—the Parmenides continued—universality and particularity

Parmenides next argues that if we have a form which covers a variety of particular cases, we will require to have a further form which covers all the cases referred to and the previous form as well. Now as far as this argument goes, there is no insuperable logical difficulty, for though this commits us to asserting the existence of innumerable forms, it is theoretically possible that there *are* innumerable forms and still participation might hold as it was said to do. Unless we require to know all these forms in order to know the first one, then the mere fact that each form implies another form creates no theoretical difficulty. But it has to be remembered that the theory of forms was put forward in order to provide a simplification of the apparent complexity of nature.[16] Now if the forms turn out to belong to just as complicated a system as that of becoming, then it may be said that the purpose of the theory has not been served. Moreover (this is the really important point) to say that a given form together with a number of particulars comes under another form is to say that the form also is a particular, that is, we no longer have an absolute distinction between that which partakes in something and that in which something partakes, in other words, between particulars and universals, and consequently we are admitting the possibility that all those things which we

---

thought Stout's position failed to clarify the role of the subject and that of the predicate in the proposition, that is, to distinguish the individual and the universal. Ramsey's article "Universals" of 1931 is included in *Philosophical Papers*, edited by D. H. Mellor, Cambridge: Cambridge University Press, 1990. Stout's articles "The Nature of Universals and Propositions" (1921) and his contribution to the 1923 symposium are included in *The Problem of Universals*, edited by Charles Landsman, New York: Basic Books, 1971.

[16][JA] Was it? So it might, and yet lead to complexities in supernatural. [Unclear]

have called particulars also exhibit universality, so that the world of becoming has all the reality that it is possible *for it* to have, and requires no external explanation.

But it may even be said that the series of forms referred to is not only implied but is actually *required for the understanding* of what is meant by the forms. In other words, we have an argument of the same type as that which is known as the "third man" and which is further developed as the discussion proceeds, namely, that the form by reference to which particular men, for example, are judged and are said to be men is not manhood as such but is that which is purely a man. It is not a pure universal but a particular, the peculiarity of which is that it has only one attribute. And then the question arises how it is to be distinguished from this attribute and how it is related to things which have many attributes.

This leads us on to one of the most fundamental criticisms from the Eleatic point of view. Socrates considered that he had overcome the separation between the two worlds by maintaining that the whole reality of any particular thing consists of the forms in which the thing partakes. Now if the thing is really nothing apart from these forms, then it is difficult to understand what it is that is said to partake in the forms. We would appear to be saying that the forms partake in one another. But this is not what Socrates wishes to maintain, since he regards the forms as separate, each having its reality by itself. The second part of the *Parmenides* shows that the question of the relation among forms creates just as great difficulties for the Eleatics as for Socrates, but this does not imply that the difficulties in the Socratic theory are in any way lessened. The Eleatics and Pythagoreans generally had assumed that their two theories were the only possibilities and that any argument against one was an argument in favour of the other. But the *Parmenides* shows that there are arguments which can be brought against both Eleaticism and Pythagoreanism. There is one thing which Socrates says of all his forms, namely, that they belong to the world of being—that they all *are*. But this implies that all the forms partake in being. And if the forms in which a thing partakes constitute its sole reality, we are driven to the conclusion that the only reality is the form of being, and that the many forms which are supposed to be have no existence apart from this fundamental form, any more than the various particular men exist apart from the form of manhood.

To meet the difficulties which Parmenides has raised Socrates proceeds to make a number of suggestions. The first is that the forms may really be thoughts, that they may exist in the mind and be applied by the mind to particular things, without the implication that they are really in particulars or are in the same region. Parmenides at once replies that a thought must be the thought of something. This in fact is the typically Eleatic position. It is not the case that Parmenides tries to determine what can be by reference to what can be thought, but he limits what can be thought by reference to what can be. If we think of the forms, then we are thinking of something, and the question is whether this can really be or not. So the position is, as before, that the theory demands forms, on the one hand, and things which participate in them, on the other; and that in order to understand the theory we require to think of both and to consider what sort of reality they can have. But if we insist on saying that the forms are thoughts, that they belong to some peculiar realm of thought distinct from the realm of being, then we will have to say (that the forms *are not* and) that the things which partake of the forms also belong to the realm of thought. And consequently we will be faced with the same problem in this new realm as before.

Socrates then makes the definitely Pythagorean suggestion that the forms may be patterns or standards, and that the participation of things in the forms may mean their greater or less resemblance to the patterns. But, Parmenides argues, if the things are like the form, the form is like the things, and consequently we will be making a statement which implies that we have brought together the form and the things under a particular pattern which will be different from the one previously referred to. And so again we require an infinite series of steps in order to understand how we come to use a particular predicate. A. E. Taylor in commenting on this argument says that this is a misunderstanding of the theory put forward, that while there is a relation of resemblance of a copy to the original which also holds between the original and a copy, the relation of copying is not itself a symmetrical one, but the original comes first and is the standard by which all the copies are estimated.[17] Now this is quite correct as far as copying is concerned, but it implies that we know that copying has taken place and that we are in a position to determine which is the original. But in experience we are confronted with both the things and the forms, according to the Socratic theory, and it is because of the perfection of the latter that we learn to make the distinction. We are not told in advance that there is any distinction, we have to find that out. In such a case we cannot tell which is the copy and what is the original. If A incompletely resembles B, then B incompletely resembles A (that is, both are "imperfect"). This way of putting the matter raises again the difficulty regarding natural kinds. We can think of a thing being a copy of one original, but not of a copy of a variety of originals at the same time. Yet it is allowed that a particular may come under a variety of forms. In fact, it is just this complex character which, for Socrates, constitutes its imperfection. But if we are presented with a thing which imperfectly resembles a number of different patterns, the difficulty is to determine which of these it is specially to be compared with, that is, to what kind the thing pre-eminently belongs. As far as the proposition goes, whether it is a statement of likeness or of any other relation we are unable to distinguish. This again brings us to the difficulty regarding the "third man", this being an objection to the Socratic theory actually raised by a number of followers of Eleaticism. The objection is stated thus (*cf.*, Burnet), "If a man is a man in virtue of partaking in the form, there must be a man who will have his being relatively to the form. Now this is not the form itself, nor the particular man who is so in virtue of his participation in the form. It remains then that there must be a third man as well who has his being relative to the form."[18]

The point is that if we have to assume this third man we cannot say either that he belongs to the realm of particulars or that he belongs to the realm of universals. He does

---
[17]A. E. Taylor, *op. cit.*, p. 358.
[18][Ed.] This seems to be a truncated quotation from John Burnet's translation of Polyxenos argument, in *Greek Philosophy, op. cit.*, pp. 259–60.

not belong to the recognised realm and yet his existence has to be assumed in order to account for the relation between forms and particulars. In other words, we can only compare things with standards, if these things have characters of their own, and if the standards have particular embodiments. If we try to take the standard apart from any embodiment as something quite abstract, then we cannot make a comparison, we cannot say how near any particular comes to having the required character. On the other hand, if we can find a perfect embodiment of the form, then that and that alone is the particular which comes under the form—the third man alone is really a man, and what we have been accustomed to call men are not men at all.

IV
The Republic

Lecture 63

The Dialogues—the Republic—ethical theories

Ethical Theories. (*Republic*, *Ethics*, Butler's *Sermons*.)

The criticisms of the Socratic theory of forms put forward in the *Parmenides* are applicable to the theories expounded in the *Republic*. The fundamental criticism was that the notion of participation failed to establish the required relation between the world of being and the world of becoming, that to an intelligible form only an intelligible particular could be related, and similarly that to a sensible particular only a sensible form could be related. If we admit either the intelligible particular or the sensible form we have broken down the distinction between particulars and universals. We have admitted that the same thing may have both characters, and we do not therefore require that the things should *strive* towards standards in order to bridge the gap. This argument which is substantially the third man argument can be exactly applied to the theory of the *Republic*.

The theme of the *Republic* is justice, particularly justice as it appears in man, but in order to find out the character of the just man it is considered advantageous to examine the just state, since it is suggested that in states justice can be more readily observed and its distinguishing marks determined than in the case of the individual. But in either case, the question is that of setting up an ideal, formulating a standard by reference to which particular men and particular states can be judged, and the ideal man so described is not the form of man, *but is precisely the third man of the Eleatic argument.* That is, he is one who exhibits perfect justice but he is nonetheless particular.[1] And similarly in order to show the nature of justice in a state, Socrates has to describe a particular state and not merely the form statehood. While he acknowledges that no historical state has ever had this ideal character, the ideal state is still not something in

---

[1] [JA] The third man = the *just* man = he who is *just* (or perfectly) a man.

which actual states participate, but is something which itself participates in the perfect form.[2] Accordingly if the ideal man and the ideal state are alone properly to be called man and state, alone have these characters in the truest sense, then the actual men and historic states, or at least those beings we describe in those terms, are not properly so described. So that in giving an account of the ideal, we have put it out of our power to give an account of the real.

This position in the *Republic* also emphasises the theory of natural kinds, which is stated almost explicitly at the end of Book I. The just man is the only one who is a man in the fullest sense of the term and similarly with the just state. Justice or goodness is in fully living up to our own nature, and thus injustice is the failure to be completely ourselves and is relative unreality. Now, as before, this doctrine neglects the fact that in order to show that anything falls short of a given standard, we must speak of it as having characters of its own. So that if a man failed to be perfectly just, he might nevertheless succeed in being perfectly unjust—the one is as much entitled to be called a perfection as the other, since it represents a definite and recognisable state of affairs. But if unjust men really possess characters other than those which are the marks of manhood and even of true manhood, this means that they belong to other classes as well as to that of man; and therefore we are not in a position to say that there is a single ideal of the nature of which we can be perfectly certain, for each of these individual things. Now it is important to notice that as a result of this theory of natural kinds and ideal standards, the notion of goodness becomes obscured. It would be imagined that in order to have a definite ethical theory, we ought to be able to state a number of definite propositions about goodness, and the things that are good, so that we could recognise them with certainty and understand the conditions under which they come about. But it is impossible to arrive at propositions of that kind if goodness means something different for every distinct class of beings—if it means, developing one's own nature. In that case we will never be in a position to predict, we will always have to wait

---

[2][Ed.] Or "commands" our philosophical allegiance, *cf.*, 591e-592b.

till after the event to see what the true nature of a thing amounts to, and even this we will never be certain of, since the ideal is never completely realised in any individual case. That is, if we were to say that A is a better man than B, this will imply that we have some conception of the ideal man, but the person who disagrees with us may do so on the basis of a different ideal man, and there will be no means of settling the dispute.

In the case of particular things, we have according to the theory of Socrates confusion arising from the fact that they participate in several different forms, and thus the approach to goodness will be marked by a reduction (of the number of characters: of complexity),[3] by the thing's coming nearer to having a single principle which dominates all its actions. But so long as it has not reached that state of perfection in which the principle operates, even assuming such a state to be precisely conceivable, we cannot tell in what direction increased consistency and fuller systematisation of action is to be found. We can form suppositions on the matter, but unless all the possible suppositions can be tested—and this is not possible in actual practice—we cannot say that we have discovered that line of development whereby conflict and confusion is reduced to the greatest possible extent. Accordingly the conception of the good man as the perfectly consistent man is one which does not enable us to settle the questions which naturally arise in practice.

But in the second place it may be doubted whether perfect consistency is the proper definition of goodness. If as far as outward practice is concerned perfect consistency is impossible (understanding by consistency, subjection to a single principle in all actions), then it is possible to *say* that if we could have this consistency we would have goodness, but it is not possible to prove it. The very hypothesis implies the attempt to consider as actual something which, it is admitted, cannot be actual. When in ordinary life we refer to good, we don't mean anything of this merely formal character, we don't mean singleness of purpose and absence of conflict, but on the contrary, we should think that everything would depend on what the purpose was. And even if as a matter

---
[3][Ed.] The student notes record here "reduction of this confusion".

of fact it turned out to be impossible for a man to be so single-mindedly evil as another man could be single-mindedly good, we could only make this discovery if we had some other criterion of good and evil than single-mindedness. When we find that Socrates represents as the good state and soul the orderly state and soul, we regard this as an insufficient criterion of good, apart from the question whether complete orderliness is possible. We should not necessarily admit that a more orderly person was better than a less orderly one. We might consider that a certain degree of conflict was desirable, possibly for its own sake, and certainly as a means to further development, so that it would be impossible to arrange lives in a series from the most the least orderly, and to maintain that this was the order of their goodness from higher to lower. We require, if we are to have a definite theory of ethics, to be able to say that men or states, exhibiting certain special qualities are good. But we cannot accept consistency or regularity of conduct as being a special quality of the kind required.

Lecture 64

The Dialogues—the Republic Book I—virtue and the arts

Republic Book I. We find that, like many other Platonic dialogues, it puts forward as the typically Socratic doctrine the theory that virtue is known, and it emphasises the Socratic distinction between knowledge and opinion. What the argument sets out to give, in fact, is a criticism of opinion for the purpose of arriving at knowledge. And so we find that in this first book Socrates is confronted with three different representatives of opinion and that the statement of their opinions leads progressively to the statement of the real problem. Thrasymachus is brought in as the typical sophist, and it is in argument with him that Socrates arrives at the formulation of the issue. But in the discussion of that issue which occupies the later books, Thrasymachus drops out and his place is taken by Glaucon and Adimantus who as students of philosophy discuss the question philosophically. Neither Cephalus nor Polemarchus is to be described as a sophist: the former represents opinion based on tradition, the latter opinion derived from a certain kind of education, particularly of the sophistic kind, while Thrasymachus represents sophistry itself.

The question introduced for discussion is under what conditions a man may be tranquil in old age, and it is suggested that riches may be of considerable importance in ensuring this tranquillity. But it is argued that while this may be very useful, it is not a sufficient guarantee of a tranquil mind, that one requires the consciousness of having acted fairly or justly towards one's fellow-man. Then Socrates wishes to know how the traditional opinions on the subject of fair dealing are to be formulated. He introduces a trivial example but one which serves the purpose of showing how difficult it is to formulate a rule which will be universally applicable. It has been suggested that justice consists of giving each man his due. But, Socrates adds, suppose we have borrowed arms from a certain person and suppose this person to become mad, then if he asks us to return these arms, would it be just to do so, considering that he might injure himself or others? To this question tradition has no answer to give, but Polemarchus then enters the discussion and proposes to support the view that justice is giving every man his own (what is due to him), taking quotations from the poets as supporting this view. And Socrates proceeds to subject this position to detailed criticism so as to bring out its weakness.

As far as this portion of the argument is concerned, we have a very close analogy with the *Euthyphro*. The *Euthyphro* was also concerned with what ought to be rendered to certain beings, but in its case, the question was what ought to be rendered to the gods, whereas it now is what ought to be rendered to men. Socrates does not regard this as a valid distinction. He considers that we cannot benefit men without pleasing the gods, and *vice versa*. The real point of criticism is that we are not entitled to pass judgement on conduct in terms of what it renders or produces. That is, we are not entitled to consider it as having a merely instrumental value (as a means to something else). The ethical problem will not be solved until we have considered, not simply what good conduct produces but what [it] is in itself. That is the fundamental objection to the position of Euthyphro and likewise of Polemarchus. But in the *Republic* the criticism is worked out more exactly by the introduction of the analogy of the arts. Is virtue an art? On this question it is often suggested that Socrates gave the affirmative answer, but, as this dialogue shows, that is not the case. He argues most definitely that virtue is not an art, and introduces the references to the arts only for the purpose of letting Polemarchus see what his position really amounts to. For the purposes of the argument, the term "art" is taken as equivalent to that which renders some service, something which is a means to certain ends, as for example the art of medicine is a means to health. No-one would think of valuing medicine for its own sake, but only in terms of whether or not it succeeded in curing disease. And similarly with other arts, such as cooking and the art of the pilot. This question of the service that is rendered by virtue is considered in detail and Polemarchus is made to admit that he cannot assign any special service to virtue, that there is no particular sphere in which it would have supreme usefulness, and further to admit that if we treat virtue as a means, then as far as we can show, it might just as well have bad as good results. Accordingly it is found necessary to drop the consideration of results, or at least not to allow it to be the main consideration, and to refer to what goodness is in itself.

But before the argument is allowed to proceed, certain further difficulties are brought forward, first of all by Thrasymachus who introduces the reference to politics and society which dominates the argument, and secondly by Glaucon and Adimantus who point out that if a satisfactory ethics cannot be based on consideration of results—cannot be purely utilitarian—then none of the prevailing systems of ethics can be considered satisfactory; that in social training and in social life generally, the utilitarian theory is absolutely dominant. Consequently Socrates, if he is going to show that this conception is false, is really committed to setting ethics on its feet for the first time and to overthrowing practically all that men have hitherto thought on the subject and certainly all that is current on the subject in Athenian society in particular. It is no doubt because of the magnitude of the task thus indicated that Socrates proposes to approach the question by means of analogy, and considers what constitutes goodness in the state prior to considering what constitutes goodness in the soul. But also in this way he magnifies his task, since, whatever is said about the soul, it would appear quite natural to hold that the state has a utilitarian basis.

Lecture 65

The Dialogues—the Republic continued

Socrates points out that if we regard virtue as something which aims at producing a certain effect, then we are treating it as an art, as a certain kind of skill, similar to the skill exhibited in games, for example, and again in such arts as medicine and cookery etc. Socrates wishes to know, if virtue is to be regarded in this way, what are the special results which it produces and which is the sphere within which it operates. We can say that medicine operates on the human body for the purpose of restoring it to health, but can we find any similar object on which justice or virtue can operate? If we take the case of medicine itself, then we should say that if we desire health, it would be better to call in a doctor than to call in a man of whom it could only be said that he was just. That is, the sphere in which justice operates is not that of medicine, the skill of the just man is not skill in curing disease. And precisely the same of any other art. In all these cases a person with special skill and special training will be more useful than the merely just man. Polemarchus suggests that justice may be useful in partnerships, that if we were seeking a partner in any enterprise, we would insist on his being a just man. But Socrates points out that we would prefer a man who was skilled in the business in hand. If he lacked that skill, then however just he might be, he would not be a very useful business partner. Finally Polemarchus is reduced to saying that the just man is he who will keep something safe for us, with whom we may safely deposit our money or any other property. Accordingly, Socrates says, the just man is useful when our property is useless, but when we want to make any use of our property, the usefulness of the just man comes to an end. Accordingly we would have to conclude that justice, the ability to keep others' property safe for them, was not of much social importance, but was inferior to almost any other art that could be named. But even this sphere (the sphere of safe-keeping) cannot be allotted to justice as a peculiar art or skill because, as Socrates goes on, an art is a capacity of opposites, that is, the man who is most skilful in producing a certain effect will also be most skilful in producing the opposite effect. The doctor who knows just what medicines will be most beneficial in certain diseases, by that very fact is bound to know what medicine will be harmful in those diseases. So, the man who is most skilful in curing is also most skilful in bringing about disease if he so desires. This holds with any art. The conclusion [is] that if the just man is good at keeping money he will also be good at stealing it. In other words justice defined as the art of safekeeping, turns out to be the art of theft. That is the consequence of maintaining that justice consists in producing certain results, or, as Polemarchus suggests, in benefiting our friends and harming our enemies. But Socrates has further objections, objections which are still connected with the distinction between what a thing is and what it produces.

The position of Polemarchus is represented as one of irresponsible opinion. Cephalus also had only been able to put forward opinions, but his opinions were founded on tradition and might be assumed to have been tested in the experience of many generations. And even if these tests had not been rigorously scientific, they might still be capable of removing certain errors. In the case of Polemarchus we have opinions without any such foundations and merely illustrating the desire of Polemarchus to show his cleverness in supporting an argument. This kind of knowledge that Polemarchus professed to have is based only on goodness of intellect, but that, Socrates considers, is a very unsatisfactory foundation. We require also goodness of character, if we are to have thorough knowledge. And even if this is not supplemented by detailed investigation, it may still express itself in a better light and more correct conceptions than are to be obtained from irresponsible speculation.

Socrates then raises the question how we are to determine who are our friends and who are our enemies, so that we may benefit the former and injure the latter. The statement is made that a man will be friendly with those he thinks good, and will hate those he thinks evil. But he may make a mistake, the persons he thought good may be actually evil, and if so he will not be doing right in benefiting them. The point Socrates is making here indicates the real basis of his distinction between knowledge and opinion. It is the case that a man may be mistaken as to the character of friends and enemies (so-called). But the important point is that Socrates is carrying the argument beyond mere friendship to the question of goodness. Friendship is a relative term, it doesn't imply any definite character in the persons who are related in that way. Or at least it is possible for friendship to exist among different sets of persons having very different characters. And if we were told an individual had friendly feelings for *another individual* we should not think we had learned much about him. No scientific theory can be based on any merely relative term like friendship, and if we take that as our starting point, we will be reduced to a mere bandying of opinion, without any possibility of arriving at exact demonstration.

In the term *good*, on the other hand, we have not a relative term but an absolute term. A man's friends may be those whom he thinks of in a certain way whether these opinions are right or wrong. But goodness must be something independent of opinion, otherwise there will be no science of ethics. In this particular case we have an argument precisely analogous to that in the *Euthyphro* regarding what is pleasing to the gods, pleasing again being a relative term, and one which does not of itself tell us what are the characters of the thing it is applied to. And just as what was pleasing to some gods might not be pleasing to others, so what was beneficial to our friends might not be beneficial to the just, and what was injurious to our enemies might be injurious to the just. Just as Euthyphro tried to get out of the difficulty by saying that piety was what was pleasing to all the gods, so Polemarchus puts forward the view that justice is benefiting those who are at once just and our friends, and injuring those who are at once unjust and our enemies. Thus in both cases the problem is incompletely solved: there remains a doubtful region within which we could not determine whether an act was just or unjust. But Socrates does not press this point in either dialogue. What he goes on to insist on is that in using terms like pleasing, or beneficial and harmful, we are already implying a knowledge of ethical predicates, and consequently we cannot use these terms to define piety and justice, unless piety and justice are subordinate ethical conceptions. And if that is so, we have the problem of determining what is the fundamental conception. But even this would hardly be satisfactory, since we understand by justice all that is good in human behaviour. Socrates takes the term *injury* and brings out its ethical character. To injure a thing, he argues, is to make it less good, and thus if it is just to injure those of our enemies who are evil, it is just to make them less good than they were before. Socrates considers naturally that this is an incoherent position, that goodness cannot consist in destroying goodness in any particular instance. It can never be just to render any sort of injury to anyone, even if that person is an enemy of ours, and even if he is an evilly disposed person. Justice will still consist in making him better, if it is possible to do so.

We find that the formula of Polemarchus cannot be accepted and that we are reduced to saying that justice consists in producing benefits, without having any clear idea of how benefits are distinguished from injuries. In fact, we may say that this position, even though it appears to give little information, has the further defect of being thoroughly confused. It is ridiculous to say that goodness consists in producing good. Goodness can only consist in being good. And so long as the emphasis is laid on the production, so long as goodness is treated as a sort of skill or art, so long will these difficulties or others of a similar character arise. The question is therefore to make a definite distinction between what things are and what they produce, or between what is good in itself and what is a means to good, and this point is made clearer in the discussion with Thrasymachus and the arguments put forward by Glaucon and Adimantus. But it is a problem which Socrates cannot completely solve, because his theory of forms commits him to the view that the reality of a thing is the end to which it is tending, that a thing really is what it aims at.

Lecture 66

The Dialogues—the Republic continued

Thrasymachus begins by demanding that Socrates himself should give a definition of justice, instead of simply criticising those given by others. He also demands that Socrates should not in formulating this definition use such terms as duty or advantage or gain or interest, because this would be a merely verbal (that is, nominal) definition, simply substituting one term for another, without making clear what either term meant. However when Thrasymachus gives his own definition, he himself employs one of these terms, interest. And the suggestion seems to be that it is impossible to define ethical terms in an unethical way, that when we are defining goodness we are not reducing it to something else which does not involve goodness, since that would amount to saying there is no such thing as ethics. The point with respect to the demand that Socrates himself should define the term is that *dialectic*, or examination of hypotheses by argument, should not be merely negative, that it should be undertaken for the purpose of formulating a positive theory and not simply for the purpose of rejecting wrong views. But Socrates could at least say in reply that in order to reject even false theories we require positive information, and while this information may not be sufficient to solve the problem we are investigating, it may indicate possible solutions, which may be further considered.

The argument developed throughout the rest of the book, while of a more positive and direct character, would not be possible apart from the critical work of which we have a statement in Book I. Socrates, then, ironically disclaiming any knowledge of the subject, persuades Thrasymachus to give his definition of justice, the point being that the latter thinks that no preliminary critical work is necessary, and that it is enough to make a positive assertion regarding the way in which the facts appear to us. Accordingly he declares that *justice is the interest of the stronger*. Socrates is able to show at once that this definition requires criticism and he eventually compels Thrasymachus to modify his definition. Even the modified definition is found to be subject to criticism. Socrates asks what precisely is meant by saying that justice is the interest of the stronger. Does it mean that what is good for the strongest person is therefore good for everyone? Thrasymachus evades this question by bringing in a reference to politics. He says that what he means by the stronger is the ruling power in the state and that justice consists in furthering the interest of that ruling power. Here again Socrates raises the question of *opinion and knowledge*. What this really implies is that the term *interest* is an ambiguous one and so cannot be a satisfactory definition. The ruling power in a state makes laws in its own interest, but it may be mistaken as to what its interest is. And consequently it may find that obedience to these laws on the part of the subjects adversely affects its interests, just as in the case of friendship we may find that following the principle of assisting our friends and injuring our enemies, we may so far fall into error as to assist those who will actually do us harm and harm those who are capable of benefiting us. If the subjects are acting justly in obeying the ruler and if he commands something which is not in his own interest, then justice will be opposed to the interest of the stronger. In fact in the definition of Thrasymachus there is a certain confusion, the stronger being regarded on the one hand as the person who *secures obedience* from the weaker, whether this obedience is to his advantage or not, and on the other hand as the person who *secures advantages* from others, whether or not these advantages come by way of obedience.

In view of this criticism Thrasymachus shifts his ground, and emphasises securing advantage, rather than emphasising obedience. Just as in the case of the arguments with Euthyphro and Polemarchus, Thrasymachus endeavours to combine the two considerations and *to define the stronger as the man who at the same time secures his advantage and is obeyed*. This leaves a number of uncertain cases, just as in the other two arguments referred to. It leaves it doubtful, in the case where there is no person who both secures his own advantage and has his commands obeyed, what justice would consist of. The line of criticism that Socrates adopts is to insist again on the divergence of the two conceptions employed, so that in the end he compels Thrasymachus to drop all reference to the question of obedience and ruling, and to come back to the more ethical and less politic conception of securing one's advantage; and also to describe the particular line of action which he prefers not as justice but as injustice.

According to the later position of Thrasymachus *injustice consists of securing one's own advantage, while justice consists of securing that of others.* Even that distinction is subjected to criticism by Socrates, but what compels Thrasymachus to make it, to praise injustice instead of justice, is that in the state of affairs which he had originally described, the state in which a ruler gains advantages from his subjects, we have not a single way of life which can be called the just life, but two entirely different ways of living, that of the ruler and that of the subject, and we cannot call them just in the same sense. Socrates insists that there must be some single sense in which the term can be employed. If we speak as Nietzsche does of master morality and slave morality, we are using morality in two different senses and we are really confusing the issues which have to be dealt with in the moral sense. Even allowing for variations in different cases we must whenever we call any sort of life moral use that term in the same sense in all the instances.

Thrasymachus then attempts to use the term ruler or the stronger in such a way as to imply both securing obedience and securing advantage. The man who enacts such laws as will lead to his own disadvantage is not really to be called a ruler. He is in so acting demonstrating not his strength but his weakness, and this is expressed by saying that the ruler in so far as he is a ruler is unerring, and being unerring always commands that which is for his own interest. The subject is required to execute his commands and consequently justice is the interest of the stronger. Socrates again uses the example of the arts to show that securing obedience and securing advantage cannot be identified in the way that Thrasymachus suggests. If the ruler is a man who acts with a certain kind of skill, and who if he is perfectly skilled cannot make any mistake, then the exercise of his skill is something quite different from the benefit he receives, even if that benefit arises from the exercise of his skill. The physician, as a skilled practitioner, has to operate on the human body, and his skill is estimated by the effects he produces on his material and not by the effects he produces on himself. Expressing personal advantage in terms of money, we do not say that the best doctor is the man who makes the most money, we say he is the man who has the greatest success in curing disease, and whether as a matter of fact he makes more money is quite beside the point and does not affect our judgment of his art. Similarly in the case of all the other arts, it is possible to gain advantage by exercising them, but we should never estimate skill in their exercise by reference to advantages gained by the person practising the art. In the same way, Socrates argues, the art of the ruler is practised on the subjects, and his skill as a ruler must be estimated by considering how the subjects behave, or the condition in which they find themselves, and not by estimating the advantages that the ruler gains. Socrates expresses this point somewhat inaccurately by saying that the ruler works in the interest of the subject and not in his own interest, and Thrasymachus naturally protests against this view. It does not follow from considering the subjects as the material on which the art of the ruler operates that that art in any way benefits the subject. All that we can say is that it works upon the subjects, affects them in certain ways, and the greatest skill in ruling is exhibited if the subjects show the greatest deal of obedience, but this obedience on the part of subjects cannot be interpreted as being necessarily in their interest. As Thrasymachus points out, the shepherd practises his art on the sheep, but we should not say that a good shepherd benefited the sheep in any sense in which the sheep *enjoyed* that benefit. In any case, one might *practise* an art which actually did harm to its material.

Lecture 67

The Dialogues—the Republic continued—the art of ruling

The distinction between the art of ruling, which is exercised by the ruler on the subjects, and the art of paying which is rendered by the subject to the ruler, depends on the original distinction of securing obedience and securing one's advantage. The argument follows the same lines as before, Socrates pointing out that a good physician is not the one who secures the greatest reward but the one who has the greatest success in curing disease. It may of course happen that these two are the same person, but we cannot say that it must be so. And similarly it may happen, as Thrasymachus maintains, that the most skilful ruler actually advances his own interests to the greatest possible extent. But we cannot say that this must be so, and so we cannot define skill in ruling by the reward which the ruler receives. Now the new position which Thrasymachus puts forward is that whereas justice is the interest of the stronger, injustice is a man's own profit and interest; and when the necessary modification, as a result of the Socratic criticism, has been made, we find that Thrasymachus' position amounts to this: that justice consists in securing the advantage of others, while injustice consists in securing one's own advantage. And that on that account injustice is better, wiser and stronger than justice.

The point may be put in a more general form by saying that the just life consists in producing goods, no matter who is going to enjoy them, while the unjust life consists in enjoying them, no matter who has produced them. And the answer of Socrates amounts to this, that it is impossible to go on enjoying goods if we do not produce any, and likewise *vice versa*. While this may be so, it does not alter the fact that there is a real distinction between producing and enjoying and that there are many problems arising on the basis of this distinction which require definite solution before we can have a satisfactory ethical theory. And that is why even though Socrates achieves a viable victory over Thrasymachus, even though he shows that Thrasymachus' solution is incorrect, further difficulties are raised by Glaucon and Adimantus with a view to a scientific statement of the whole position. It has also to be pointed out in criticism of the Socratic theory of the interrelation between the production and the enjoyment of good, that what is produced and enjoyed is not necessarily good, and thus we require a more definite ethical criterion than the mere association of men for mutual benefit.

As Glaucon points out, this association may be based on motives which are anything but good, and which allow of the possibility of all sorts of deception and trickery.

We find at the very beginning of the criticism of the second position of Thrasymachus, that an important issue is raised and a dangerous confusion pointed out. Socrates asks Thrasymachus if he is prepared to call justice virtue and injustice vice. And Thrasymachus replies that of course he is not prepared to do so, since he regards the unjust life as the better. But when Socrates goes on to ask him if he would call justice vice, he replies that he would rather call it simplicity, whereas injustice is discretion. Now all this indicates a confusion of ethical conceptions. If what has been called justice is not entitled to be described as a virtue, then it could not be justice at all. The point is emphasised by the unwillingness of Thrasymachus to call it a vice. The point is that it is commonly taken for granted in ethical discussion that there is no dubiety about what is good and what is bad, and that the only important question is how the good is to be secured and the bad avoided. Now this as Socrates has indicated reduces virtues to the level of an art, with all the paradoxical consequences that follow therefrom. It is incorrect therefore in estimating human behaviour to set on one side the various rewards that can be obtained or pains which can be suffered, and on the other hand the various lines of action that can be adopted in relation to these ends in the way of getting good and avoiding evil—as if human life could be divided into two separate parts, one of which was subordinate to the other. What Socrates wishes to show is that no line of action can be considered as a mere means to an end, that it has characteristics of its own, one of which may quite well be goodness, so that it can be ethically judged in the same way as the end itself. And secondly (a point emphasised by Aristotle) that we cannot treat the end as a mere result to be achieved, as a mere passivity of mind, but we must regard it as something also of an activity, that is, of being capable of producing further results in the same way as the action which led up to it. If all human actions have both results and characters of their own, then they can all be considered both as means and as ends. That point is more fully brought out in the statements of Glaucon and Adimantus. In the meantime Socrates considers more directly the assertion that injustice is better, wiser and stronger than justice.

It is to be remembered that injustice has been defined as securing one's own advantage or enjoyment, while justice is to be taken as securing advantage and enjoyment in general both for ourselves and for others. Injustice is something which is opposed to cooperation, and it is on that account that Socrates maintains that it can be neither wise nor strong nor good. It cannot be wise, because wisdom essentially consists in something which can be shared. The unjust man, Thrasymachus admits, endeavours to overreach everyone, whereas the person who has wisdom in any particular line, while he will claim to excel those who have not wisdom, will be found to be in complete agreement with others who have wisdom. For example all skilled musicians are agreed as regards the correct tuning of an instrument, and, as Socrates puts it, they don't try to go beyond one another in the tightening and loosening of the strings. Similarly skilled physicians are agreed about what is just right in the case of a particular disease, whereas the unskilled will disagree both with the skilled and with one another. The argument amounts to this: if on any subject wisdom is possible, if there is a truth of the matter to be discovered, then all who are entitled to be considered wise will be in agreement. But according to the admission of Thrasymachus the unjust disagree with one another, as much as with the just. The just are found to be in general agreement. So that as far as wisdom is concerned, it would seem to reside in the just man and not in the unjust.

Again as regards strength, there is obviously, Socrates considers, greater strength to be found among people who agree than among people who disagree. A man who is the enemy of every other man cannot be said to be in a strong position. Even among a band of robbers, we require to have certain rules, agreements to support one another's interests, if the band is to have any strength at all and to be able to carry out its projects. Only in so far as they have a kind of justice among themselves are they able to take any action and to secure what they desire. And in an exactly similar way even in the mind of a single person, unless his various desires and impulses are subordinated to some common rule, it will be impossible for him to lead any sort of settled life and to provide for his wants. In so far as he simply gives rein to his impulses, his life will be not wise and strong and good but the opposite of all these. Now while we can say that the position of Socrates here is more scientific than Thrasymachus', while we can say that agreement, regularity or consistency is a criterion not only of a definite kind of life but of any settled scientific theory, we cannot say that this condition is sufficient. We cannot say that mere agreement is an indication of wisdom or that mere regularity of conduct is a guarantee of goods. As Glaucon points out at the beginning of Book II, it is possible for people to adopt a common means to diverse ends and in general it is possible for people to agree and yet be wrong. Even if error involves some inconsistency, so that perfect consistency would be a guarantee of truth, the fact that perfect consistency is unobtainable then makes this criterion of little value. And in the same way we cannot say that the Socratic ideal of an orderly state and an orderly soul provides a solution for all ethical and political problems.

Lecture 68

The Dialogues—the Republic continued—justice and the form of the good

In this argument with Thrasymachus Socrates endeavours to show that serving oneself or securing one's own advantage cannot be a better life (and similarly wiser and stronger) than serving other people or aiming at advantage in general. The unjust life as described by Thrasymachus cannot be wise, because people who have real knowledge agree with one another, whereas unjust men disagree with one another. In the second place, since this unjust life implies discord, it cannot be strong: the unjust man has everyone else opposed to him and even among his own activities there is conflict[4] because he tries to secure the object of every desire without subordinating these desires to some fundamental principle

---

[4] [JA] That is, Socrates is really contrasting chaos and order *as principles*: but "that which is essentially chaotic" is really nothing at all: no more is "that which is essentially orderly"

which could be universally accepted. According to Socrates, if unjust men are to achieve anything, if they are to have any power, they must agree with one another. And to the extent of their agreement, of their subordinating their immediate desires to some common plan, they are not unjust but just. Their injustice consists in their opposition to the rest of mankind.

This is the position which Glaucon thinks is insufficiently demonstrated. It involves the supposition that the test of justice is agreement, that the more widely agreement extends, the more just the activity in question is. And in the end it involves the supposition that justice is a principle to which every action can be subordinated, one which covers the whole of life and unifies it—a supposition which appears again in the theory of the Form of the Good. The just life is the unified life, the life which has been most completely brought under a single principle. And the degree of unification in any particular life is its degree of justice. This position is further exemplified in the final argument of Socrates against Thrasymachus. Justice must be *better* than injustice as well as stronger and wiser, because only the soul which is in harmony with itself can live well. Now when a soul knows its true end or good, it is performing its function and is in harmony with itself. But the function or good of the soul cannot vary from one soul to another, so that when many souls live well by knowing their own good or end, they must be in harmony with one another. Thus the just or harmonious life is the best.

This is substantially the same view as is put forward in the account of the form of the good. The reality of a thing is what it strives to be, and the end of this striving is the thing's good. This as we saw implies a theory of natural kinds such that one soul cannot really be different from any other soul. Ultimately they are all alike and have a single good, and they are bound therefore to cooperate in pursuit of this good.[5] And the completion of the Socratic theory is that there is one ultimate good of all things—a good at which all things aim—and which is thus the true reality or law of the universe. We have already seen in what way this position may

---
[5][JA] Third man (what is just or perfectly a man).

be criticised from the Eleatic point of view. If this universal law is the only thing which is ultimately real and if all things are defined in subordination to it, then not only must they all be said to be indistinguishable from one another, but they cannot be said to be separately real. So that these things and all their strivings must simply be said not to exist. On the other hand, if we do say that particular things exist, then we cannot say that there is a single reality or a single end to which things are tending. That alternative may be derived from the Eleatic criticism just as much as Eleaticism itself. All that has been shown is that there is not room in the same theory for ultimate reality and for immediate or particular reality. But that alone does not tell us which of the two to reject. Now these being the general logical objections to the position of Socrates and indicating that he cannot arrive at a completely satisfactory ethics, it is still possible for him to solve certain particular ethical problems and so to advance the science. And that is what is done in the discussion of the ideal state and soul which occupies Books II to IV.

The argument is developed by Glaucon with respect to the distinction between means and ends or between production and enjoyment which has been emphasised in the previous book. Glaucon begins by putting forward a certain theory of the nature and origin of justice, a theory which is the original of later conceptions of the social contract. According to Glaucon's argument, men set up laws which become the criterion of justice, not because they think that the just life—the life of obedience to law—is better than the unjust life for an individual who can practise it, but because they are afraid of suffering injustice at the hands of others. Glaucon contends that there is more evil in suffering injustice than there is good in inflicting it, and consequently the setting up of laws takes place as a practical compromise, as a kind of insurance against injustice; but does not imply that the citizens *prefer* justice or that there is any real agreement on fundamental good(s). That is, this social contract is a means to the best result which is possible on the whole but not to the best results possible to the individual, if he can evade the injustice of others. And Glaucon supports this contention by pointing out that those who practise justice do so unwillingly and that if there was opportunity for practising injustice without suffering any social penalty, then the person who did not take advantage of it would be considered a fool. And thus, Glaucon contends, in support of the position he is upholding merely for argument's sake, this is a perfectly correct conclusion because the unjust life is really the better. The just life must be something which has its advantages in itself, whereas the unjust man is free to take all the advantages he can get. Comparing the unjust life with every possible advantage with the just life without any such addition, we see that the unjust life must be better.

Here Adimantus enters the argument and points out that the case as stated by Glaucon is still incomplete. He points out that justice is commonly praised not for itself but for its results—that is, it is supposed to be the best way of getting certain advantages, but is not supposed to be advantageous in itself. It is the results (or supposed results) that are really praised, and not the just life itself. This reinforces Glaucon's conclusion that if we could be unjust without being detected, that is, if we could get the advantages which are supposed to accrue from justice without going to the trouble of being just, then this would be very much the best thing to do. Now, Adimantus argues, injustice does not really have bad results because social penalties depend not on what we do but on what people think we do, and thus the unjust man who has taken care to gain a reputation for justice will get all the advantages of an unjust life and also all the social advantages that are supposed to follow from justice. On the other hand, the just man will be quite indifferent to reputation, he will have none of the social advantages which are given to the man who is thought just and none of the advantages gained by the man who is unjust (pursues his own interest). The problem as put by Adimantus to Socrates is to show that justice in itself without any reward whatever, justice simply as operating in the soul of the just man, is better, that is, procures its possessor a better life, than one which is enhanced by every possible external reward, by everything whatever that can be given to a man. We have the fundamental contrast between what goes on in a man's own mind and the circumstances in which he is placed.

Lecture 69

The Dialogues—the Republic continued—theory of the good based on forms and the doctrine of natural kinds

We saw that Glaucon and Adimantus developed further the arguments put forward by Thrasymachus. Though they are not in agreement with Thrasymachus, they think that the answer given by Socrates is inadequate. Stating the position again in terms of the production and enjoyment of goods, the Socratic view was that it is impossible to concentrate on mere enjoyment, because in order that the enjoyment should be secured, a certain amount of cooperation is necessary. That is, in order that we may be able to enjoy goods, we must join with others in their production and not always be considering our own interests (*cf.*, Butler on "disinterested" passions). As Socrates says, even a band of robbers, in order to be successful, requires to have a certain amount of cooperation. Each individual robber must subordinate his interests to the common interests of the band, since otherwise they could not carry out any of their exploits. Or to put it more generally, organisation of some kind is necessary for a secure life whether of a society or of an individual. Yet Socrates in admitting the possibility of organisation for evil purposes, has shown that we cannot take it as a simple criterion of goodness, that we have to enquire more fully into the characters and conditions of organisation, into what assists and what hinders it. What Glaucon's argument amounts to is that even society as a whole may be organised for evil purposes or, at least, for purposes that are not specifically good. It may simply be, he argues, that each man is following out his own interests and that, granted that he has to subordinate them to some extent to the common interests, he does so to the least possible extent, so that there is very little really in common among the members of the society. While they profess to cooperate to produce in common and to enjoy in common, in reality each man may be endeavouring to gain as much as possible for himself and to give as little as possible. But with all this there may be such a degree of cooperation, however small, as will enable the society to persist. As Adimantus points out, we may find that many men only profess to be assisting in production, while in reality they are consuming without producing.

The method by which Socrates works out his theory of goodness is connected with his theory of forms and of the natural kinds to which particular things belong. If we say that a certain character of a thing, or a certain form under which it falls, is the only ultimately real thing about it, then we seem to be compelled to deny the reality of the various other characters which the thing appears to have. In order to reconcile his theory of the peculiar form or end or good in relation to which each thing has to be estimated with the multiplicity of characters which the thing exhibits and with the fact that the thing has a history, Socrates has to concede that the thing may have these characters in a subordinate sense. In other words, the characters of a thing belong to one definite order leading up to and culminating in its supreme character. The characters form not a multiplicity but a hierarchy, and similarly the organisation of society must take the form of a hierarchy. It must be a system of functions, some of which are subordinated to others and all of which are subordinated to one ultimate or central function. It is this system of subordination that constitutes the organisation of a thing and in relation to which the thing can be called good or bad. In the case of a good thing, the soul for example, we have strict subordination of all minor functions to that function in virtue of which it *is* a soul—pursuit of the good.[6] On the other hand, in the case of a bad soul, we have no single order of functions, but we have a number of conflicting principles, striving for complete dominance, but being unable to secure it. And on this account, the man whose mind is not completely organised in subordination to the good is bound to be unhappy—to be striving for something he cannot secure.

The difficulty in relation to this position is that souls being particulars must all according to Socrates fall short of perfect organisation, and consequently they must all be unjust and unhappy. In every soul there must be conflict. So that ethics would appear to deal with pure suppositions without any relation to actuality. It is impossible for us to say how near a particular conflict comes to complete absence of

---
[6][JA] Orderly.

conflict.[7] It is impossible for us to arrange states and souls in a definite order from that which exhibits the greatest conflict to that which exhibits the least. Moreover, if it is necessary to strive towards the good, then it must be necessary to introduce conflict for the sake of avoiding conflict. It would appear on the face of it that that man lives the best life who refuses to strive and takes things as they come. Out of the Socratic philosophy, then, as a theory of higher and lower qualities or higher and lower realities, we can find no positive ethical results. And similarly we cannot accept the Socratic logic as giving a sufficient reason for the organisation of a state in a particular way with certain classes performing the highest functions and certain others performing the lowest. It would appear, even on his own showing, that a state of this kind would exhibit a very low degree of cooperation. The classes to which the lowest tasks were allotted could have no appreciation of the real ends for which the state existed. And therefore they would be in the position of persons who produced without enjoying. Their work would be necessary for whatever goodness was to be found in the state, but whatever enjoyments they had would not be enjoyments of that goodness.

So that the very hierarchy which Socrates proposes, involves elements of conflict, involves an association between different classes not because they have common ends to pursue but because each can serve the purposes of the others. And when we take the highest class into consideration we find that Socrates regards them as living in equality with one another. So that in this particular part of the state the principle of hierarchy is abandoned. Socrates, then, cannot even consistently work out his peculiar theory of social organisation. It has the same sort of defects as his general theory of the nature of particular things, as expounded in the *Phaedo* and elsewhere. And it is open to the same sort of criticisms as are brought in the *Parmenides*. The fundamental difficulty is to bring this ideal of pure organisation and complete absence of conflict into relation with any description with actual affairs. As soon as we attempt to apply the ideal, we fall into contradictions. On the

---
[7][JA] Hidden harmony.

other hand, if we make no attempt to apply the ideal, then we have failed to account for our ordinary ethical judgments, for the fact emphasised in *Republic I*, that no matter how we try to avoid doing so, we find ourselves committed to making ethical distinctions, that is, to regarding one thing as really better than another.

Lecture 70

The Dialogues—the Republic continued—the nature of the state

To sum up the state of discussion as we have so far considered it, we can say that the three persons with whom Socrates argues in the first book each put forward a theory which Socrates would consider to be based merely on opinion, and what he points out in the first part of the argument is that virtue or goodness cannot be a mere matter of habit, because we are necessarily confronted with situations in which habits conflict, and we must have some way of making the necessary distinctions. That is, we require to exercise our intelligence. But in the second place virtue is not a mere matter of intelligence. It is not suggested in the argument that Polemarchus is a person of outstanding intelligence, but the point is that he tries to solve ethical problems by mere irresponsible theorising, without paying proper attention to facts of life. It is one of the chief points of Socrates, in his general support of the theory that virtue is knowledge, that we can have no real knowledge and no real understanding which is not based on a certain kind of character. It is only the man who has the proper attitude who is capable of finding out the truth, not only on ethical questions but on any scientific question whatever.

Now we find that Aristotle makes a distinction between goodness of character and goodness of intellect,[8] corresponding to the distinction referred to in the *Republic*, and this distinction is connected with the theory of education given in Books II to IV of the *Republic*, an education which is a training in character without being a definitely intellectual training. On the other hand, the system of education which is expounded in Book VII is a definitely intellectual one. But

---
[8][Ed.] *Cf., Nicomachean Ethics*, Book VI.

Socrates does not wish to make an absolutely hard and fast distinction. He would insist that the persons who are able to profit by the intellectual training can only be persons of good character. Again while the training of character does not of itself lead to intellectual eminence (though it must be undertaken by intellectual persons) there are intellectual elements in it. The man of good character must be able to discriminate; he must know what social tendencies he ought to assist and what he ought to resist. So that on the whole Socrates does not make such a hard and fast division between the two types of excellence as Aristotle does, but insists that each is to some extent necessary for the other. Now the more definite the division is made, the more definite will be the distinction between a ruling or legislative class and the class which is subject to that rule. And in Aristotle's *Ethics* the problem is entirely that of training citizens. It is assumed from the beginning that there are thoroughly competent legislators who will do everything that is required to make the state as good as possible. And it follows that the mass of citizens would be quite unable to criticise the legislators, since they did not belong to the ranks of the wise and good. Even if as a matter of historical fact there was an intellectual division of this kind in society, it would be something that could be discovered only if we had a definite knowledge of what wisdom and goodness consisted in. And therefore Aristotle is not entitled to make the distinction, unless he is prepared to state a positive theory of goodness, and not merely to say that when we come to any actual problem, the good man will know what ought to be done.

We find that the only positive account of goodness which is given by either Socrates or Aristotle is that it is to be found in the speculative or intellectual life. But it would appear that prominence is given to this life because intellect is required for the regulation of society or of the life of the individual. So that it appears almost as if intellect also were a mere means to good and that what goodness consisted in, what the good life would be like when it had actually been reached, has not been determined. This difficulty is obscured by the fact that throughout the argument both in the *Republic* and *Ethics* reference has been made to certain specific virtues, such as courage for example, and though these are treated as subordinate to the goodness of the whole system, the mere fact of their presence in the system gives us a reason, which we should not otherwise have, for calling it good.

The third point, which arises in the discussion with Thrasymachus, is that virtue is not a mere matter of *results*, that is, that we cannot regard it simply as a means to an end. If there is to be any ethical system at all, Socrates considers, we must be able to evaluate ends as well as means, and we cannot give one account of the meaning of goodness in relation to what we choose to call ends and a different account of its meaning in relation to means. And Socrates supports this argument by showing that even those who tried to make virtue a mere means to an end are compelled to use language which implies that they regard the end also as capable of evaluation. Now, allowing that this criticism is sound, it is pointed out by Glaucon and Adimantus that the view in question is not confined to the sophists, that the public generally and moral teachers in particular all praise virtue not for what it is in itself but for the gains that it brings. And thus we find that in a later part of the *Republic* Socrates described the public itself as "the great sophist".

Sophistical views of knowledge and conduct, that is to say, the view that there is nothing absolute in either knowledge or conduct but that they are entirely relative, these views are quite widespread, and in fact are the views which the ordinary citizen seems naturally to adopt. And this is one of the reasons why Socrates emphasises the importance of education. The uneducated man is the one who is quite unacquainted with standards or forms and who takes everything in a relative way. Now while the criticism passed by Socrates on the ordinary distinction between means and ends is quite valid as far as it goes, it cannot be worked out to its logical conclusion because Socrates himself is to some extent influenced by this distinction. As we have seen, he considers that the ultimate reality of anything is the end at which it aims. And thus he is not capable of entirely overcoming the difficulties that this division entails, but he seems to be working out a theory of social organisation as a means to an end which can only be defined as social organisation also. In fact his argument on society shows that he considers the good society to be the one which is alone really social, and thus, having determined the kind of relation which in his opinion constitutes society, he simply carries that to an extreme in determining what is the good society. And in view of the way in which he begins his exposition, it is not surprising to find, at the end of the argument, that goodness or justice consists in the fulfilment of function. In this way the end, or outcome, of the argument has really been assumed from the beginning, but this particular line of argument is important to Socrates, because, as he puts it, goodness is more readily recognisable in the state than in the soul, or, as we may put it, because it is easier in considering society to justify a system of subordination, a hierarchical system, which alone is in accordance with the Socratic theory of the ultimate reality of things under which their relative realities or appearances must be brought. And thus having set up classes in the state Socrates is able to argue by analogy that there are certain distinct principles or faculties in the soul, and that virtue consists in having these faculties in their right order. And when these faculties are expounded, as to the nature of their working and the specific character exhibited by each, we find that they are the three faculties of the soul, or the three types of human activity, which are implied in the Pythagorean doctrine of the three lives. This doctrine is one which Socrates must have held from an early period in his thinking. And thus we can say that it is really prior to the theory of the three classes, and that the state has been divided in the way in which Socrates divides it, not because this is a natural division, but simply in order to support the Pythagorean account of the three divisions of the soul.

Lecture 71

The Dialogues—the Republic continued—goodness as fulfillment of function—three classes within the state

To a certain extent we may say that the conclusion at which Socrates arrives as a result of his analysis of the state is simply the original assumption that he had made, in a rather more developed form. At the end of Book I we are told that the goodness of a thing consists in its fulfilling its function, and the nature of justice as stated at the end of Book IV is simply that of the fulfilment of function. The difference between the two statements is that in the former case the function is thought about as something simple, something about which all persons possessing wisdom and goodness will agree. But in the later statement emphasis is laid on *difference* of function, though all the different functions are supposed to contribute to and to be constituted of, one total function which is the goodness or reality of the thing which is functioning. Again in introducing the discussion of the state in Book II, Socrates employs as his principle of construction the conception of a particular form of work which each member has to do. The implied argument is that if all members of the community performed the same sort of work, then their association would be no benefit to them. Instead of a number of persons together performing work which satisfies the needs of all, we might as well have a situation in which each person looked after his own needs. The fact that they associate in this way indicates, Socrates contends, that individuals are not self-sufficient, but one individual requires something which another individual is best able to provide. So that we have as the condition of social life, a certain division of the latter, the first illustration of which is the division existing among different trades. But when the theory of society is fully worked out, we find that the tradesmen are classed together in one division while the other divisions have functions of a different kind. Now in connection with this argument, it is necessary to point out the advantages of simple cooperation, that is, cooperation in which the various associations all perform the same kind of work. Now we find that when this is so, the amount of work that can be done by a number of men working together is greater than the sum of their products would be if they were all working separately. It is only after simple cooperation of this kind has gone on, that division of the latter can be developed. So that though undoubtedly there are social advantages in the division of labour, it does not have quite the importance that Socrates attaches to it. There certainly must have been societies before division of labour could take place, apart from that which is implied in the different functions of the sexes.[9] Socrates, on the other hand, argues as if a number of tradesmen, each skilled in his craft, had come together and arranged to supply one another's needs. Whereas that skill could only have been developed within an already existing society. Now the main point of criticism of the procedure of Socrates is that, while it may be admitted that division of labour is socially valuable, it does not follow that every distinct social task should be performed by a distinct social class.

The main classes into which Socrates divides the state are the legislative class (guardians), the military class (auxiliaries) and the producing class (tradesmen). Allowing that legislation is necessary in the state and that legislation is different from trade (though perhaps only in "degree"?) it does not follow that legislation should not be the work of tradesmen, or that separate classes are required for the three main social functions. What we find is that this division corresponds to the doctrine of the three lives, and that it is by means of the various theories worked out in that connection that Socrates supports his social and ethical views. That is, he would consider that a division of classes is required, corresponding to the division of principles of action in the human soul, namely, reason (which corresponds to the function of the guardians), spirit or temper (auxiliaries) and desire (tradesmen).[10]

What Socrates is particularly anxious to show and what his whole argument turns on, is that these three functions of the soul are distinct, that we must recognise reason to be different from spirit, and both to be different from desire. Now if the matter is expressed in terms of the three lives, it would appear that such a division is necessary. The life which is lived for the sake of wisdom is quite different from that whose guiding principle was honour, and both are distinct from the life devoted to gain. But while this is so, it is still possible to argue that theoretical activities, practical activities and productive activities don't require to be carried out by

---

[9][JA] Simple cooperation (social contract) like division of labour implies existing society.
[10][JA] Tradesmen as sheer *wanters* (and *givers*); supply and demand. *Cf.*, Hegel's bourgeois society, as contrasted with hierarchical society, in which we have *standards*. Hegel as a feudalist. *Cf.*, contemporary petit-bourgeois view of tradesmen or artisans. In fact, Hegel is *not* the fine flower of bourgeois philosophy: Locke or Kant [Unclear: "L. or K."] would have better qualifications for that position.

different persons, but that they even gain from being the activities of a single person; that the person who produces is capable, if his theoretical aptitudes are developed, of being a better theoretician than the man who devotes his whole life to theory. Whether or not this is so, the opposite is not proved by the conventional distinction of the three lives. What lies at the basis of the Socratic theory is that we can distinguish in the state the framing of a public policy from the carrying out of that policy, and we can distinguish both from the economic activities of the citizens. But we cannot therefore say that there must be those three classes that Socrates refers to or that tradesmen or producers are incapable of formulating and carrying out a public policy. Assuming, however, that we have those three classes in the state, the question is what virtues are they capable of exhibiting and how can they work together to form a just state.

Socrates answers these questions by reference to the four commonly recognised virtues of wisdom, courage, temperance and justice. Wisdom is the special virtue of the legislative and courage of the military class, but, according to the Socratic theory, temperance is not peculiar to the productive class but is a virtue of all three classes;[11] and is required to operate throughout the state if justice is to be possible. Temperance in the state consists in universal agreement as to who are to be the rulers and who are to be ruled. It consists, that is, in each member of the community recognising the function of the others and not attempting to interfere with it in any way. In this way temperance corresponds *negatively* to justice, the latter being dependent on each person's carrying out his own function, while the former involves his not interfering with others. So we come back to a definition of justice which is very like that which was proposed at the beginning of Book I where justice was regarded as rendering to every man his own. But in place of that passive way of regarding it, we now have an expression in regard to a man's own activities, justice consisting in his performing his own function or minding his own business. This is obviously connected with not minding other people's business (though legislators have in

---

[11][JA] That is, tradesmen are only bits of men; partly human.

a sense to mind everybody's business), so that temperance and justice are not very readily distinguishable. But we make a general distinction between (of) temperance as implying a willingness to cooperate but as not amounting to the positive and developed activity which justice requires.

We find that there is no special virtue of the trading class, and that at least leads us to question whether wisdom and courage are peculiar to the legislators and the warriors respectively. It would rather seem, from the discussion of virtue in the soul, which Socrates works out on the analogy of justice in the state, that no man can be really just, and consequently no man can adequately fulfil his social function, unless he has all the virtues. (Or, he cannot have one unless he has all.) It would certainly not be said that legislators should be lacking in courage and they must be temperate. On the other hand, the military class must have a certain amount of wisdom in order to know how to perform their functions and in order to be able to recognise the moral authority of the legislators. And the same will apply to the trading class. But if we require to have all the virtues in each of the classes then it would appear that there can be no fundamental division among the classes. Instead of being a difference of kind, it will be at most a difference of degree, those who happen to have developed goodness to the greatest extent being placed at the head of others being graded according to their goodness. But this implies that we can admit degrees of goodness, can consider a person good in spite of many deficiencies, and it also implies that it is possible so to grade people from the best to the worst. It appears then that there is something arbitrary about the Socratic theory both of policics and of ethics.

Lecture 72

The Dialogues—the Republic continued—parts of the state and parts of the soul

In attempting to prove that there are three fundamental faculties or parts of the soul, Socrates proceeds on the basis of the principle of consistency or non-contradiction, which he has taken to be the main criterion of reality and goodness. If we do not make the distinction between the faculties which Socrates names then, he argues, we will fall into contradictions. That is, from the principle of consistency alone we can deduce the organisation of the soul and of the state. Actually when any attempt is made to derive concrete consequences from the abstract principle of non-contradiction, it will be found that that which had to be proved has already been assumed. Socrates concludes that because reason and desire act in opposition to one another, they must be different faculties. But unless we had known to begin with that there were different faculties, we could never have discovered that they could conflict. The general principle that the same thing cannot act at the same time in contrary ways does not tell us anything about the specific faculties of reason and desire, and apart from a knowledge of actual things with their peculiar characters and differences, we should not know what ways of acting were contrary to one another. That is something we can find out only by experience.

In treating of desire Socrates assumes that the object of desire is a pure particular, something considered in absolute isolation. For example the object of thirst is drinking and that is considered as a simple object apart from interrelations with other things and possible internal differences. If that were so, then any faculty which considered the relations among things would have to be a faculty other than desire, and it might be that faculty which Socrates calls reason and which has as its object not something particular but something universal. But if that were so, it would be difficult to see how desire and reason could conflict, that is, how a pure particular could be opposed to a pure universal, or again how something particular could be distinguished from others as being in accordance with the universal. This is a difficulty similar to that which arises in Butler's theory as regards the relation of conscience to particular passions. If conscience alone is capable of passing a judgment, and if the particular passion has as its object an isolated thing which cannot be expressed in the form of a proposition, then we cannot explain in what way conscience can conflict with passion or find that the latter's object was wrong. If the objects of the two faculties are of different types, if they belong to different orders of reality, then we cannot explain, not merely how they could conflict, but how they could be related in any way. In the case to which Socrates refers, of a man thirsty and yet unwilling to drink, it must certainly be admitted that another tendency besides thirst is operative in the man's mind. But we cannot infer that the tendency which opposes drinking is different in kind from the one which urges drinking. Socrates considers that the former must be rational because it has the power of forbidding, that is, of taking into account not merely the object which is desired but also the other faculty which desires it, and the general circumstances of the case. But he himself has to admit that while reason can overcome desire, the reverse is also possible—so that in that case the desire will have forbidden the object of reason and must be considered capable of acting in relation to a complex situation and not merely an isolated particular. If we examine human behaviour without prejudice we find that any tendency which operates, operates in relation to a situation; and not to any simple and separable entity, whether we call it a pure particular or a pure universal. All that this proves is that we have a number of different tendencies, all of which may be described as desires, and that these tendencies are capable of conflict with one another and trying to prevent each other's object from being realised.

This conception of the case, namely, that all the tendencies belong to a single order and have objects of a similar kind, that is, some situation to be brought about—that conception is supported in this discussion of the faculties of the soul by the recognition of the third faculty, spirit or temper. In recognising this faculty and distinguishing it from both desire and reason, Socrates has admitted that what is opposed to desire in a particular case may itself be passionate. If we admit this, then we are admitting the possibility of an activity which exhibits both the character which Socrates has attributed to reason, namely, the ability to weigh up a situation, and the character he has attributed to desire, namely, the determination to bring about a certain object. If then a rational activity may have a particular object, and a passionate activity may take account of the circumstances of the case, it is possible that pure reason and pure desire to which Socrates has previously referred, are arrived at simply by abstraction, that is, by taking separately a number of characters which are found together in ordinary human activity. If Socrates is to prove that there are really three faculties, he would have to indicate a situation in which all three were operating separately, and we could determine what was the contribution of each to the outcome of the situation. But actually Socrates can only compare them two at a time, and even then he cannot clearly show that spirit is ever opposed to reason. We may say therefore that the supposed purely rational activities of the human mind really involve a certain amount of passion or emotion, and that the passionate activities do not make it impossible for us to take account of the facts of a situation. Without denying that a person has different motives, and that some of these may be dominant, and that some may be better than others, we can still object to the classification made by Socrates and to the arrangement of motives in an ascending scale according to the reality possessed by the object in each case. If we deny that there are different degrees of reality, if we assert that all real things are real in precisely the same sense, then we cannot accept either the psychology of Socrates or his ethics.

The account which Socrates gives of the virtues corresponds with the division of mind into faculties. Wisdom is the virtue of reason, courage of spirit, though it participates in reason to a certain extent in that it involves knowledge of what is to be feared and what not; but temperance is not a virtue peculiar to desire, it is a state of harmony among the three faculties such that wisdom rules, spirit carries out the dictates of wisdom, and desire provides the material on which the other faculties are to operate. But even this agreement among the faculties, this subordination of desire to spirit and reason and of spirit itself to reason, implies that the subordinate faculties, including desire, must know that they ought to subordinate themselves and consequently desires would have a certain amount of wisdom. But if we take the division as it stands, if we think of wisdom, courage, temperance as being different sorts of operation, then we seem to have different kinds of goodness. And also if desire and spirit, each in its proper degree, exhibit a certain wisdom which does not amount to the wisdom of which reason is capable, then we seem to have three different types of knowledge, and, correspondingly, of goodness.

Again it has been determined about reason that it ought to rule, but we have not discovered any criterion whereby we can determine whether reason does rule in a particular mind or not, because we have been given no specific information as to what reason seeks, as to what are the good objects which it is a mark of wisdom to pursue. We have simply the vague criterion of harmony, but we have nothing to show how progress towards harmony may be made. Even the account of the form of the good, given in Book VI, does not tell us what particular things are good, and consequently doesn't indicate what reason in the soul, or the ruler in the state, is to aim at. And this same difficulty appears again in Aristotle's *Ethics* where he maintains that if there are legislators who know what is good, then they can train the citizens so as to follow the good, they can impose virtuous habits on the natural desires which men have. But *unless* those wise and good legislators are present, our ethical theory cannot be applied, and it cannot even tell us how to recognise wise and good legislators. Certainly in Book X Aristotle recognises a definitely good life, namely, the speculative life, but he does not apply the results of this view to the detail of his ethics, and as far as that is concerned, it would appear that knowledge is praised not because it is a good thing but because it is a useful thing, that is, because it helps us to arrive at goods which are otherwise determined.

Lecture 73

Consequences of the theory of justice in the state

We have three classes—rulers, warriors and the productive class—and they are all required for the state to be just. But according to the Socratic theory of justice in the soul, it is impossible for members of those classes all to be just since only the ruling class possesses wisdom and wisdom is essential to justice. According to the theory of the state that he has expounded the warriors have learned to act in accordance with wisdom, that is, have come to know what social tendencies to support and what to oppose, but the kind of education they have had doesn't give them an exact understanding of this distinction, they have only been trained in good habits, and while these are preserved, the warriors will not oppose the rulers. But we may ask how this is possible, how the warriors can courageously carry out the tasks imposed by the rulers, when according to the theory of justice in the soul courage is taken to be the virtue of the spirited part of a just man and can operate only in obedience to the wise commands of his own reason and in preventing his own desires becoming insubordinate. (Socrates seems to suggest that warriors don't *possess* reason, but are subjected to the reason of others! Similarly tradesmen have *only* desires! This does away with tripartite division as a psychological theory, and is certainly not what Socrates means to convey, but it is what would appear from a comparison of different parts of his theory.) If the warriors lack wisdom, then they cannot even have the necessary courage. Courage, it should be remembered, is identified by Socrates not with fearlessness but fearing the right things and not being afraid of other things. If the warriors don't have any wisdom of their own, then they will be unable to retain their courage—that is, make the proper distinction between what is and is not to be feared. They will become *rash or foolhardy*, and in that way interfere with the perfect justice of the state.

And again it may be questioned, even in accordance with the theory of virtue expounded by Socrates himself, whether a man can be trained in good habits without acquiring wisdom in the process. This would be possible only if the habits were habits of the body and not of the soul. But if they are habits of the soul, then their exercise involves the recognition of the peculiar characters of different situations, that is, involves understanding.[12] Thus training in good habits is really training in understanding, and the warriors to carry out their functions would have to be wise in the same sense as the rulers.

In the case of the *productive class* we find they are not supposed to have had even the education given to the warriors. All they require to learn apparently, apart from learning their own trade, is to do what the warriors tell

---

[12][JA] Knowledge as discrimination, different reactions to different situations, or reaction to differences. The more differences—or changes—a thing reacts to, the more it knows.

them. But this again would imply that they had intelligence to see the desirability of doing these things, unless we are to presume that they are simply terrorised by the warriors, in which case we could hardly consider they were living a temperate life, even apart from consideration of the Socratic theory that true temperance is only to be found in the just soul (similarly true courage), that is, in the soul which has both wisdom and courage. If we say the tradesmen lack wisdom and even good habits, that they have had no real training in virtue, then we will have to admit there is a constant tendency on their part to break the laws of the state. And even if they don't actually break them, there will be constant friction in keeping them subordinated. This seems to be admitted by Socrates when he says that the meaner desires of the many are held down by the virtuous desires and wisdom of the few (Book IV, §431). This holding down can hardly be called *agreement* as to who are to be the rulers, so that we come to the final conclusion that, unless the trading class are also wise, they are not even temperate. Or if we attempt to apply the theory of the just soul to the theory of the just state we are bound to come to the conclusion that only that state can be just in which all the members are wise, that is, in which there are no such distinctions of function as are here alleged.

All these difficulties are connected with the general difficulty of treating the state or the soul as a hierarchy of functions, and in general with the conception of a supreme function which is the reality of any particular thing, and to which all its other functions must be subordinated. We can criticise his position on this question in the same way as the Eleatics criticised the Pythagorean position, that is, if we are going to admit a supreme function, then we cannot allow of the existence of any other function of the thing, and that means we cannot even distinguish the thing itself from the supreme function it is supposed to have. So we are brought back in this case to the ideal or form of man or justice, without being able to fill it in in detail. Even then we have the further difficulty that in recognising these many forms which all partake in being or which are all subordinated to the form of the good, we are forced to deny the existence of anything but the ultimate being, and we cannot justify our description of it as *good*. It is from the recognition of some of these difficulties that Aristotle in his *Ethics* criticises this conception of *the form of the good* and insists on discussing a good really obtainable by men. *The form of the good* being quite apart from human life cannot give us any information about the regulation of human life. It may be said in criticism of Aristotle that his objections to the form of the good are formulated in such a way as to imply there is no such thing as universal goodness, and not merely ultimate goodness, and this is connected with the fact that Aristotle thinks that each particular thing or species has its own good which may have nothing in common with that of any other species. Aristotle's own conception of happiness is itself a vague way of conceiving this good in the case of the human species. And his theory showed that he himself is partly under the influence of the Socratic theory of natural kinds—that the reality of a thing is its end or what it aims at, and this is how goodness in the case of that thing, is to be understood. And we find Aristotle also adopts in his own particular way the theory that virtue is knowledge, that though he emphasises even more than Socrates the distinction between habit and understanding, and correspondingly goodness of character and intellect, he really derives his views on this question from the *Republic*, and continues to think, as Socrates had done, that knowledge is of the utmost importance in the good life.

We may say, as regards the Socratic doctrine that virtue is knowledge, that the arguments by which he supports it really only go to show that ethics is a science (unless, as above suggested, we treat knowledge as equalling habit, and in that case vice also would be knowledge). He opposes the sophistic theory that goodness is relative and that we cannot make any statements about good activities conformable to those which the pre-Socratics make about physical activities. The sophists denied not merely that there was a *nature* of absolute character of human things but even that there was a nature of things in general. On this view not only could there not be a rigorous ethical science but there could not be a rigorous physical science. And Socrates in supporting the demands of science attacked them on the ground where they considered themselves strongest, that is, human behaviour, and pointed out that even the statements the sophists made implied there were ethical realities and that these could be known. But the possibility of ethical science, of knowing what is good, does not imply that goodness itself in any way consists in or depends on our knowing it. And again the practical outlook, in which a particular end is chosen and we take steps to bring it about, is also supposed to be of the greatest importance for ethics. Ethics is supposed to be specially concerned with ends, and goodness is taken as the characteristic of an end, as being that for the sake of which something is pursued, instead of simply being a quality of certain processes or activities whether it is pursued or not.

V
Aristotle's Nicomachean Ethics

Lecture 74

Aristotle—ethical theory—the good life as that which is aimed at

We find that Aristotle at the very beginning of the *Ethics* formulates a theory of goodness in terms of ends or things pursued. From that point of view, the good life is that which men aim at, though we have to make a distinction between better and worse aims, the criterion being whether or not we are satisfied with the object of our pursuit when we attain it. But just like Socrates, Aristotle thinks of the good for man as being something which he can consistently pursue throughout his life. This in itself creates a logical difficulty. If we define good as something aimed at, then we are defining it in a relative way, and it does not seem possible on that basis to determine precisely what goodness is. If on the other hand we begin by considering what things are good, whether pursued or not, then we could go on to consider how these good things come about. But even that will not be strictly a part of ethical theory, it will be an application of it. Ethics itself will be concerned only with what things are good. When we have defined good as something pursued, we naturally think of it as something capable of giving satisfaction, and also as something about which deliberation will take place. But if we approach the subject without that prejudice, we might find it possible for a person to be good even though he did not take any special thought about his activities and in particular about whether they were good or not, and even though he did not look for any satisfaction from having these activities. If we consider then general activities of men, we find that the objects they have in view are for the most part external to the men themselves—a view which is supported by Butler's theory of particular passions, which aim at producing certain results without considering whether these will have the further result of bringing pleasure to the doer. And though, in the course of experience, we can determine what effects the attainment of particular objects will have on us, it remains true that for the most part we pay attention to these objects and don't think about their effects on our minds. If this is so, and if goodness is to be regarded as characteristic of what is pursued, then we would have to regard all sorts of situations in "the external world", situations which have no mental character, as being good. But on the other hand we do commonly assume, in speaking about goodness, that it is something which belongs to minds (or to the life of the mind) and not to other things.

Accordingly it would seem desirable to recognise that goodness is not defined as being an end, and that as far as our general activities are concerned their goodness does not depend on the goodness of the things they bring about. From that point of view if the term *virtue* is retained, it will mean the sort of activity which is itself good (or which is in *harmony* with good activities?) whether the results it brings about are themselves good or not, and not that kind of activity which brings about good, whether it itself is good or not.

Having taken goodness to be some end, Aristotle inquires what is the supreme end at which men may aim, and defines it as "happiness". This term *happiness* is an ambiguous one. According to Aristotle it is not to be confused with pleasure, that is, he does not adopt the theory of the utilitarians who identify happiness with pleasure. But this does not mean that his own theory is not, strictly speaking, a utilitarian one; or that what John Stuart Mill means by *pleasure* is not largely similar to Aristotle's *happiness*. The main difficulty is that Aristotle regards happiness as an activity, that is, not as something which is merely received by the mind, a final result beyond which it is impossible to go, but as a way in which the mind behaves and which is capable of producing further results. But Mill and Aristotle agree in that they regard happiness as something to be aimed at, and that they consider that for that reason it is ethically important, that is, they are both utilitarians because they adopt the principle of utility—they regard the relation of means to an end as of supreme importance in human life. They make a division among human activities, some of which are to be estimated by the character which they have and not by the effects which they produce, while others are to be estimated by their effects and not at all by their characters. In fact deliberation is a human activity which is defined in these theories entirely by the effects which it produces, its own character is considered to be that of aiming at something else. Obviously no human activity can be defined by its relation to other things. It must have some characters of its own, and in virtue of these characters it could be said to be either good or bad without reference to what it was going to produce.[1] Aristotle and Mill also agree in taking happiness as something *final*, the state of *happiness* is that in which we are quite satisfied and don't desire anything else. This is a negative definition. It doesn't tell us any of the positive characteristics of happiness and consequently it cannot tell us whether or not that happiness is good. In connection with this question Aristotle criticises the theory of goodness which was current in the Platonic school and appears in the *Republic*. Is there such a thing as the *Form of the Good*, that is, as a universal and absolute goodness? And he arrives at the conclusion that there cannot be, that there can only be a good for man.

In so far as his arguments are directed against *the form of the good* as an entity apart from all other things, and as a thing which the whole world aims at[2] his criticism may be accepted. But if we carry them to their logical conclusion, we find that the denial of *the form of the good* involves the denial of particular ends or special functions of particular things. If we once grant that every real thing has an end and this end presides over the thing and directs its operations, then we are bound to formulate the theory of an ultimate end which equally presides over all these particular ends. And if we likewise reject *the form of the good* because it is apart from any particular thing, we would be bound to reject a *human* good conceived in a similar way. Aristotle does insist on finding goodness in particular human activities and not above them, but he retains from the Socratic theory the conception of this goodness as an end and the conception of it as simple. Apart from the theory of forms there is no reason

---

[1] [JA] Good things can cause bad. That is, acting on a "bad character", good activities can occasion a bad activity in reaction to them. Hence communication does not mean that goods cause goods, only and always; *or* that goods are caused by goods, only and always.

[2] [JA] The col... [unclear] of the universe! [Ed.:] JA's manuscript in this sentence literally reads "the whole wld aims at". The student notes here have "the whole would aim at".

for thinking that goods form a *totality*—and that there is any supreme good. But it is just this supreme good which the term happiness is intended to convey. If we take goodness simply as a quality of human activities, then we would expect to find that there are many different good activities and that the goods of which one man is capable are quite different from those of which another is capable, so that there can be no *good for man* acting as a standard to which every particular man has to conform. And this is the objection to any system of moral rules or precepts. The notion that certain acts are commanded implies that all men are equally capable of performing these acts, but if we have any positive theory of goods and if we recognise as a definitely good activity the production of beautiful works of art, we cannot say that this is obligatory on men, because we know that some men are not capable of producing these. But this does not imply that these men are not perfectly capable of entering on other good activities. The conclusion would be that there is not any single sort of life which is capable of being described as the good life. (The only *command* could be "do good": *cf.*, Kant.) But on the other hand all the various activities which we call good must be good in the same sense. And as far as it has that implication, as far as it implies that good must have a single definition if it means anything at all, the Socratic theory of forms is to be supported against Aristotle's criticisms. Aristotle actually criticises the theory on the ground that the term *good* is applied to qualities and relations as well as to substances, and that it cannot possibly be applied to all of these in the same sense. But if this is so, then we don't really have a single term *good* but we have many terms for all of which the same word is employed. The question will be then to determine which of these terms is relevant to ethics, and we have no reason for supposing that they all are. But even if they all were, we would require to distinguish one from another and, if we continued to call one *good*, to find other names for the others. The fact is, however, that it is owing to *confusion* that *good* has come to be used in all these ways and that if we understand it correctly, we will apply it only in one way (that is, as a character of things) and reject the other uses entirely.

Lecture 75

Aristotle continued—emphasis on the practical and achievement of happiness

Aristotle is concerned in the *Ethics* with actual goodness and the ways in which it can appear in actual things. Though this way of looking at the matter makes it possible to have a positive science of ethics, it is also connected with a certain confused conception of ethics whereby it is regarded as a peculiarly *practical* science—it being considered that we study ethics not merely in order to know what goodness is but in order to bring it about. As far as this distinction is concerned, we should not be able to base on it any real distinction between practical and other sciences. Any science whatever may be studied for a certain purpose (even "the acquisition of knowledge", which is as much a "particular", "practical" object as anything else). We may study mathematics because we wish to solve engineering problems but this does not make mathematics a practical science. Our purpose in studying it does not enter into the science itself, and unless we could study it objectively without reference to what we are going to do with the knowledge once we obtained it, we could never really obtain it. If we allowed our purposes to affect our mathematical beliefs, we would introduce confusion into the science. What we require is to be able to give a mathematical proof of certain propositions. In the same way with ethics, if we are to be able to use ethical knowledge in order to bring about certain results, we must *have* that ethical knowledge, that is, we must have discovered certain propositions which are true in exactly the same sense as those of mathematics are true. Certainly if we are to be able to apply our ethical beliefs, they must deal with actual things with which we come into practical relations, but there is nothing in the study of ethics itself to say how the propositions which it embodies are to be applied. This emphasis on the practical aspect encourages Aristotle to adopt the rough and ready criterion of happiness and in general to think that ethics is concerned with ends or with things that can be brought about by calculation. It is quite legitimate to ask how far calculation can assist us in bringing about good things, but we cannot *approach* ethics from that point of view. We must first of all have inquired in a quite detached manner what things are good.

Again, Aristotle's treatment of goodness as having several meanings is connected with this theory of ends and also with his general logical and psychological views. We find that in this discussion goodness is regarded in three distinct ways. In accordance with the opening statement and with the theory of voluntary action worked out in Book III, we have good practically identified with what is aimed at, that is, what a man thinks good and what he aims at are treated as absolutely equivalent. But among these aims some are higher than others and in order to make that distinction we would have to use *good* in a different sense—of "that which is capable of giving the most complete satisfaction". And it is from that point of view that goodness is identified with happiness. It is thought of, that is, not simply as something aimed at but as something the securing of which would leave us perfectly satisfied, so that we should not require to aim at anything else. And yet the supremely good state is regarded by Aristotle as being necessarily an activity. Happiness, he says, must be regarded as an activity—we do not call a man happy unless he is exercising his faculties in some way, namely, in the way which brings him the greatest satisfaction. But if the man is active, he must be aiming at certain things: he cannot be completely satisfied. (Though here the notion of good as activity which *sustains itself,* a way of living in which we can *continue*, is shadowed forth. Even so, that is a formal distinction, and one which (a) doesn't of itself tell us what is good, and which we discover only after knowing goods; (b) is not properly led up to as the *limit* of a series of things which *don't* "completely satisfy", that is *sustain themselves.*) And this is connected with the fact that whereas things aimed at are in general not mental at all, that which can be called *good* must be mental, and could quite well not have been aimed at. The assumption is that whatever is aimed at by any particular thing must for that reason be estimated to be superior to the thing itself. It is suggested that what is pursued must always be better than the pursuit of it, since, unless this was taken for granted, the pursuit would not take place. But this view depends entirely on the identification of goodness with an end and when we recognise that certain mental activities are good, if we are not dominated by this theory of ends we may quite well consider that the things that these mental activities bring about are not good at all.

This way of regarding goodness as belonging to things in virtue of their own characters is what is required to justify the view that certain mental activities are good. But it is not in accordance with the identification of good with the object of desire. Again, in comparing certain different objects of desire, so as to find what is the highest or most satisfactory, we have according to Aristotle to rely on the opinions of the *wise and good*. This means that we are using goodness in a third sense, and that this would be the fundamental sense, that it would be that by reference to which other forms of goodness could be estimated. The question then is, how is the goodness of a particular activity related to the goodness of a man who is given this superior position? We find that Aristotle's definition of happiness is that it is an activity of the soul according to goodness[3] and if there are more kinds of good than one, in accordance with that which is best and most complete—all that is what Aristotle calls the good for man. Unless this is a circular definition, we must be using good in two different senses.

We have to inquire what is this goodness with which the activity is to be in accordance. And we find that Aristotle defines it as a certain condition of soul. He distinguishes between three features of the soul—feelings, capacities and conditions. And he argues that goodness, that is, that which entitles us to speak about a *good man*, cannot be either a feeling or a capacity, but must be a condition. Apart from the question of how it is shown not to be a feeling or a capacity there is a difficulty in treating it as a condition, similar to the difficulty in treating happiness in the same way. As Aristotle says, we do not call a man happy when he is asleep. Similarly we cannot call him good when he is asleep. If he is to be described as good, it must be in virtue of his activities, and we cannot distinguish between

---

[3] [JA] Peters: "excellence" in contrast with Burnet's "goodness". *The Nicomachean Ethics of Aristotle*. by F. H. Peters, Oxford; London: Kegan Paul, 1881.

the condition which makes certain activities possible and the activities themselves. The condition, if it really belongs to the mind in question, must actively appear. We find, then, that it is impossible to maintain the distinction between a good condition of soul and a good activity of the soul. And so the definition of the *activity* as being in accordance with the *condition* really gives us no information. What Aristotle would have to show would be that certain activities are called *good* in virtue of having some definite characteristics, but these characteristics must appear in the activities themselves. That is, they cannot be anything static on which the activities could be based or by which the activities could be measured. To make it possible for them to measure activities, they must themselves belong to the same realm of existence. Now in addition to this criticism it is possible to criticise Aristotle's arguments to show that goodness cannot consist of feeling. Aristotle says that we are not praised or blamed for our feelings, but only for having these feelings in a certain way. A man is not blamed for anger alone, but only for being angry to a particular extent and under particular circumstances. But even under those circumstances, what is regarded as blameworthy is the particular feeling exhibited. We cannot really distinguish between feeling and *feeling in a certain way*, because every feeling must be of a certain kind, it must have various special characteristics, such that it is possible to distinguish one feeling of anger, for example, from another, even though we admit that they are both called anger in the same sense. So it is quite possible that we should regard one species of anger as blameworthy and another as praiseworthy. It is also possible that we should reject Aristotle's simple statement—unsupported by evidence—that anger as such is not blameworthy, and consider that in every case anger is bad. It is certainly impossible to solve ethical problems simply by taking all the judgments of praise and blame that people pass and trying to make a coherent system out of them. We can only obtain a coherent ethics by considering not what everybody believes but which are the facts themselves, what are the real characteristics of our feelings and what differentiates one group from another. We find then that Aristotle's views are largely determined by the peculiarities of his logical and psychological theories with their distinction between activities and passivities, capacities and conditions, instead of dealing with the positive characteristics of the various processes which we are investigating.

Lecture 76

Aristotle continued—the theory of the mean

Right mean. Aristotle's theory of the mean as determining the goodness of actions is connected both with Pythagorean theories in general and with the Socratic theory of the relation of virtue to knowledge, that is, in the notion of the right mean we have a recurrence of the Pythagorean conception of configuration. According to the Pythagoreans goodness in the soul, just like health in the body, consists in a correct arrangement of the elements of the soul. Aristotle's view of what these elements are differs from the Pythagorean view. From the Pythagoreans we obtain only the theory of the parts of the soul, a theory which is worked out in detail in the *Republic.* The right condition of the soul is that in which these parts are placed in a certain order, where desire is subordinated to spirit and spirit to reason. And though he gives many practical illustrations of his views, the theory of Socrates does not appear to go much beyond this Pythagorean basis. Aristotle on the other hand had worked out a detailed psychological theory, and it is in relation to this theory, or to as much of it as he considers fits his present purpose, that he formulates his theory of the right mean.

As we saw, he makes a distinction in enumerating the features of mental life between feelings, capacities and conditions. And from his theory of the good for man we can see that he further distinguishes *activities* from all of these. Not only is it difficult to justify these distinctions, even if we allow that some distinction among mental faculties must be made, but Aristotle's formulation of the question also introduces ambiguity into his conception of goodness which, as we have seen, is associated at one time with activity and at another with the condition or state of the soul, and again is taken to be specially related to desire or appetition.

Aristotle himself has pointed out that we don't ordinarily consider a condition to be of any value unless it is actively manifested. But it may be further contended that unless it is active, it is not truly to be regarded as a condition of the soul. We certainly do not expect to see any individual engaging in all his activities at the same time, but it is possible for us, if we take a sufficiently broad view, to see how a number of distinguishable activities contribute to some wider activity including them all. It is ethically important to take this wider view, because it is possible to divide up a person's activities into such small parts that any one of these taken by itself couldn't be called good. But even though these are all the parts it is not possible to infer that the person has no good activities at all, because the parts don't exist separately but in certain series and arrangements, and when we take a number of activities together in that way, it is possible to find qualities which we should have overlooked if we had simply taken the parts separately.

In connection with this possibility of division, Aristotle considers whether anything short of a complete life can be called good. It is possible that a life might be good up to a point but that after that point it might become bad. Now does this mean, Aristotle asks, that until a life is completed, we cannot pass judgment upon it? If that were so, we could only judge that a life was good when it had ceased, and therefore ceased to be good. Secondly, in order to judge it good, we have to refer to certain characteristics which could just as easily be exhibited in particular activities as in a whole life. Thus it seems to be possible to have judgments of goodness only if we can refer to specific activities which, if we like, we can call *ways of life*, but not to life as a whole. The conclusion is, then, that it is certain human activities that are called good, whether or not these activities cease at a certain point and give way to something which is bad. The difficulty that arises on this question is due to Aristotle's treatment of good in terms of means and end, and his consequent formulation of a complete good which would be the ultimate end. The assumption is that if there are goods, there must be a best, and that it is in relation to that thing which is best that anything supposed to be good has to be judged. But this would mean that nothing is really good but the best—a view which is illogical since unless we know what is really good, we cannot know what is best; and since also, in order that there should be a best, there must be many goods; and likewise a view which implies that goodness is actually unattainable in human life, that is, which is subject to criticisms similar to those brought by Aristotle against the Socratic theory of *the form of the good*. A similar difficulty appears in Utilitarianism, where *the good* is taken to be the greatest possible pleasure and to be the only thing ultimately worth pursuing. But if it were attainable at all, it could only be by the pursuit of particular pleasures, and secondly there is nothing to show that there is such a thing as the greatest possible pleasures. (*Logic* as studying the sort of things that can be and the sort of things that *can't* be: for example, "averages".) In the same way we couldn't show that there is such a thing as complete happiness or, in general, that any theory of goods implies the conception of a superior good. By an exactly similar argument it might be contended that because some distances are greater than others, there must be a greatest distance, and it is in some such sense that the term *infinity* is often used, infinity being taken to be the actual measure of the greatest distance; whereas what the use of the term implies is precisely that there is *no* greatest distance. It cannot be said then that if a number of things are good and some are better than others, there must be something which is better than all others.

This conception of completeness is connected with the conception of good as something to be pursued, and so also is the conception of the right mean. It is asserted or implied that goodness arises as a result of our taking up some attitude or entering into some course of activity, and the question to be considered is whether this is the best possible course to pursue or not, that is, Aristotle makes the assumption that because moralists deliberate about goodness, therefore the person who is actually behaving well must also deliberate about goodness. That is, he approaches the view of Socrates that in order that ethics should be a science, virtue must be knowledge. And he considers that if any person performs virtuous actions, then if he has not deliberated about these himself, it can only be because he has been trained by someone who has, that is, that he has been taught good habits without understanding them. But this training is also considered to be necessary for the development of understanding, and virtue is considered to be incomplete until understanding has been developed. Aristotle supports this view by distinguishing between goodness of character and goodness of intellect—a distinction which he connects with that current in the Platonic school between the rational and the irrational parts of the soul. But just as there is reason for doubting the correctness of this division in the soul, so there is reason for doubting the correctness of the distinction between goodness of character and goodness of intellect. In the first place a man's intellect is just as much a part of his character as anything else and consequently his goodness in that direction will belong to the same category as any other goodness he may exhibit. But in the second place, if Aristotle means by goodness of intellect what is ordinarily conveyed by the expression, that is, if he means being *good at thinking*, then he is using the term goodness in the relative sense and not in the strictly ethical sense. In so far as intellect is a part of a man's character, it will be capable of being judged good or not good in the absolute or ethical sense. But there is no reason for passing that judgment from the mere fact that a man is good at thinking—and not even if he happens to be good at thinking about ethics.

Lecture 77

Aristotle continued—goodness of character

Aristotle distinguishes between goodness of character and goodness of intellect in a way which would not be possible if the term were applied in a single and unambiguous sense. If there is anything good in intellectual activity, then that will be a part of goodness of character. On the other hand, if a good intellect is simply one that produces certain results, then it is not good in the ethical sense. So that all that can be justified by the argument as far as it has gone, is a reference to goodness of character, and even that, if we take other parts of Aristotle's argument into account, should really be expressed as goodness of activity, and this activity, as we have seen, might quite well be considered to take an emotional form. In emphasising the question of character, Aristotle is thinking particularly about education. The good character is the one which is produced by training, and we more naturally think of the object of training as a general state or quality of the mind than as any particular activity. But this distinction is really an incorrect one—we certainly cannot select one particular act as being what the training was for, but we can take as the object and result of training a whole series or class of acts which would not have been possible if the training had not taken place. We certainly cannot say that a person has been properly trained unless he not merely can but *does* enter upon these activities. And similarly we cannot speak of his character as something lying behind his activities, it simply is his activities considered as a system. Aristotle's emphasis on character, which is to be the result of training, is connected with his theory of the importance of *knowledge* in goodness, just as it was in the theory of Socrates. Good habits are produced by the teaching of some person who knows what is good. Regularity of behaviour (it seems to be argued) is something inconceivable apart from knowledge and intention, just as Socrates had argued (as indicated in the *Phaedo*) that we could only have regularity in nature, if things were arranged for the best. So that we could conceive the creator of nature as having endowed it with good habits. While the importance of mind and knowledge as securing regularity is thus emphasised, Aristotle also emphasises its importance for the opposite reason, namely, that in different circumstances, different kinds of action are required, and that therefore for true goodness we require knowledge of the situation and of that which precisely fits the situation. Mere habit would not be sufficient, for certain minor differences would be overlooked, and what was exactly fitting, what precisely struck the right mean, would be neglected. Taking this position in general as suggesting a contrast between mind and nature, we can say that if there is such a thing as nature at all, if there are definite things in the world, then they must always act in accordance with their character and also in accordance with the situation in which they find themselves (that is, with *what* and *where* they are: the thing's *situation* being its *subject* and *character* its *predicate*: that is, things *act* as middle terms). So that we cannot say that mind is required unless we are prepared to deny that there is anything at all which is not mind, and we cannot say that this reaction to circumstances, this preservation of a persistent character by acting differently in different situations, is anything peculiar to goodness. The general position is that if there are definite goods in existence, they will have definite ways of acting, and that these ways will be different in different circumstances, but that there is nothing in all this which specially implies knowledge, and certainly nothing which implies knowledge of what is good. And, moreover, there is nothing to show that the mode of reaction which is good under certain circumstances can always be described as action in a mean.

Aristotle's theory of a mean is connected both with the Pythagorean theory of configurations and also with the Socratic theory of definition and with the Socratic method generally. Goodness, Aristotle seems to say, is a certain arrangement of elements, a certain configuration of feelings and acts which together make up a good whole. But there is nothing in this to tell us what things particularly are good. The theory of configuration is one which applies to anything which exists, and unless we are going to say that good things have certain peculiar characters, the doctrine of the mean will not help us, because what is bad will exhibit configuration of the same order. In fact Aristotle seems to some extent to adopt the Pythagorean view that only what is good or harmonious has complete reality and that other things fail to arrive at complete reality. But this is really to divide reality into parts (N.B. if there cannot be *parts* of reality, there cannot be a *whole*, reality is not a *thing*) which afterwards cannot be connected, as the Eleatic criticisms show. Now if as a matter of fact we give any definition of what is good, if we show precisely what distinguishes it from what is not good, then we are at the same time showing quite as definitely what is opposed to good, as what goodness itself is.

Lecture 78

Aristotle continued—theory of action in a mean continued—ways of acting—emphasis on activities

This theory of action in a mean, or of determining what is the right configuration or arrangement, that is, on what arrangement virtue is based, is in accordance with the Socratic theory of virtue, but is somewhat more fully worked out, and just because it is more fully worked out, its defects become more apparent. Socrates, discussing what is meant by particular virtues, argues that the distinguishing mark of virtuous conduct in any sphere is precise knowledge. As we saw in the *Euthyphro* he points out that in piety we have a division of acts into those which are pious and those which are not pious, and the question is how we are to distinguish between the two, and he argues that it is by finding some characteristic which belongs to all pious acts and to no acts which are not pious. The definition of piety so obtained is important precisely because it enables us in any particular case to determine whether piety is present or absent. In the same way, in regard to courage, Socrates contends that this consists in drawing an exact distinction between what is to be feared and what is not to be feared. We can assume that things are divided into things to be feared and things not to be feared, and the courageous man is the man who knows where to draw the line. If he draws it in another place, then he has not true courage. If he does not fear some things he should fear, he is rash or foolhardy: but if he fears things which should not be feared, he is a coward. (That is, the rash man *extends* the class of things not to be feared beyond the proper limit, the opposite for the coward.) In accordance with this way of expressing the matter, we could say that courage is a mean, and the "right mean" in the case of courage is the right distinction between what is to be feared and what is not to be feared; what is dangerous and what is not. Now as regards this division, it may be pointed out that we still have the confusion between ethical theory and moral behaviour. It would seem natural to say that a courageous man is one who *is not* afraid of anything of which he should not be afraid, and *is* afraid of all the things of which he should be afraid, assuming that there are such things. But it is another matter to say that a courageous man *knows* what he ought and what he ought not to fear. It is quite possible that without having formulated any theory on the subject, he is so constituted that he reacts directly to each situation as it arises (though this would be opposed to knowledge as discrimination—here knowledge is taken as judgment or, more precisely, as being able to *say* what we know). On the other hand, it is equally possible that a man who recognises that a certain thing should not be feared may nevertheless be unable to prevent himself from fearing it. Socrates thinks this impossible only because he identifies regularity of behaviour with knowledge. The point being that if we know certain things (regularities) by acting in certain ways, we don't therefore know *that way of acting.* But if there are any things whatever that do not have knowledge, they must nevertheless have a certain character or constitution, and in virtue of that character, they must act with a certain regularity. If this were not so, no science of nature would be possible, and the only real things would be those things which had knowledge. Now we find in Aristotle the similar assumption that regularity of behaviour is induced by knowledge, that is, is the result of training. But whatever it is the result of, this regularity, according to the theory of habituation, need not imply knowledge on the part of the agent itself. And consequently we are forced to admit the occurrence of regular behaviour without knowledge on the part of the thing which is behaving. And we find that at a later stage Aristotle suggests that knowledge or thinking is required in order to meet different situations in different ways (universals as differences). But this again will be true of anything whatever which has a definite constitution, granted that it *does* enter into different situations. So that the first difficulty in regard to the theory of the mean is that no reference to knowledge is required.

In the second place, as Aristotle admits, there are certain kinds of activity which do not admit of a mean (which are always blameworthy, for example), and in regard to the particular question of fear, it may quite well be considered that there is nothing which ought to be feared, that fear, even if we cannot prevent its occurrence, is always an evil. But this question is obscured by the theory of the mean, and it must be so because it indicates that that theory is incorrect. Now Aristotle carries the theory even further than Socrates had done. Not only has it to be determined what are the things to be feared and what not to be feared, but in the case of those things which are to be feared we have to determine what is the right amount of fear to feel under those circumstances. There will be a certain amount which will be too much and a certain amount too little, and between these we find the right amount of fear—that which is appropriate to the occasion. The same applies to anger and all the other feelings that we can have, allowing, as even Aristotle admits, that there are a few exceptions in the form of feelings which are always excessive or defective.

We find that having formulated the theory of the right mean, Aristotle is unable to apply it exactly to any situation, to show, in other words, how definite ethical results may be derived from it. He has to say that the mean can be determined only in relation to the particular situation, and that the right mean is the one which the wise man would consider right. So that, as far as ethics is concerned, we, unless we are wise men, are still left in a position in which we can only apply guesswork. Now Aristotle tries to argue that the indefiniteness of the mean is something peculiar to moral behaviour. He says that if 10 is much and 2 is little, we take 6 as the mean in relation to the object, for 6 exceeds and is exceeded by an equal number and is therefore the arithmetical mean. But it is different, he says, in relation to ourselves: if 10 pounds of meat are too much for a man to eat and 2 pounds too little, it does not follow that 6 pounds will be the correct amount. But it has to be pointed out that the same applies to any particular case whether we ourselves are concerned in it or not. The fact that 10 is considered much and 2 little, would not imply that 6 would be considered neither too much nor too little. Any number whatever between 10 and 2 could be the correct answer here. Of course if we are asked to find the arithmetical mean between 10 and 2, there will only be one correct answer—6. But that will also be the correct answer if we ask a similar question about pounds of meat. So Aristotle has not succeeded in proving that the mean has any special relation to ourselves or that there is any special ethical importance in describing certain feelings or actions as excessive or defective.

Now Aristotle goes on to consider in detail how the mean is to be attained, and he puts forward certain general rules which cannot from the nature of the case be quite exact, but which are important from his point of view as showing the necessity of deliberation. The mean is something that we have to deliberate about, and similarly we have to deliberate about means to ends. That is, the term *mean* appears to be used in two different senses in these two cases, but there are certain common features. We can select the means which is the right one relatively to a given end. Also we can find that there are a number of necessary features of anything which is to be capable of leading up to an end. We may find that in selecting a means to an end we have failed to provide for some particular necessity, that is, the means we have chosen is too little. On the other hand, we may provide for something which is not really required and which we were not particularly aiming at, and in that case we were selecting something excessive, always granted that we have a specific end in view. In that case we can do either too much or too little to bring it about.[4]

Now as regards this possibility we have to recognise that Aristotle's division is not exact, since the very same act or means might be both excessive and defective. It is almost bound to be excessive, because in any act whatever that we propose to do, there are always, when it comes about, features which we did not anticipate, and in many cases, these are such that, if we had known about them in advance, we would have chosen some other course. (Of course Aristotle admits that fuller knowledge—"the wise man"—is required for selection: but even the wise man doesn't know "all" the results and "all" the possibilities.) But also, besides exhibiting these superfluous features, the particular line of action entered upon may be in certain respects insufficient to bring about the desired result. Exactly the same applies to the Socratic theory of courage, that is, it is quite possible that the same person should fear things which he ought not to fear and not fear things which he ought to fear. So that

---
[4][JA] Ambiguity here? So *much* that we *don't* bring it about: or that we bring about so much *more*—which interferes with our plans?

his behaviour would have to be said to be *both* excessive and defective. (But not at the same time? Yes, quite possibly. This applies at least to "drawing the right line": we can draw it in several different places.) In other words, we cannot think of modes of action as forming a single series from the greatest to the least in respect of some special feature. But we find them varying in a number of different directions. So that the notion of drawing a line of division turns out not to be a perfect illustration by any means. (But who used it?)

Now the practical rules which Aristotle gives for attaining the mean depend on this notion of a continuous series. Of the two extremes (which are either just as "total" or "individual" as the mean: *or* can be extreme in both directions at once) we generally find one to be further away from the mean than the other, and that is the one we ought to be most on our guard against. (The theory of *safety* or protection.) In the second place, we find that our natural tendencies may be stronger in one of the two directions, and in the third place we may find that one of the two extremes is more associated with pleasure. And for these reasons also we ought to be more on our guard against that particular extreme. But when all these things have been allowed for, the exact mean is by no means (!) determined, and we can only react as directly as we can to each particular case. So that this quantitative way of expressing things is actually taken as a reason for not giving exact qualitative distinctions which would be the only way in which the science of ethics could really progress.[5]

Lecture 79

Aristotle continued—comparisons with Bishop Butler's sermons

Aristotle's theory of deliberation is connected with this view that goodness is a matter of calculation, that it is something which specially concerns an agent, and that if we do not think of it in action, then we can neither be regarded as behaving morally nor as being sound moral theorists. In acts of will which are those acts in which we weigh up a situation and act in accordance with what we find it to be, there are,

---

[5][JA] Note how... [unclear] has to fall back on ... [unclear], authority, for example, when it tries to be definite: availing itself of "the ideal" as guarding against any accusation of being merely quantitative!

Aristotle considers, two distinct elements. (Another dualism.) There is the element of deliberation which is intellectual, and which is concerned with the selection of means, and there is the element of wish, which is appetitive and not intellectual, and which selects the end. There can, Aristotle asserts, be no deliberation about ends, but only about means to ends, because in order to formulate a new end, we would require to have a new wish which was directed to that end. It may be argued that both of these distinctions are incorrect, that is, the distinction between the appetitive and intellectual factors in the mind, and the distinction between means and ends. It has to be admitted that in a particular case we may have a means to a given end, but it does not follow that that means can never be an end (for example, that we could have selected it as a *means* at all, unless we had had it as an end: *cf.*, Butler on interested and disinterested), or that that end can never be a means. Actual experience would suggest that this is not so, but that what is a means at one time is an end at another, and *vice versa*. It also shows that the ends we have in view vary at different times and at different periods of our lives. If this were not so, the training which Aristotle refers to would be ineffective. All that it could do would be to make us better at calculating, but the fundamental direction of our outlook would remain unaffected—we should really have the same ends in view from first to last. (Of course it might be argued that education shows us what are our ultimate ends, or *is* our ultimate end. But this does not get over the fact that we come to *want* things we didn't want before, and the same criticisms as before of "happiness" or "single function" remain in force.) This is not so, as we can see from experience. And thus we cannot make the required distinction between means and ends. Similarly we cannot make the distinction between appetite and intellect, since as we also saw in connection with the Socratic theory in the *Republic*, if it is to be possible to bring the aims of two faculties into relation, these aims must be of the same order. They must all aim at some *situation*, and if the fact that they can take that situation into account would justify us in describing them all as intellectual, the fact that they *aim* at these situations, or *strive* to bring them about, would justify us in calling them all appetitive. Now if we take this view, if we reject the distinction that Aristotle has made, we may likewise reject his description of the objects of wish as good because they are ultimate. We find in fact that when goodness is discussed in relation to our aims and pursuits, an ambiguity invariably creeps in, the term *good* being applied indifferently to what we aim at and to our aiming at it. Now if we are to have a definite ethical science, we cannot use the term goodness in this double sense. And we find that when Aristotle discusses the goodness of the contemplative life, he considers it to be good, not in virtue of its being pursued or of any relation that we have to it, but in virtue of its own characters. But if this is to be the method of ethics, namely, inquiry into the characters of things and pointing out which are good and which are not, then the question of pursuit or aiming at things is one which need not arise. Aristotle has deliberately set out to find how goodness may be promoted. But in the first place, that is not strictly a part of ethics itself, and secondly it can only be determined if we already know what goodness is, or what things are good. And the confusion which is present throughout the argument, between the attitude of the moral theorist and that of the person behaving morally, would justify us in casting a certain doubt on Aristotle's conclusion that the theoretical life is the best one. Not, of course, in doubting that theoretical activity is a good thing, but only whether Aristotle clearly conceived what its goodness consisted in.

Comparisons of Socratic and Aristotelean Ethical Views with Bishop Butler.

Butler in his *Sermons on Human Nature* takes a view of moral behaviour which very closely resembles the views of Socrates and Aristotle. Like them he considers that thinking about goodness and acting well are closely connected. And like Socrates again he thinks that goodness in men consists in their realising their true nature. And further like both his predecessors he thinks that there is an end which all pursue and which can be described as happiness. But in his theory of *conscience*, granted that it is defective in certain respects, he makes allowance for certain points overlooked or controverted by Socrates and Aristotle, and he prepares the way for a more positive theory of ethical truths. The faculty of conscience is not one which is primarily concerned with action, in the sense of being an agency. What it does, according to Butler, is to approve or disapprove of the actions of other faculties, that is, what it does, though primarily in relation to the actions of the person whose conscience it is, is to pass moral judgments which will be either true or false, and on the basis of which we might be able to build up a definite ethical science. And this conscience is also something which everybody possesses. It is not taken to be anything peculiar to the theorist, and the theorist is not considered to have any advantage over others in the moral life. But conscience, as Butler conceives it, resembles reason as conceived by Socrates in that it is an authoritative faculty. Its authority does not consist in controlling the other faculties, but in pointing out the way they ought to go. And a person who was living the good life would know that this was so from having the approval of his conscience. Its authority resides in the fact that it is a peculiarly critical faculty, that it is capable of passing judgment on all others, while they are not capable of passing judgment on it. They merely pursue their particular objects, whatever these happen to be, but it can say whether these objects are good or not. Now in this theory we find difficulties similar to those which we found in the Socratic theory. Taking simply the relation between conscience and the particular passions or inclinations, we are bound to say that if they can come into conflict at all, the objects which they pursue must be of the same order. If the passions pursued mere particulars, simple entities, and not complex situations, then these particulars could not conflict with the complex situations expressed in the judgments of conscience. And again if we consider inclination as pursuing a thing apart altogether from its goodness, then the judgment of conscience that the thing was bad would have no effect whatever on the inclination. We could have no such thing as a moral appeal, a demand that we should mend our ways, but the inclination would go on pursuing its simple object as before, and the conscience would go on passing its judgments. But, actually, this is not the case. We can not only recognise that we have made mistakes (though this might mean: done what we didn't intend) but we can try to correct these mistakes. And that implies that our inclinations can and do deal with complex situations, and if we recognise that conflict among our different faculties and tendencies is possible, then we cannot assume (and this implies a criticism of both Socrates and Butler) that it is always the same faculty that exercises criticism, but we should rather expect to find that the criticism might be reversed. And this is actually the case in human experience; there are different things that we take as our major objects at different times and employ in criticism of minor objects.[6] We cannot say then that there is only one critical faculty, whether we call it reason or conscience. Butler tries to get over this difficulty by bringing in another reflective faculty, namely, that of self-love, and also a faculty of benevolence, which he sometimes treats as a reflective faculty and sometimes as a particular passion or inclination. But when those reflective faculties come into relation with one another, as well as with inclinations, then the same problems arise, and we cannot say that either of the conflicting faculties has a peculiar authority and is more entitled to pass judgments than any other.

Lecture 80

Aristotle continued—comparisons with Butler continued

The way in which Butler presents his theory is connected with the particular purpose that he had in view. His sermons were addressed to people who were not particularly theoretical and to whom, Butler thought, the need for behaving virtuously had to be brought home in a very emphatic way. (Who were bad examples?) We are to think of them as sophisticated persons who had fashionable views about virtue and vice, and considered themselves superior to the untutored person who simply followed the promptings of his nature. They are addressed to people who in Butler's opinion are leading an unnatural life, and who require to have the claims of simple virtue presented to them. In his preface Butler acknowledges that this is only one way of dealing with ethics, that there is another more direct way

---

[6][JA] And rejection of the view here suggested depends on the mere *demand*—the Leibnizian postulation—that our "whole history" *should* be capable of unification under a single "principle"—*cf.*, Kant's ideas of reason: Kant's criticism of which leads him to infinite regress, which like Leibniz he treats as a *sort* of unity—"taking the place of a reason". So A. E. Taylor on the *good* regress shows his Pythagorean affinities.) Monism as *ideal*: both unnecessary and insufficient.

which consists in "inquiring into the abstract relations of things", instead of into the particular constitution of human beings. And he considers that the two methods of inquiry lead in the end to the same ethical conclusions, but that while the more formal method may give a more satisfactory theoretical proof, the more concrete method may be more valuable for convincing people of the importance of the subject. According to the formal theory, vice consists of opposition to nature in general. On the other view, it is taken as a violation of our own nature, but since our own nature is bound up with nature in general, since a thorough analysis of either requires an investigation of the other, the results cannot be different in the two cases. In the theories of Socrates we have a greater emphasis on the nature of things, on the general conception of form or function, which is supposed to be immediately applicable to human nature. Aristotle on the other hand has insisted on considering the good for man, though he also expresses this good in terms of a general theory of ends.

Now in putting his position in the way he does, Butler is probably thinking more of the theory of his immediate predecessor Shaftesbury than of these Greek theories. Shaftesbury approached the matter in terms of the conception of nature in general, and Butler seems to suggest that this method of approach is not sufficiently convincing to the average human being, even though it may be logically more fundamental. We see then that Butler also considered that the inquiry into ethical problems was to be undertaken from a practical point of view, that is, that it had as its purpose the encountering of virtue rather than the mere discovery of truth. And though he distinguishes between the two methods, it would appear that he to some extent confused the two and so considered that the special character of goodness was to be an end. When we set up this doctrine of ends, or of something ultimate to which other things are to be taken as relative, the natural consequence is that we should distinguish a faculty which is concerned with what is ultimate from those which are concerned with what is relative. And thus, just like Socrates, Butler is bound to think of some authoritative faculty, or else like Aristotle to think of certain persons who are to have authority and who are to guide other persons to goodness.

Now when a view of this kind is taken, the difficulty immediately appears of finding a relation between the authoritative faculty and that which comes under its authority (Socrates' metaphysics of "obedience") and this is the same problem as appears in regard to the Socratic theory of forms, namely, of finding a relation between what really is and what is subordinate to that real being—the particulars. As we have seen, particularly in relation to the *Parmenides*, this problem cannot really be solved, that is, we cannot think of any connection, whether of conflict or of support, between a pure particular and a pure universal. Butler endeavours to overcome this opposition by means of a theory of reflective faculties, that is, faculties which are not mere inclinations but can take account of complex situations, but which are also distinguished from the reflective faculty of conscience. This in particular is the position of *self-love* in Butler's theory. The object of self-love is the happiness of the individual, and it pursues this object by working on and controlling the inclinations. Butler opposes the hedonistic theory that the object of every inclination is the pleasure or interest of the agent. Strictly speaking, he says, these inclinations are perfectly disinterested, that is, there is some external object which they aim at bringing about, and it is only when, operating in this way, they have succeeded in bringing it about, that we can tell whether the object will bring us pleasure or not, and that, if it does, the inclination can have the support of self-love. If, on the other hand, it is argued that all inclinations are interested, and not disinterested, in that their aim is one which we *wish* to bring about then, Butler points out, even benevolence must be regarded as interested. If we are benevolent, then benevolence is something to which we are inclined, and in that case would be interested action in the same sense as our inclinations in general are interested. But what Butler wishes to insist on and what entitles him to say that the inclinations are really disinterested is that our own happiness or pleasure is something perfectly specific and distinct from other things, that the hedonists in saying that we always pursue pleasure are confusing between *our mere activity in pursuing* and *a particular result which we may arrive at*, and that when we define pleasure in the latter sense, instead of leaving it vague as the hedonists do, we must regard it as the object of a particular inclination or faculty, and not of inclinations in general. What we pursue, then, need not be in any way a state of ourselves, but what we bring about does have effects on ourselves, and consequently we have to take these effects into account. Though Butler doesn't take the object of self-love as goodness, his theory of the way in which it controls the passions or inclinations is open to objections similar to those which can be brought against the Socratic theory of relation between reason and desire. That is, in order that self-love may be able to conflict with a passion, the objects pursued by both must be of the same order. If the one is a complex situation—a situation involving relations—then the other must also be complex. And if we regard all objects of inclination as complex, if we consider every inclination as being able to take account of the circumstances of a case, then the fact that self-love can take account of circumstances does not show it to be a peculiarly reflective faculty, but merely entitles us to class it along with the other inclinations. The function of self-love in Butler's system is to control the particular passions in a way which he admits conscience or the mere judgment of good and evil cannot do. So he has really broken up the Socratic faculty of reason into two faculties—one of which has the function of passing moral judgments, while the other has the function of controlling inclinations. The object of the one is goodness—the object of the other is pleasure, and the question is how these two rational faculties are to be related in the mind. Conscience, being the faculty of moral judgment, is capable of passing judgments upon the operation of self-love just as upon that of any inclination, but it is not capable of controlling self-love as self-love controls the inclinations. At the same time self-love must be able to take account of judgments passed by conscience, if any connected thinking on moral questions is to be possible. Here again there is a difficulty regarding the nature of the relation, because if self-love passes judgments in the course of its pursuit of pleasure, there seems no reason why conscience should not *pursue* goodness as well as pass judgments about it. If the two are to be capable of being harmonised, then they must act harmoniously, that is, self-love must take pleasure in goodness and conscience must find goodness in pleasure. In that case the doctrine of a peculiarly authoritative faculty would seem to break down. In order to support it, Butler would have to say that conscience is in some way *more* reflective than self-love, that it deals with further complexities in the situations into which men enter. But even this would not justify us in placing it on a higher level than self-love; the objects of the two would still require to be related, that is, they would have to be capable of dealing with the same situations.

Now Butler admits that they do deal with the same situations but he considers that while conscience can pass judgments about them, which have absolute certainty, the judgments of self-love only have probability, and consequently in any case of conflict, the former ought to be preferred. On the other hand, if the precepts of conscience were ever found absolutely to conflict with the agent's happiness, then, Butler considers, conscience would have to yield. But owing to the uncertainty of happiness as contrasted with the certainty of goodness, this problem can (would) never arise. And we can go on believing, and are indeed bound to believe, that if we always act with the approval of our conscience, then we are taking the best possible steps to secure our happiness.

Lecture 81

Aristotle continued—comparisons with Butler continued

In distinguishing between a faculty which can give certainty and one which can only give probability, Butler admits that they can both deal with the same things, that is, no matter what degree of certainty we had as to the judgments passed by these faculties, they certainly could not conflict, their objects could not be treated as alternatives, unless they both dealt with goodness. If self-love simply aimed at pleasure, and if there were no question of confusing pleasure and goodness, then the calculations of self-love would be quite irrelevant to the immediate judgments of conscience. What is implied is that we may mistake pleasure for goodness, and this is made plausible by the general conception of goodness as something which pertains to an end, instead of simply being a special character of certain particular things, no matter what our attitude to these things may be. And from that point of view, conscience is regarded as being able to formulate an ultimate end, an end to which any other object of choice could be regarded as merely a means. In order to substantiate this view, Butler would have to show that the objects pursued by the other faculties are always subordinated to the good which is pursued by conscience (that the objects which various tendencies desire are taken by them to be "desirable"). But in fact, he admits that this is not so, that in some cases the promptings of conscience are not attended to. (*Cf.*, idealists: that a less is preferred to a greater good.) That means that in these cases, the object of conscience is subordinated to other objects, such as pleasure, for example.

This appears to imply that conscience has not the authority which Butler claims for it. Butler tries to avoid this difficulty by distinguishing between conscience and power. He says of conscience that "had it strength as it has right, had it power as it has manifest authority, it would absolutely govern the world". But if its authority can be overruled, then that really means that we allow some other faculty to have authority over it. Another way of representing the same difficulty is that while Butler regards *following conscience* as leading a life in accordance with our nature, it is not really to be supposed that any life which we may lead can be contrary to our nature. If a particular man follows after pleasure in preference to any other object, then we are bound to say that it is his nature to do so, allowing that a person's nature may be influenced by his surroundings, that is, we have the same difficulty as appeared in the Socratic theory, in connection with the view that the good man is the only one who is truly a man. But that means that the other beings whom we call men are not really men, so that the command that we are addressing to them to follow their own nature and be men has no real application to their case.

Again, the assumption that conscience has authority because the judgments that it formulates have a peculiar certainty, cannot be reconciled with the fact that different persons, or the same person at different times in his life, take different things to be good. If once we admit, as some commentators on Butler have suggested, that conscience is capable of development, then we are treating it as a particular faculty with a particular aim, that is, on the same level as the passions or inclinations. But the facts seem to be better explained by considering that different faculties or (motives, tendencies)[7] are dominant in a particular mind at particular times. This does not necessarily introduce confusion into the notion of good, so long as we do not identify good with what any person happens to prefer or to pursue. If we think of good as a predicate of certain propositions which are either true or false, we have no reason for supposing that persons in acting well or badly formulate any such propositions. As Butler develops his theory, we find that he maintains that certain modes of behaviour, such as truthfulness or justice, are absolutely good, that is, independently of whether we pursue them or not, and also of whether they bring us happiness or not. In suggesting that goodness must always be in accordance with happiness, Butler really introduces a double standard of morality, that is, one which necessarily leads to insoluble problems. If, on the other hand, we consider the position of self-love, that is, of a faculty whose object is some condition of our own needs, then we find that there is no more reason for considering it to be capable of passing only probable judgments than for saying the same about any other faculty. Granted that we do not know all the consequences of a particular act, we are capable of knowing some of the particular consequences, and that particular consequence may be the object that we have in view; because if there is such a thing as the pursuit of happiness, it cannot be the pursuit of happiness in general but only of happiness in particular instances. Provided that that is a clear idea, then it is just as possible to pronounce on it with certainty as to pronounce with certainty on truthfulness or justice.

Butler's theory of self-love, and also his theory of benevolence, are connected with his identification of good

---

[7][Ed.] The student notes record "faculties or inclinations" here.

with something pursued, the object of action. In that way he speaks of self-love as the pursuit of our own good, and of benevolence as the pursuit of the good of others. But he is then using the term *good* in a different sense from that in which it is taken to be the object of conscience, and applied in particular to truthfulness or justice. If then we do not accept that description of the objects of self-love and benevolence, we would have to think of what Butler calls self-love as simply the pursuit of certain conditions of our own minds, whatever these might happen to be. Or, in Shaftesbury's language, of *affections towards affections*, the question of goodness not directly arising. And in the same way we should think of benevolence as meaning the pursuit of certain conditions of other people's minds, whether these could be called good or not. These tendencies or affections, united under the name self-love or benevolence, are just as particular as the tendencies to produce non-mental situations, and we cannot say either one or the other is more likely to produce conditions of goodness, prior to an examination of the whole situation in general. Butler partly recognises this in admitting that the passions are quite capable of producing good, even though there may have been no reflection about the goodness of the situation that was to be produced. This is further recognised in the treatment of benevolence (which had been first taken as a reflective principle) as a particular inclination to be subordinated to the general principles of conscience and self-love. This is more in accordance with Butler's view that benevolence is not any more disinterested than any other inclination. Like them it has a particular object and in both cases the object is one that the agent desires to bring about. This point becomes clearer still if we remember that benevolence as Butler uses the term covers all actions which take effect on other persons, no matter what that effect may be. The general position is that we have to distinguish our various inclinations which all have particular objects and which are capable of conflict with one another and of overcoming one another, from any view that we may hold about ethical questions, as well as about the questions arising in any other science. Butler shows the necessity of making the distinction, but he is still sufficiently dominated by the theory of goodness as man's nature, and the connected theory of goodness as an end of action, to fail to make these distinctions clear and thus to fall into contradictions.

Appendix

Books on Greek Philosophy in the Anderson Family Collection

Pre-Socratics and General

John Burnet (editor and translator), *Early Greek Philosophy* London: Adam and Charles Black, 1948.

The copy includes marginal notes, most particularly on Heraclitus and Burnet's decision to translate *kosmos* as "world" rather than "order" in Fragment 20 (i.e., "This world, which is the same". JA asks "Why?" to Burnet's footnote declaration that *kosmos* must mean "world" in this context. He also writes "order" over "world" in the text.)

Karl Reinhardt: *Parmenides und die Geschichte der Griechischen Philosophie.* Bonn: Verlag von Friedrich Cohen, n.d. Owned/signed: Norman Porter, University of Sydney 1929.

John Burnet, *Greek Philosophy: Part I, Thales to Plato.* London: Macmillan 1914. Also a second copy signed by A. J. (Sandy) Anderson.

Plato

The Dialogues of Plato, translated into English with analyses and introductions by B. Jowett In 5 volumes. Oxford: Clarendon Press 1892. Includes Book Plate indicating it was acquired on graduation in 1917 from University of Glasgow.

Platonis Opera recognovit brevique adnotatione critica instrvxit Ioannes Burnet Volume 1 only. Oxford: Clarendon Press, n.d. Book Plate: Stanley Raymond Phippard

Crito of Plato, edited by A. S. Owen. London: Blackie and Son, 1903. Signed by Jas. B. Hutton Class VI W. D.

Robinson Class VII; M. W. Robinson Class VII; (Kinross-shire Committee on Secondary Education).

Plato and Xenophon: Socratic Discourses. Introduced by A. D. Lindsay. London: J. M. Dent and Sons, 1910 (latest imprint 1954).

Plato: Last Days of Socrates, Translated by Hugh Tredennick (Euthyphro, Apology, Crito, Phaedo). Harmondsworth: Penguin 1954 (latest imprint 1979).

Plato: The Republic, translated by H. D. P. Lee. Harmondsworth: Penguin 1955 (latest 1965).

Platonis Dialogi secundum thrasylli tetralogias dispositi. Post Carolum Fridericum Hermannum recognovit Martinus Wohlrab. Leipzig: B. G. Teubneri, 1921. In 6 volumes.

Plato's Euthyphro, Apology of Socrates and Crito. Edited with notes by John Burnet. Oxford: Clarendon Press, 1924.

Platonis Opera: Phaedo. Edited with introduction and notes by John Burnet. Oxford: Clarendon Press, 1911 (latest 1949).

Five Dialogues of Plato bearing on Poetic Inspiration. Introduced by A. D. Lindsay. London: J. M. Dent, 1910 (latest 1931).

Plato: Republic. Translated and introduced by A. D. Lindsay. London: J. M. Dent 1906 (latest 1942). Includes 2 quarto pages in JA's hand on Thrasymachus.

Platon's Dialog Parmenides neu Uebersetzt und Erlaeutert von Otto Apelt. Leipzig: Verlag von Felix Meiner, 1919.

Plato: Philebus and Eponimis. Translated and introduced by A. E. Taylor. Edited by Raymond Klibansky. London: Thomas Nelson and Sons 1956.

The Education of the Young in the Republic of Plato. Translated into English with notes and introduction by Bernard Bosanquet. Cambridge: Cambridge University Press, 1901. Owned/signed: M. W. Robinson. 1912.

Plato: Gorgias. Translated by F. G. Plaistowe. London: University Tutorial Press, n.d.

Plato: Republic of Plato. Translated by John Llewelyn Davies and David James Vaughan. London: Macmillan, 1882.

Theaetetus of Plato. Translated by M. J. Levett. Glasgow: Jackson, Wylie and Co., 1928.

The Republic. Translated by A. D. Lindsay. London: J. M. Dent, 1906 (latest 1965).

WORKS ON PLATO:

David G. Ritchie, *Plato.* Edinburgh: T. and T. Clark, 1902.

A. E. Taylor, *Plato: the Man and his Work.* London: Methuen, 1926. Includes marginalia and 4 quarto pages of very rough notes. 2nd copy of this work owned/signed by A. J. Anderson.

John Burnet, *Platonism.* Berkeley, University of California Press, 1928.

Aristotle

The Works of Aristotle, translated into English under the editorship of W. D. Ross. Volume 1 and Volume 8 only:

Volume 1: *Categoriae and de Interpretatione,* E. M. Edghill; *Analytica Priora,* A. J. Jenkinson; *Analytica Posteriori,* G. R. G. Mure; *Topica and De Sophisticis Elenchis,* W. A. Pickard-Cambridge. Oxford: Oxford University Press, 1928 (latest 1950). Includes marginalia and notes.

Volume VIII: *Metaphysica.* Oxford: Clarendon 1908. Signed M. W. Robinson 1909.

The Ethics of Aristotle Illustrated with Essays and Notes by Sir Alexander Grant. 3rd Edition, in 2 volumes. London: Green and Co., 1874. Owned/signed: L. Owen. New Cole January 1884.

Aristotelis quae ferunter Problemata Physica edidit Carolus Aemilius Ruelle recognovit Hermannus Knoellinger. Leipzig: Teubneri 1922.

Aristotelis Ethica Nichomachea recognovit Franciscus Susemihl. Leipzig: Teubneri, 1912.

Aristoteles De Anima edidervnt G. Biehl and O. Apelt. Leipzig, 1926.

Aristotle's Poetics Translated by Benjamin Jowett, introduced by Max Lerner. New York: Modern Library 1943.

Aristotle: *Nichomachean Ethics*. London: J. M. Dent, 1911 (1942).

Aristotle: *Metaphysics*. Edited and translated by John Warrington. Introduced by Sir David Ross. London: J. M. Dent, 1956.

Aristotle: *Nichomachean Ethics*. Translated with analysis and critical notes by J. E. C. Weldon. London: Macmillan, 1908. Includes Book Plate indicating John Anderson awarded 3rd Prize by Gilbert A. Davies for an essay at the University of Glasgow in 1912 (his second year).

Aristotle on Education: Extracts from Ethics and Politics by John Burnet. Translated by John Burnet. Cambridge: Cambridge University Press, 1905.

WORKS ON ARISTOTLE:

W. D. Ross *Aristotle*. London: Methuen, 1923. Owned/signed: John Anderson.

William Barrett, *Aristotle's Analysis of Movement: Its Significance for its time*. New York, 1938.

Index

Adimantus, 206, 208, 212, 217, 219, 223, 224, 229
Anaxagoras, 66, 108, 110–113, 117
Anaximander, 13, 18, 21–32, 34, 35, 39–45, 68, 77
Anaximenes, 9, 13, 23, 30–35, 37, 44, 45, 65, 77
animism, 5–7, 53, 56, 66, 167, 183
Anytus, 159
appearance and reality, 10, 15, 32, 34, 52, 56–58, 60, 65, 72, 75, 108, 112, 113, 119, 120, 129, 132–134, 162, 191, 192, 194, 222, 225, 230
Aristotle, 13, 21, 27, 51, 183, 218, 227, 228, 238, 241, 243–256, 258–263, 266
    Nicomachean Ethics, 203, 228, 238, 241, 243, 247
Atomism, 9, 10, 33, 48, 56, 92, 101, 108, 110, 117, 120, 132, 174, 183
authority, 84, 85, 143, 146, 154, 155, 234, 261, 264, 265, 267, 270, 271

beauty, 174, 179, 181, 182, 187
being and becoming, 21, 26, 28, 55, 57, 60–62, 64, 81, 95, 98, 101, 103, 108, 113, 118, 119, 129–132, 163, 165, 167, 171, 175, 176, 180, 181, 184, 187–189, 191, 198, 203
being, single way of, 7, 10, 11, 13, 15, 19, 22, 26, 28, 37, 44, 54, 56, 58–63, 68, 73, 74, 79, 95–98, 101, 111, 119, 130, 171, 188, 189, 196, 200
belief, 12, 42, 98, 132, 135–138, 140, 141, 143, 146, 160
Bergson, Henri, 62, 95
Berkeley, G., 197
Bosanquet, Bernard, 194
boundless, the, 13, 22, 24–33, 35, 40, 45, 69, 96
Burnet, John, 8, 13, 18, 30, 33, 48, 49, 58, 82, 86, 87, 110, 111, 119, 129, 131, 145, 165, 173, 191, 195, 201, 249
Butler, Bishop, 224, 235, 243, 262–272
    Sermons on Human Nature, 203, 263

capacities, 39, 84, 85, 249, 251
categories, 60
causality, 13, 21, 114, 149, 171–174, 177
Cebes, 168, 170
Cephalus, 206, 210
certainty, 39, 41, 86, 142, 269, 271
Church, F. J., 172
classes, 16, 17, 33, 39, 55, 97, 114, 135, 147, 153, 156, 177, 182, 188, 204, 205, 237, 257
complexity, 8, 46, 56, 63, 64, 66–68, 70, 79, 83, 87–92, 95, 97, 101, 109, 110, 116, 117, 172, 192, 199, 201, 205
contemplation, 55, 97, 130, 138, 166, 179, 188, 263
Copernicus, N., 28
copula, 97, 105, 140

definition, 125, 137, 138, 140, 144, 146,

147, 149, 151–154, 156, 158, 162, 205, 213, 214, 234, 245, 246, 249, 250, 256
democracy, 84, 85, 159
dependence, 91, 165
Descartes, Rene, 92, 120
determinism, 83, 84
dialectic, 92, 157, 164, 172, 213
disinterestedness, 224, 262, 267, 268, 272
division of labour, 231, 232
doubt, 8
dualism, 46, 58, 61, 65, 66, 78, 81, 98, 262

education, 76, 143, 159, 207, 227, 229, 239, 255, 262
egalitarianism, 84–86, 226
Eleatics, 9, 17, 28, 43–46, 53, 55, 56, 61, 66, 74, 89–92, 96, 98–109, 111–113, 115, 117, 119–121, 123, 129, 130, 132–136, 155, 163, 180, 187, 191, 192, 194, 195, 199–201, 203, 222, 240, 256
emotions and feelings, 237, 249–251, 255, 256, 259, 260
Empedocles, 18, 56, 66, 103, 108, 110–113, 116, 117, 129
ends and means, 82, 208, 218, 220, 222, 229, 242, 243, 245, 248, 249, 260, 262, 266
Engels, F., 188
essence, 79, 116
Euthyphro, 145, 149–158, 207, 211, 214
existence, 15, 16, 26, 30, 31, 33–35, 58, 59, 68, 70, 92, 97, 98, 133, 172, 241
explanation, 8, 10, 11, 37, 40, 58–61, 91, 107, 120, 172, 174–178, 187

facts, matters of, 5–8, 10, 12, 38, 44, 52, 61, 110, 113, 132, 141, 173, 213, 237

faculties, 39, 136, 139, 151, 230, 234–238, 248, 251, 262, 264, 265, 267–271
forms, the, 14, 16, 20, 56, 57, 106, 115, 120, 125, 129–131, 134, 138, 153, 160, 163–165, 167, 169, 171, 175, 176, 179, 180, 182–189, 191, 192, 194–203, 205, 212, 225, 229, 240, 245, 246, 267
Freud, Sigmund, 61, 80, 150
friendship, 211, 214

geometry, 46, 49–51, 53, 119, 129
Glaucon, 206, 208, 212, 217–224, 229
gods, 5, 21, 38, 41, 68, 145, 146, 152–154, 156–159, 207, 211
good, the, 54, 75, 80–82, 86, 87, 146, 150, 155, 158, 160, 185, 192, 195, 204–206, 208–214, 217, 218, 221, 222, 224–231, 234, 238, 240–249, 251–254, 256, 262–273
Gorgias, 105, 108, 111, 119, 120

happiness, 81, 241, 244–246, 248, 249, 253, 262, 263, 267–269, 271
harmony and attunement, 50, 54, 67, 69, 81, 85, 87, 170, 185, 221, 226, 237, 238, 244
Hegel, G. W. F., 232
Heraclitus, 19–21, 26, 44, 46, 54, 56–80, 82–96, 102, 106, 109, 110, 112, 113, 118, 183
historical view of things, 19, 42, 56, 60, 63–65, 67, 73, 74, 76, 80, 82, 83, 92, 95, 102, 110, 165, 175, 176, 181, 184, 189–193, 225
Hume, David, 6, 155
hypotheses, 6, 38, 143, 149, 150, 158, 173, 213

idealism, 22, 270
ideals, 119, 179, 180, 188, 191, 194, 195
identity, 7, 73, 78, 79, 88, 95
illusion or false belief, 16, 98, 120, 132

imitation (mimesis), 130, 132, 153, 162, 163, 169, 181
infinite regress, 83, 265
inquiry, 5–7, 22, 36, 37, 59, 60, 64, 68, 92, 93, 150, 151, 263
intellect, 169, 210, 227–229, 241, 254, 262

Jowett, B., 172
justice, 69, 148, 156–158, 160, 161, 203, 204, 207, 209, 210, 212, 213, 215–221, 223, 230, 231, 234, 238, 239, 241, 271, 272

Kant, Immanuel, 96, 232, 246, 265
knowledge and opinion, 11, 37, 40, 42, 53, 61, 63, 67, 92, 98, 104, 132–136, 140, 146, 160, 206, 207, 211, 214

laws of nature, 7, 15, 61
Leibniz, G. W., 92, 265
Leucippus, 9
limit and unlimited, the, 13, 22, 24, 28, 44, 45, 48, 52–54, 56, 60, 82, 129, 140, 148, 155, 248
logic of events, 35, 37, 43, 58, 59, 61, 68, 80, 85, 253

mathematics, 19, 28, 35, 36, 44, 45, 68, 125, 178, 195, 247
matter, 9, 10, 22, 24, 96, 110
Melissus, 103, 108
Milesians, 7, 9, 13–16, 18–20, 23, 30, 31, 33–37, 40, 43–46, 51, 58, 65, 70, 72, 73, 75, 76, 88, 91, 153
Mill, John Stuart, 244, 245
misology, 157, 171
modern physics, 10
Monism, 14, 36, 37, 107, 110–112, 265
music, 45, 48–52, 54, 219
mythological thinking, 5, 8, 10, 11, 14, 18, 21, 30, 33, 36, 41, 43, 60, 61, 83, 153

Nietzsche, F., 215

number, 46–53, 60, 129–131, 174, 175, 177, 186, 260

Parmenides, 9, 10, 14, 15, 20, 22, 26, 46, 48, 53, 56, 88–96, 98, 100–112, 117, 120, 130, 132, 194, 196–198, 200
participation, 163, 174, 175, 186, 187, 196–198, 200, 201, 203
perfection, 20, 169, 201, 204
Peters, F. H., 249
philosophy, 5–11, 13, 17, 20, 22, 28, 30, 32, 35, 40, 43, 53, 54, 62, 68, 91, 111, 143, 154, 206
Plato, 27, 28, 54, 58, 90, 93, 105, 106, 130, 140, 163, 179, 192, 194, 206, 245, 254
    Apology, 158–160
    Euthyphro, 145, 146, 149, 150, 152, 207, 211, 257
    Meno, 159
    Parmenides, 55, 93, 105, 163, 192, 194, 199, 203, 226, 267
    Phaedo, 70, 131, 134, 138, 141, 162, 164–166, 179, 189, 191, 193, 226, 255
    Phaedrus, 191
    Republic, 54, 55, 192, 203, 204, 206, 208, 227–229, 241, 245, 251, 262
    Sophist, 90, 93, 105
    Theaetetus, 137, 163
pluralism, 112
pluralists, 36, 108, 109, 111
Polymachus, 206–212, 214, 227
posivitism, 120
powers, 5, 6, 18, 37, 38, 56, 114, 154
predicate, the, 89, 97, 104–106, 111, 117, 134, 135, 140, 148, 163, 165, 171, 175, 180–182, 185–191, 193, 194, 196–198, 200, 212, 256, 271
process and change, 17, 19–21, 26, 28, 29, 32, 34, 38, 40, 55, 57, 59–64, 69, 70, 74, 78, 81, 83, 95, 102, 106, 108, 112, 115, 184,

188
production and enjoyment of goods, 71, 212, 216–218, 222, 224–226, 231, 233, 245, 246, 254, 272
progress, 6
proposition, the, 59, 81, 90, 92, 97, 105, 106, 117, 134, 136, 138–141, 148, 156, 163–165, 172, 173, 177–183, 186–191, 194, 197, 235
Protagoras, 108, 119, 137
psychoanalysis, 154
psychology, 119, 237, 239, 248, 251
Pythagoras, 36, 44, 45, 48, 49, 54, 56, 58–61, 63, 88, 108
Pythagoreans, 24, 27, 28, 30, 35, 40, 43–69, 74, 78, 81, 83, 85, 86, 88, 90, 91, 95, 96, 98–101, 104, 106–111, 113, 118–125, 129–134, 136, 140, 151, 155, 162–165, 170, 183, 191, 192, 199, 200, 230, 240, 251, 256

qualities, 9, 10, 15, 16, 20–22, 24, 30–34, 46, 65, 89, 100, 109, 110, 112, 113, 115–117, 183, 194, 196, 198, 206, 226, 242, 246, 252, 261

Ramsey, F. P., 197
rational and irrational, 51, 55, 59, 101, 107, 111, 131, 254
rationalism, 52, 154
reality as historical, 9, 13, 20, 58, 68, 118
relativism, 157
reminiscence, 162

scepticism, 8, 10, 11, 20, 28, 36, 43, 44, 67, 105, 138, 157
science, 5–8, 10, 11, 14, 15, 17, 27–30, 43, 44, 52, 86, 106, 110, 133, 150, 151, 158, 160, 165, 175, 177, 188, 194, 210, 211, 247
Shaftesbury, third earl, 266, 272
Simmias, 166, 168, 170, 175, 176, 183–185

social classes, 41, 226, 228, 230–234, 238–240
Socrates, 9, 11, 19, 28, 56, 61, 62, 70, 90, 91, 106, 125, 129, 131–134, 136–141, 143, 145–148, 150–168, 170–181, 184–197, 199–201, 203, 205–237, 239–241, 243, 251, 253, 255, 257–259, 263–267
sophists, 11, 12, 28, 36, 43, 44, 108, 119, 120, 125, 132–140, 142, 143, 145, 146, 149, 151, 155, 158, 160, 187, 191, 192, 207, 229, 241, 242
space, 9, 13, 24, 27, 29–31, 34, 35, 37, 39, 42, 45, 53, 55, 96–101, 104, 117, 118, 122, 124, 125, 134, 174
space and time, 34, 37, 96–98, 100, 102, 117, 118, 122, 124, 125
Spinoza, Baruch de, 92, 120
Stekel, Wilhelm, 150
Stout, G. F., 197
substance, 9, 13–15, 20–22, 29–34, 37, 45, 73, 92, 101, 103, 106, 108–110, 116, 120, 139
syllogism, 176, 177, 186, 190

Taylor, A. E., 146, 154, 200, 265
Thales, 9, 13, 17–24, 26, 31, 34, 35, 65
third man argument, 199, 201–203, 221
Thrasymachus, 206–208, 212–221, 224, 229
time, 97, 99, 102, 107, 116, 125, 132
totality, 14, 74, 77, 83, 112, 231, 246, 261
tradition, 149, 207, 210

ultimates, 16, 28, 37, 38, 45, 46, 50, 52, 53, 56, 57, 60, 63, 67, 72, 74, 79, 89, 99, 103, 109, 118, 229
unconscious, the, 183, 190
universals, 78, 166, 169, 186, 187, 191, 192, 198, 199, 201, 203, 235, 236, 258, 267
utilitarianism, 208, 209, 244, 253

utility, 244

ways of life, 54, 215, 252
Whitehead, A. N., 97

Xenophanes, 36–44, 51, 52, 65, 142

Zeno, 28, 46, 96, 99, 108, 118, 120–125, 130, 134, 135, 137

www.ingramcontent.com/pod-product-compliance
Lightning Source LLC
Chambersburg PA
CBHW050854160426
43194CB00011B/2147